The Novels of Nadine Gordimer

The Novels of Nadine Gordimer

Private Lives/Public Landscapes

John Cooke

Louisiana State University Press
Baton Rouge and London

Excerpts from the works of Nadine Gordimer are reprinted by permission of Viking
Penguin Inc., New York, and Jonathan Cape Ltd., London: *Occasion for Loving*,
copyright © 1960, 1963 by Nadine Gordimer; *The Late Bourgeois World*, copyright
© 1966 by Nadine Gordimer; *A Guest of Honour*, copyright © 1970 by Nadine
Gordimer; *The Conservationist*, copyright © 1972, 1973, 1974 by Nadine
Gordimer; *Burger's Daughter*, copyright © 1979 by Nadine Gordimer; *July's
People*, copyright © 1981 by Nadine Gordimer; *Selected Stories*, copyright © 1952,
1956, 1957, 1959, 1960, 1961, 1964, 1965, 1968, 1969, 1971, 1975 by Nadine
Gordimer; *A Soldier's Embrace*, copyright © 1975, 1977, 1980 by Nadine
Gordimer; *Something Out There*, copyright © 1979, 1981, 1982, 1983, 1984 by
Nadine Gordimer. Also reprinted by permission of Viking Penguin, Inc., is the
excerpt from *Writers at Work: The Paris Review Interviews*, sixth series, edited by
George Plimpton. Copyright © 1984 by The Paris Review, Inc. Excerpts from
Melvyn Bragg's interview "The Solitude of a White Writer" are reprinted by
permission of the author; Roy Campbell's poem "On Some African Novelists" is
reprinted by permission of Fransisco Custodio and Ad. Donker (Pty) Ltd.

LIBRARY OF CONGRESS CATALOGING IN PUBLICATION DATA

Cooke, John, 1946–
    The novels of Nadine Gordimer.

    Bibliography: p.
    Includes index.
    1. Gordimer, Nadine—Criticism and interpretation.   I. Title.
PR9369.3.G6Z63   1985   823   85-9692
ISBN 0-8071-1247-X

For my father and
in memory of my mother

The novelist in South Africa does not live in a community and has begun to write from scratch at the wrong time. Don't think I am patting down the red earth of Africa over his grave—I am not. He survives, and will survive, but the going is not easy for him. The word is prickly, but full of juice, like some of the plants of Africa, and the low cultural rainfall forces it to take on certain forms and shapes and not others.

—Nadine Gordimer
"The Novel and the Nation in South Africa" (1961)

Contents

The Novels of Nadine Gordimer

1

"Only Pursue": The Novelist and the Situation

I

Nadine Gordimer's third novel, *Occasion for Loving*, was greeted in 1963 as yet another example of the problems presented to the novelist by the intractable South African situation. A typical response appeared in *Commonweal*, where the reviewer noted "the atmosphere of daily melodrama which makes South African writing its own category" and concluded that "the book is only as good as it honestly can be." His judgment that the South African novel was limited by its separate category was echoed by Martin Staniland, who went on to surmise the consequences: "It is because of the frustration which the present South African system presents to the novelist as humanist that I think Miss Gordimer's work may stand as the ultimate in the South African novel for some time . . . perhaps as its epitaph." Gordimer's humanism had been based on Forsterian liberalism—in South African terms, the belief that blacks and whites would overcome the country's racial divisions through personal contact across the color bar. As she reflected in 1980, "during the 1950's, we believed very strongly in the personal relationship, in the possibility that in changed circumstances blacks would view us as fellow human beings . . . the Forsterian 'only connect' lay behind what we believed in." With the increasingly truculent application of apartheid by the Nationalist government through the early sixties, Gordimer and many of her contemporaries had found connection, the informing principle of their novels, less and less possible. By 1963 Gordimer, then only forty, seemed a likely candidate to assume from E. M. Forster the unenviable role of oldest living ex-novelist.[1]

The frustrations Gordimer encountered as a novelist drew particular attention because of her early success as a writer of short fiction. Born in 1923 within the white enclave of Springs, an East Rand mining town forty miles outside Johannesburg, Gordimer had been writing stories from the age of nine, when she was barred from normal childhood activities due to the suspicion of a heart ailment. By her late teens she was publishing what she would later call "master-servant stories," accounts of the distortions in personal relationships caused by a racist society, in the small liberal magazines *Forum*, *South African Quarterly*, and *Trek*. By 1949, a small Johannesburg press had published a volume of short stories titled *Face to Face*. She gained the early recognition so difficult for a South African writer to get outside South Africa when, through the efforts of the Afrikaner poet Uys Krige and a remarkable agent, Sidney Saterstein, her work was accepted by American journals. In 1950 the *Yale Review* published a story, and the following year Gordimer began her long association with the *New Yorker*. By the mid-fifties she had two short story collections and a largely autobiographical novel, *The Lying Days* (1953), to her credit.

Her development had no doubt been fostered by the unusually vigorous literary activity in South Africa since World War II. Indeed, the proceedings of the conference of writers and critics who met at the University of the Witwatersrand in 1956 reads like an official stock-taking of the achievements of South African literature since the war. Alan Paton, whose *Cry, the Beloved Country* (1948) was the most widely recognized product of this outpouring, drew an apt contrast between the pre- and postwar periods by designating the latter not a renaissance but a "first birth." And the Anglo–South African William Plomer described the accomplishments of South African writers in a way which would have seemed absurd a decade earlier. "South African literature in the English language," he said, "is in such a flourishing state that there is no longer any need to keep bending over to see if it is

1 Samuel Hynes, "The Power of Hatred," *Commonweal*, LXXVII (1963), 667–68; Martin Staniland, "Apartheid and the Novel: Desperation and Stoicism in a Situation Which Frustrates," *New African*, IV (March, 1965), 15; Johannes Riis, "Nadine Gordimer," *Kunapipi*, II (1980), 21.

growing. We now have to look up to it." Plomer overstated the case only slightly. Paton and Peter Abrahams seemed well on their way to becoming major figures, and a spate of other writers had produced at least one work of promise.[2]

The promise was rarely fulfilled. Indeed, the conference proceedings served as not just a record of this literary outpouring but its epitaph. Some of the writers, like Paton, turned to nonfiction or political work; even more, most notably Abrahams and Dan Jacobson, expatriated. By the early sixties Gordimer was almost the only member of the postwar group to continue producing fiction from within the country. That she should be the survivor was not altogether surprising, for she was in essential ways more a product of South Africa than her contemporaries. She attended university at home, not in England as colonial writers so regularly have; she did not travel abroad until she was thirty. When she did consider exile, she found "that the roots of other countries, however desirable, were not possible for a plant conditioned by the flimsy dust that lies along the Witwatersrand."[3] Gordimer's development into the writer who would eventually fulfill the promise of the "first birth" in the 1970s derives most fundamentally from this simple but, in the context of her writing community, radical act: she remained to examine how she and her countrymen had been "conditioned" by their "flimsy dust."

Gordimer seemed particularly unsuited to prosper as a writer in her arid land because of the disjunction between her temperament and the situation she confronted. More than any of her contemporaries,

2 Alan Paton, "The South African Novel in English," in A. C. Partridge (ed.), *Proceedings of a Conference of Writers, Publishers, Editors, and University Teachers of English* (Johannesburg, 1957), 145; William Plomer, "South African Writers and English Readers," *ibid.*, 56. Paton's novels were *Cry, the Beloved Country* (London, 1948) and *Too Late the Phalarope* (London, 1953). Abrahams had published five novels, most notably *Mine Boy* (London, 1946) and *Wild Conquest* (New York, 1950). Accomplished novels on public themes included Dan Jacobson's *A Dance in the Sun* (London, 1955), Jack Cope's *The Fair House* (London, 1955), Phyllis Altman's *The Law of the Vultures* (London, 1953), and Harry Bloom's *Episode in the Transvaal* (Garden City, N.Y., 1955). Notable novels with a more private focus included Charlotte Webster's *Ceremony of Innocence* (New York, 1949), Daphne Rooke's *A Grove of Fever Trees* (New York, 1950), and Marris Murray's *The Fire-Raisers* (London, 1953).

3 Nadine Gordimer, "Johannesburg," *Holiday*, XVIII (August, 1955), 49.

Gordimer was initially drawn to private themes, which appeared so unreconcilable with a land where, as she said in 1974, "the creative imagination, whatever it seizes upon, finds the focus of even the most private event set in the overall social determination of racial laws."[4] At the Witwatersrand Conference Paton had used *The Lying Days* as an example of one of the few South African novels which had avoided public themes, and both it and Gordimer's second novel, *A World of Strangers* (1958), were contrasted, generally unfavorably, with Doris Lessing's more political treatments of Southern Rhodesia. As Gordimer herself stated in 1965, "I am not a politically-minded person by nature. I don't suppose if I had lived elsewhere, my writing would have reflected politics much. If at all."[5]

By the mid-sixties it appeared that Gordimer's major achievement would be in the short story form, in which her private themes could be developed with only tangential treatment of the broader South African social fabric, that "overall social determination of racial laws." Her early, well-received short story collections—*The Soft Voice of the Serpent* (1953), *Six Feet of the Country* (1956), *Friday's Footprint* (1960), and *Not for Publication* (1965)—centered largely on those private themes. So much did her early work seem suited to the short story form that the *TLS* reviewer of *A World of Strangers* found that "it is a conclusion in no way to Miss Gordimer's discredit to say that her novel would have made an excellent collection of short stories." The same assessment, clearly a discredit to Gordimer as novelist, was made more forthrightly and comprehensively by Robert F. Haugh in his study of Gordimer's fiction through 1970. After an appreciative consideration of the short stories, he concluded that "the novels are something else. Frequently, the trouble is that in seeking a more sustained story structure, Miss Gordimer is drawn into the sort of direct racial confrontation that she avoided in her most successful short stories."[6] While the causes were more various than Haugh indicates, his judgment applies

4 Nadine Gordimer, "Literature and Politics in South Africa," *Southern Review: An Australian Journal of Literary Studies*, VII (1974), 208.

5 Arthur Ravenscroft, "A Writer in South Africa: Nadine Gordimer," *London Magazine*, V (May, 1965), 23.

6 Review of Nadine Gordimer's *A World of Strangers*, in *TLS*, June 27, 1958, p. 357; Robert F. Haugh, *Nadine Gordimer* (New York, 1974), 161.

well to the three novels through *Occasion for Loving* and her short fourth novel *The Late Bourgeois World* (1966). Gordimer herself accepted valuations such as Haugh's in a typically self-deprecatory comment on her fiction in 1965: "I don't consider myself a short-story writer primarily—whatever other people may think—because I really do want to write novels. That is, I want to write both. I have written a few stories that satisfy me, but I've not written a novel that comes anywhere near doing so."[7]

By the mid-sixties Gordimer had in fact written more than a few satisfying short stories. She found the novel form more difficult, and in this respect she was like other South African writers. The typical creative profile of the South African novelist—Olive Schreiner, William Plomer, Pauline Smith, and Harry Bloom, to cite but a few—is of a promising first novel, then decline or silence. For those novelists who continued to write, the primary difficulty was fashioning a comprehensive view of a society even more impoverished than Henry James found Hawthorne's. More accurately, in South Africa there has been no society at all, only separate worlds yoked together by violence. The severity of the problem they confronted can be represented by Forster's useful description in *Aspects of the Novel* of the novelist's territory. South African novelists needed not just to depict the mountain range of history that Forster said bounded the novel on one side; they needed to create it. In the terms Gordimer employed in "The Novel and the Nation in South Africa" (quoted in my epigraph), the novelists needed to fashion distinctive "forms and shapes" appropriate to an arid land with "low cultural rainfall." Gordimer's depiction of her native mountain range, her creation of novel forms fully consonant with her land's conditions, is her most notable accomplishment—and thus my major concern in this study—because it is unparalleled in South Africa. Indeed, the successful transition from shorter to longer forms late in a career is rare for a writer anywhere, in any time.

Only in 1970 with *A Guest of Honour* did Gordimer show her readers, as James said Turgenev showed his, that there are possibilities in a large, dry land that no one wants to visit. Only then did the predictions of her demise as a novelist, such as those made in 1963, begin to seem

7 Stephen Gray, "Landmark in Fiction," *Contrast*, XXX (April, 1973), 83.

premature. *A Guest of Honour* and her subsequent three novels—*The Conservationist* (1974), *Burger's Daughter* (1979), and *July's People* (1981)—received substantial critical acclaim and brought her exposure as a novelist to a wider audience than she had previously enjoyed. The critical reception is reflected, in brief, in literary awards: the James Tait Black Memorial Prize for *A Guest of Honour*, the Booker Prize for *The Conservationist*, a South African CNA Literary Award for *Burger's Daughter*, and the French international award, the Grand Aigle d'Or. Such recognition no doubt prompted the wider dissemination of her novels. Her early novels, long out of print, were reissued from 1976 to 1978 by the English publishing house of Jonathan Cape. In America, she has begun to get belated attention. Penguin has reissued all her novels except *The Lying Days* in paperback, and she has become a regular contributor to the *New York Review of Books* as well as the *New Yorker*. Her novels have been translated into Spanish, Italian, and most recently, Polish. Even in South Africa all her novels are now in print. For various periods, three had been banned, a fact which is itself a kind of left-handed literary award.[8] Her standing as a novelist, abroad and at home, is now secure.

For Gordimer to reach this point required the longest trek in the history of South African literature. The problems in describing its course are suggested by Roy Campbell's well-known quatrain, "On Some South African Novelists":

> You praise the firm restraint with which they write—
> I'm with you there, of course:
> They use the snaffle and the curb all right,
> But where's the bloody horse?

Few critics have placed Gordimer with those novelists of Campbell's who have style but no theme to convey. That bloody horse exists, but

---

8 The banned novels were *A World of Strangers* (twelve years; only the paperback edition, presumably because it was more accessible to Africans), *The Late Bourgeois World* (two years), and *Burger's Daughter* (a few months). Gordimer responded in the final case with an item-by-item response to the charges against the book leveled by the appeal board in *What Happened to "Burger's Daughter," or How South African Censorship Works* (Emmarentia, S.A., 1980). Gordimer has written over a dozen articles on banning and censorship legislation, most often focusing on black writers, who have been the most severely affected.

what it looks like—the shape of her novels, taken as a whole—has been elusive. This is partly because Gordimer's output has been so large and so varied. By mid-1984, it included eight novels; one novella, "Something Out There" (1984); ten collections of short stories, including the 1976 *Selected Stories*; a book of criticism, *The Black Interpreters* (1973); more than a dozen reviews and over fifty uncollected essays on diverse subjects—travel, South African censorship, African culture, and the craft of fiction; a few dozen published interviews and lectures; and, recently, seven films, for which she served as advisor, based on her short stories.

The shape of Gordimer's career has been elusive for a more significant reason: she has not quite fit into any of the contexts her critics have used. Some have seen her as simply a European writer who happens to live in Africa. Reviewers have recurrently begun their assessments with comparisons to the great nineteenth-century Russians, and, to take a more concerted treatment, Robert F. Haugh places her short stories solely in a tradition epitomized by Flaubert, Chekhov, and Mansfield. To others she has been a white colonial writer. In a 1965 essay, "Les Grandes Dames," the South African critic Lewis Nkosi placed Gordimer with Lessing on the same pedestal, and in a recent book Abdul R. JanMohamed juxtaposes three "colonial" novelists (Gordimer, Joyce Cary, and Isak Dinesen) with three "African" novelists (Chinua Achebe, Ngugi wa Thiong'o, and Alex La Guma).[9] To yet others, like that *Commonweal* reviewer, she has been a product of a South African tradition, which is "its own category." It is a category, unfortunately, which has been destroyed by the banning, censoring, forced exile, and even imprisonment of two generations of black writers. Moreover, as there is as yet no legitimate South Africa, there can be no "South African literature"; there can only be the separate literatures of the separate societies, which would make Gordimer a "white South African writer," a label she rejects. Finally, there are others, myself among them, who agree with Gordimer's own assertion that she and other whites shaped by an African experience are fundamentally African writers.

9 Lewis Nkosi, "Les Grandes Dames," *New African*, IV (September, 1965), 163; Abdul R. JanMohamed, *Manichean Aesthetics: The Politics of Literature in Colonial Africa* (Amherst, 1983).

That each of these categories has been useful, if not sufficient, in describing Gordimer at different times suggests yet another problem she presents: the change which has characterized her writing career. Gordimer has recorded the radical change of her society over three and a half decades; more importantly, she has redefined her view of her society's direction and her position in it. Such change is not as common as one might expect, partly because so few novelists have remained concerned with contemporary South Africa for long periods. There are exceptions, most notably André Brink and Es'kia Mphahlele, and the new direction taken by J. M. Coetzee in *The Life and Times of Michael K* (1983) suggests that he might, if he persists, join their number. But Alan Paton is more characteristic. *Ah, But Your Land Is Beautiful* (1982), his first novel in thirty years, shows his continuing preoccupation with the liberal opposition of the fifties. With Paton and most other South African novelists we too often find ourselves stepping into the same river twice.

The problem of placing Gordimer extends to the private sphere as well. She has been reticent, until recently sometimes even misleading, when questioned about her private life. As she wrote in 1965, "Autobiography can't be written until one is old, can't hurt anyone's feelings, can't be sued for libel, or, worse, contradicted."[10] Only since her mother's death in 1976 has she begun to discuss the highly unusual details of her upbringing, which, I will suggest, has had a decisive effect on her fictional themes. In both public and private terms, then, Gordimer has been a moving, and elusive, target.

Most critical studies of Gordimer have treated single novels. Attempts to describe the whole body of her work are rare. These are often of the general kind advanced by Margaret Daymond, appropriately in *Bloody Horse*, one of the many small magazines which have sprung up during the recent "second birth" of South African literature. "Most serious writers," she asserts, "have a subject around which their work revolves. Nadine Gordimer's is failure in relationships and the recognition of isolation which comes to those who fail."[11] Only two critics have attempted in book-length studies to provide more precise defini-

10 Ravenscroft, "A Writer in South Africa: Nadine Gordimer," 25.

11 Margaret Daymond, "Disintegration, Isolation, Compassion," *Bloody Horse*, IV (March/April, 1981), 91.

tions than ones like this. In a 1974 Twayne study centering on the private themes in the short stories, Robert F. Haugh holds that the novels are increasingly unsatisfying because Gordimer is temperamentally unsuited to treat the public subjects which become more and more her concern. Michael Wade's 1978 study in Gerald Moore's Modern African Writers series is in essential ways the antithesis of Haugh's. Wade focuses on the novels (through *The Conservationist*), and his concern is a public theme. Dorothy Driver summarizes his approach well in a review in *English in Africa*. Wade, she writes, "argues that a major theme in Nadine Gordimer's fiction is the collapse of the romantic hero. Whether romantic rebels, liberal democrats, or new pragmatists, whites in Africa who hold on to a European context and do not give themselves to Africa are considered irrelevant. So Europe-in-Africa falters and fails."[12] Wade's study leaves one wondering what Gordimer implies *will* succeed and how later Gordimer protagonists like Rosa Burger and the white revolutionaries in "Something Out There" could be accommodated by his focus on defeated romantic heroes. Still, Wade's is a more than useful discussion of one of Gordimer's major themes.

Gordimer has not often helped her readers to picture her bloody horse. She has been as reticent as Faulkner in discussing particular themes or approaches in her work. She does not, for example, admit a feminist impulse in her fiction. Nor does she acknowledge that women, as the examples of Schreiner, Sarah Gertrude Millin, Pauline Smith, and Lessing might suggest, have a better—or even substantially different—vantage point on the Southern African world than men. Such refusals to be categorized typify Gordimer's response to those who would do so. She acknowledges no specific political affiliation. She claims no ethnic or religious influences. (The daughter of Jewish parents, she briefly attended a convent school.) She champions no aesthetic doctrine. The contemporaries she admires are diverse, the influences on her work eclectic.

But Gordimer does return again and again to her fundamental belief—an unequivocal repudiation of apartheid. As she said of apartheid in 1965, "Whether I like it or not, this has been the crucial experience

---

12 Dorothy Driver, Review of Michael Wade's *Nadine Gordimer*, in *English in Africa*, V (March, 1978), 77.

of my life, as the war was for some people, or membership in the Communist Party for others. I have no religion, no political dogma—only plenty of doubts about everything except my conviction that the colour-bar is wrong and utterly indefensible." What Gordimer emphasizes here—indeed, in the vast majority of her numerous essays and lectures—is this indefensible condition of her society. Only occasionally, as later in the same essay, will she note that "my private preoccupations remain, running strongly beneath or alongside or intertwined with the influence of the political situation."[13]

I want to approach Gordimer through the ways she has tried to intertwine these private preoccupations with her political, more generally, public themes. Then I will turn to the pervasive change in her style brought about by the merging of these themes in *A Guest of Honour* and the following novels.

The four novels through *The Late Bourgeois World* serve as a kind of protracted apprenticeship in unifying Gordimer's private and public themes. Like many of her contemporaries, Gordimer's initial tack was through the subject of interracial sex, a private relationship prohibited by a series of "Immorality Acts" in South Africa. But she finally achieved this unification in two reciprocal ways. One was the gradual accretion of public resonances around her private themes. Her fiction shows, as the Stilwells realize at the close of *Occasion for Loving*, "the personal return inevitably to the social, the private to the political." This transformation develops in Gordimer's novels from a private theme—I would say her major one—which has not been widely apprehended: the liberation of children from unusually possessive mothers. This theme takes its impetus from the formative event of Gordimer's childhood, her mother's abrupt sequestering of young Nadine at the age of nine on the pretext of what the daughter later learned was a very minor heart ailment. In recent years Gordimer has referred to this event as "extraordinary," even "tragic," and in her *Paris Review* interview, she indicates how dominant her mother's influence became thereafter in the bald statement, "I simply lived her life."[14] In Chapter Two,

---

13 Ravenscroft, "A Writer in South Africa: Nadine Gordimer," 22, 23.
14 Jannika Hurwitt, "The Art of Fiction LXXVII: Nadine Gordimer," *Paris Review*, LXXXVIII (Summer, 1983), 90.

my concern is not how this private event is reflected in the novels but rather how Gordimer endows it with public associations. Again and again, she develops her public themes from this private kernel, but the progressively greater liberation of daughters from possessive mothers is most central in her three long novels with predominantly feminine perspectives. *The Lying Days, Occasion for Loving,* and *Burger's Daughter* form an extended *Bildungsroman* in which the daughters learn that complete liberation from private, familial restraints requires challenging the dominant political order as well. In the terms used repeatedly in these novels, the daughters learn that truly leaving "the mother's house" requires leaving "the house of the white race."

The other, complementary development was the increasing recognition of private concerns in novels that take their impetus from the public sphere. While a public focus is most pronounced in *A World of Strangers* and *The Late Bourgeois World,* which define "worlds," in all her early novels Gordimer sought, as she said in 1965, to provide "a background of self-knowledge" for her largely unexamined society. The centrality of this background in Gordimer's novels is evident, in brief, in the recurrent depiction of three representative landscapes, which reveal her changing perception of her world's shape. At the outset of her career, the Witwatersrand mining communities, the basis of white power since the 1890s, are the center of her world. The first of the three sections of *The Lying Days* is titled "The Mine," but by the novel's close and in the subsequent novels through the mid-sixties, Gordimer is increasingly preoccupied with a second "background," the city of Johannesburg. Initially, she portrays the city as a place where a more egalitarian multiracial society was being forged, but as the racial separation there actually increased through the sixties, Johannesburg came to represent for her what Dublin did for Joyce, "the centre of paralysis." With *A Guest of Honour* the vital center of Gordimer's world becomes the veld. Here, she finally focuses on the development of a resurgent African culture which had its roots partly in a mining system which antedated the one created by the white magnates. Her most recent conception of the history reflected in the South African landscape is set forth in the closing lines of "Something Out There." With the occupation of an ancient mine dump by black saboteurs, she writes, "a circle was closed: because before the gold-rush prospectors of the

1890s, centuries before time was measured, here, in such units, there was an ancient mine working out there, and metals precious to men were discovered, dug and smelted, for themselves, by black men."[15]

I am partly concerned with the way Gordimer uses her landscapes to convey a changing picture of South African history, from the colonial mine and city to the African veld and the ancient roots of African culture. But I am more interested in the radical transformation in the interaction between the private character and the public landscape which occurs during the course of her career. Chapter Three shows how Gordimer's novels of the fifties and sixties are a record of what she called the "outward signs" of her society. As not only the prominence of the three landscapes but Gordimer's recurrent use of the landscape as the source of her metaphors suggest, the signs in the physical world are the locus from which these novels, particularly the two named after "worlds," develop. The characters in these early novels remain observers of those signs. They fail to develop a linkage between their private lives and the public landscape. Indeed, their very means of perceiving the landscape in photographic terms, as a repository of signs discrete from themselves, prohibit engagement. By contrast, as I show in Chapter Four, Gordimer's later novels, which take their impetus from the landscape—*A Guest of Honour*, *The Conservationist*, and *July's People*—depict the growing interaction of observer and world observed. The characters, often unwillingly, become embedded in the landscapes they wish to hold "out there." The landscape the protagonist of *The Conservationist* inhabits is typical. "This place," he thinks, "absorbs everything, takes everything to itself and loses everything in itself."[16] He and the other later protagonists can no longer confront discrete public worlds outside themselves; their landscapes become "something inhabited in imagination."

These two reconciliations of the private and public are not, of course, worked out as separately and schematically as they are adumbrated here. The South African situation is depicted in the novels of daughters' liberations, and rejection of possessive parents is an important

15 Nadine Gordimer, *Something Out There* (New York, 1984), 203. Subsequent references in the text are to this edition.
16 Nadine Gordimer, *The Conservationist* (New York, 1974), 189. Subsequent references in the text are to this edition.

secondary concern in *The Conservationist* and *July's People*. But the concerns with which these two sets of novels originate and the emphases from novel to novel differ markedly. If Gordimer has, as she has commented on more than one occasion, written one novel throughout her life, she has done so through a twofold process, the private life accreting public overtones, the public situation inhabiting private conditions.

Chapters Two through Four describe how the resolution of private and public themes was effected; my concluding chapter examines how these thematic resolutions are reflected in the transformation of Gordimer's style, broadly defined, over the course of her career. (This view of style as a function of content is one that Gordimer herself has often used.) The changes in Gordimer's style are wide-ranging, but they center on the novelist's distance from her world. As Gordimer herself put it succinctly in the late seventies, "style is the point of view, or the point of view is style."[17] It is natural that point of view would preoccupy Gordimer, for apartheid is the most elaborate system yet devised to keep a society's groups so separate that presuming to look from the perspective of groups to which one does not belong—in Gordimer's case, these comprise over three-quarters of her countrymen—is all but impossible.

So it is appropriate as well that Gordimer would find it difficult to fashion an effective point of view—a style, as she said—in these conditions. She was increasingly frustrated as racial separation was more rigidly enforced during the fifties and sixties. Her response was to withdraw from her world, to examine it from an increasingly detached perspective. The detachment of Gordimer's early protagonists from their landscapes is but one of the many signs of the novelist's own detachment from the world she depicts. Gordimer was often, and justly, praised, in Campbell's phrase, for the "firm restraint" with which she recorded the South African situation in her early novels. But she was more often viewed as too cold and clinical. In the novels after 1970, this criticism ceases to be apt. Indeed, Gordimer's own repeated references to the need for the artist's involvement with her world reveal a very conscious attempt to alter her perspective. In 1976 she depicted

17 Hurwitt, "The Art of Fiction LXXVII," 111.

her intention well when she wrote that the "double process" of detachment and identification "makes a writer."[18] Beginning with *A Guest of Honour*, Gordimer's novels are informed by a tension between these two impulses; she at once observes her world from without and envisions it from within. Through this double process, the fruit of her long apprenticeship, Gordimer creates masterful forms and shapes despite the "low cultural rainfall" of her world.

II

It is necessary to state, even belabor, the obvious: Gordimer has a private life, and it counts in her fiction. In 1981, she herself allowed that she was often distressed when interviewed in America or England "because the interest there tends to be only in my life vis-à-vis the apartheid society in which I live. The other side—what happens to you as an individual, as a woman, as a writer—nobody is very interested in that." Her complaint was warranted, for she has been approached relentlessly as, in the title of a recent essay, a "Woman of Fiery Conviction." The recurrence of headings like "South Africa after Revolution" in reviews, of subtitles like "Strains in South African Liberalism" in articles suggests how often her novels have been approached as documents about the South African situation. While Gordimer has acknowledged again and again the impact of the highly politicized South African world on her work, she has adamantly refused to accept it as the sole or even dominant factor. In 1965, she characteristically referred to her concern for "'my' Dreyfus affair (bannings and detentions without trial) or 'my' war (against apartheid)," but she went on to affirm that hers was a "writer's morality," not one based on a cause. She continued, "I honestly don't think I've ever sacrificed the possible revelation of a private contradiction to make a political point." A decade later she used even stronger terms when she concluded in "A Writer's Freedom" that "all worthwhile writing . . . always comes from an individual vision, privately pursued."[19]

18 Nadine Gordimer, Introduction to *Nadine Gordimer: Selected Stories* (New York, 1976), 11.

19 Stephen Gray, "An Interview with Nadine Gordimer," *Contemporary Literature*, XXII (1981), 269; Ravenscroft, "A Writer in South Africa: Nadine Gordimer,"

Gordimer's individual vision has had a remarkably distinct, one could even say obsessive, focus: the liberation of children from overly possessive mothers. From the very start of her career, Gordimer focused on the problems of children claiming their maturity. Indeed, her first short story collection, *Face to Face* (1949), took its title from the well-known *I Corinthians* passage

> When I was a child, I spake as a child
> I understood as a child, I thought as a child:
> but when I became a man, I put away childish things.
> For now we see through a glass, darkly;
> But then face to face: now I know in part;
> But then shall I know even as also I am known.

The passage is an apt metaphor for the transformation Gordimer's children attempt and, with Rosa Burger, finally succeed in making. Theirs is a long fight to "put away childish things" by renouncing the parents who strive so regularly in Gordimer's fiction to prolong a childish dependence. Attaining full maturity in Gordimer's fictive world requires that they learn, in the words of the biblical passage, to trust also in what they know, as well as how they are known by others. But even this private liberation is incomplete, as *Occasion for Loving* so clearly demonstrates, unless it is infused with a political liberation from *herrenvolk* views. The metaphor of achieving religious understanding applies as well, for this double liberation is the closest thing to the attainment of religious knowledge in Gordimer's fiction. That Rosa Burger completes this process is the best explanation for Gordimer's acceptance of Conor Cruise O'Brien's claim that *Burger's Daughter* is "a profoundly religious book."[20]

Not until recently did the motivation for Gordimer's almost obsessive preoccupation with maternal domination become a matter of public record. Only after her mother's death did Gordimer speak publicly, in a 1976 interview with Melvyn Bragg, of the most significant event of her childhood:

22; Nadine Gordimer, "A Writer's Freedom," *English in Africa*, II (September, 1975), 49.

20 Susan Gardner, "'A Story for This Place and Time': An Interview with Nadine Gordimer about *Burger's Daughter*," *Kunapipi*, III (Fall, 1981), 111.

Bragg: When did you start writing?

Gordimer: When I was about nine. I wanted to be a dancer, and I went to dancing class like all little girls. I was an acrobatic dancer. Then I got some strange heart ailment, and had to stop dancing, and it was about then that I began to write. I time it to this illness, you see. Otherwise I wouldn't know so precisely.

Bragg: It's unusual to remember so clearly, and start so young.

Gordimer: Well, I had a very strange childhood, because from that age I really didn't go to school. This mysterious ailment is something I can talk about now, because my mother's dead; as long as she lived, I couldn't. I realized after I grew up that it was something to do with my mother's attitude towards me, that she fostered what was probably quite a simple passing thing and made a long-term illness out of it, in order to keep me at home, and to keep me with her.[21]

Gordimer's few earlier autobiographical fragments make no mention of this event. Even in the 1963 "Leaving School—II," which covers her life from roughly age eight to twenty-two, she sedulously avoids the incident. This essay seems strangely disjunct, for Gordimer discusses her early education, then jumps to her first "adult" story, written at the age of sixteen. Of the interim, she notes only that she attended school infrequently because she was a "bolter" and "various other factors had continued to make attendance sketchy." There is, in short, a hole in this account, the years between nine and sixteen when Gordimer's mother used the "illness" to keep her daughter at home. Even in her 1976 exchange with Bragg, Gordimer speaks almost disinterestedly of this incident, perhaps because her mother had so recently died.

Only in interviews conducted in 1979 and 1980, which appeared in the summer 1983 *Paris Review*, does Gordimer return at greater length, and with greater emotion, to her "very strange childhood." Dancing was, she says here, "my passion, from the age of about four to ten," and after the heart ailment was uncovered, "the dancing stopped like that, which was a terrible deprivation for me." Gordimer suggests that her unhappily married mother used her ailment to gain attention from the

21 Melvyn Bragg, "The Solitude of a White Writer," *Listener*, October 21, 1976, p. 514.

family doctor. But her mother's subsequent actions indicate her need to retain control over young Nadine, her youngest child, "the baby, the spoiled one, the darling." For, as Gordimer says,

> When I was eleven—I don't know how my mother did this—she took me out of school completely. For a year I had no education at all. But I read tremendously. And I retreated into myself. I became very introspective. She changed my whole character. Then she arranged for me to go to a tutor for three hours a day. She took me there at ten in the morning and picked me up at one. It was such a terrible loneliness—it's a terrible thing to do to a child. There I was, all on my own, doing my work; a glass of milk was brought to me by this woman—she was very nice but I had no contact with other children. I spent my whole life, from eleven to sixteen, with older people, with people of my mother's generation. She carted me around to tea parties—I simply lived her life. When she and my father went out at night to dinner she took me along . . . I got to the stage where I could really hardly talk to other children. I was a little old woman.

Here, the emotional effects of this treatment emerge clearly. What wasn't discussed in 1963, what was "very strange" in 1976, becomes "terrible." Gordimer returns to this word twice, as well she might: a "whole character" was changed; an "acrobatic dancer" became "a little old woman." On learning at the age of twenty how insignificant the ailment really was, Gordimer's resentment toward her mother was pronounced. A stage of resentment, she notes, "happens to many of us, but I *really* had reason." Gordimer eventually came to understand and pity her mother, and she has stated that "by the time she died in '76 we were reconciled. But it was an extraordinary story."[22]

The story had an extraordinary impact. Most generally, it led Gordimer to read and to write. The sequestered girl "read tremendously," a fact she returns to at length in the interview. And she began to write early; she had a substantial portfolio of juvenilia by the time of her first "adult" story at sixteen. More specifically, the extraordinary story prompted what has been a career-long concern with unusually intense attachments between parents and children. The compass of such bonds

22 Nadine Gordimer, "The Bolter and the Invincible Summer" (rpr. of "Leaving School—II," 1963), *Antaeus*, XLV/XLVI (Spring/Summer, 1982), 109; Hurwitt, "The Art of Fiction LXXVII," 89–90.

is wide, including the distortions in father-son relationships as well. In *The Conservationist*, the failed relationship of Mehring and his son seemed so crucial to Christopher Ricks, for example, that he titled his review "Fathers and Children." In such relationships, as in those with mothers, Gordimer is drawn to the most terrible conflicts. Indeed, she researched perhaps the most terrible of those publicized in modern times in order to write the 1984 "Letter from His Father," an imagined rejoinder from the grave by Kafka's father to his son's bitter "Letter to His Father."

But far more often Gordimer's concern is with mothers. It is no surprise, for instance, that Camus and Proust, writers with pronounced attachments to their mothers, are (with Forster) her major acknowledged influences. And Gordimer is often drawn to review works on this subject, such as Carson McCullers' *The Mortgaged Heart* in 1972 and Wole Soyinka's *Aké: The Years of Childhood* in 1982. In the latter, she begins with a reference to Proust which suggests her two major fictive uses of mother-daughter relationships: "It is not always possible to find the child again. Proust did, not only by reason of his genius but because the emotional force of the child-parent relationship was never exceeded by any other in his strange life."[23] Gordimer's fiction is replete with attempts to find the child, the young dancer she had been to the age of nine. Gordimer has commented that she likes to live alternative lives, and the one she was suddenly denied is the one she returns to again and again. There are cameo appreciations of young women dancers from Ann Boaz dancing in the streets in *Occasion for Loving* to the revolutionary Joy dancing away her tension and celebrating her fellowship with her soon-to-leave African compatriots in "Something Out There." In *July's People* this autobiographical element surfaces clearly. Maureen Smales—the rhyme with "Nadine" is suggestive—often thinks of her youthful ballet training in a mining community much like Gordimer's own, and when she fails to adapt to the new world into which she is suddenly thrust, she seeks solace at the novel's close by dancing into the bush. For all of these women dancing is a release, a celebration, a joy to be treasured.

Gordimer's second, and much more central, concern is the continu-

23 Nadine Gordimer, "The Child Is the Man," *New York Review of Books*, October 21, 1982, p. 3.

ing "emotional force of the child-parent relationship." It was never exceeded by Proust but, an essential distinction, it finally was by Gordimer. She did not simply define and recapture the emotional force of this past relationship, although Proust amply reveals the worth of doing so; she finally mitigated the emotional force of her mother's hold on her. The three novels in what I have called her extended *Bildungsroman* (and, less centrally, *The Late Bourgeois World* and *July's People*) are a record of progressively greater liberation—and finally freedom—from the mother's confining world. Gordimer's use of her difficult childhood is expressed well by Camus' generalization, when thinking of his Algerian childhood, that "each artist preserves deep down a unique spring which, throughout his life, feeds what he is and what he says."[24] Gordimer's "unique spring" is her protracted childhood. The child-parent relationship feeds her art in five novels, and in the process of writing them she liberates herself from what she feeds on. Through the treatment of mothers and daughters, Gordimer rises on stepping stones of her dead self to higher things.

Gordimer's "unique spring" has not been apprehended because specific correspondences with her upbringing are rare in her novels. To be sure, three of her heroines come from mining communities broadly similar to Gordimer's own, and Jessie Stilwell in *Occasion for Loving* recalls being sequestered because of a "heart ailment." But, on the whole, the autobiographical elements are hidden, not simply, as Gordimer has stated, out of a desire not to hurt her mother, but because Gordimer could not directly confront them herself. As she noted of her up-bringing in the *Paris Review* interviews held in 1979 and 1980, "It's really only in the last decade of my life that I've been able to face all this." Gordimer returns continually in her early novels to the background she wasn't "able to face" directly until the 1970s. It is, I will argue in Chapter Two, the presence of a highly charged, but submerged emotional affect which has made the earlier novels, *The Lying Days*, *Occasion for Loving*, and *The Late Bourgeois World*, seem perplexing, even flawed to many readers. In each novel, as in the 1963 "Leaving School—II" article, there is a hole at the center, namely the motivation for the animus of daughter toward mother.

24 Germaine Bree (ed.), *Camus: A Collection of Critical Essays* (Englewood Cliffs, N.J., 1962), 5.

The 1976 and 1979–1980 interviews explain the motivation; the fiction itself reveals the preoccupation, the suppression of children by domineering mothers. The most concerted treatment of this condition—and thus my major concern—occurs in the three long novels *The Lying Days, Occasion for Loving,* and *Burger's Daughter.* In them, the daughters are increasingly successful—Rosa Burger finally fully so—in their attempts to escape the mother and establish mature personalities of their own. The daughters all begin powerless, confined in protracted childhoods which resemble Gordimer's own. All are observers who, having remained subject to the mother's will, rarely express themselves. They are solitary; except for Rosa Burger, whose siblings are absent from that crucial age of nine, they are only children. None has a childhood friend. Most generally and most importantly, the daughters' lives are typified by stasis and disconnection because of their inability to break free from "the mother's house," as it is referred to in each of the novels. In *The Lying Days* Helen Shaw, who never leaves her mother's house, is conscious only of the symptoms—what she terms "the gaps" in her life—that afflict her. The later protagonists learn that their malaise derives from the failure to escape from the child's world of the present which the mother has prolonged. They seek what Jessie Stilwell calls "a coil from the past," from which commitments to the future—from marriage to political activity—can grow.

It is from these struggles for private lives informed by individual pasts and futures that Gordimer develops her political themes. Not surprisingly, these children initially fasten on the mother's house as the means for overcoming the racial division of their society. They seek to bring Africans inside. The failure of this gesture in all three novels serves as a public parallel to the dominant private theme; both the private life and political change must be fashioned outside the mother's house. Fittingly, it is black children outside who herald political change. In the lines of Gordimer's favorite poem in the 1950s—used repeatedly in *The Lying Days* and as the epigraph to *A World of Strangers*—she seeks "a black boy to announce to the gold-minded whites / the arrival of the reign of the ear of corn." And he finally does. The mournful and longing song of African children, a reflection of Helen Shaw's withdrawn state at the close of *The Lying Days*, becomes the rebellious shout of the 1976 Soweto children in the final pages of *Burger's Daughter.* Rosa Burger, acting to further their rebellion, ends in a women's prison where, she says, "My sense of sorority was clear." Her claiming a personal and political maturity outside the mother's house best explains why Gordimer has called *Burger's Daughter* her first "inspirational" novel.

July's People carries this development further; the novel opens with the mother's house already vacated, probably burning with the other suburban houses in a Johannesburg largely in control of African liberation forces. In the veld, where the Smales have sought refuge with the family of their former servant July, the children become part of an African family. Indeed, the entire Smales family is offered this prospect—they have all perforce become "July's Children," in an early title of the work—but only the Smales children can accept this new house. They are last seen receiving fishing string from July with cupped palms, the traditional African means of receiving a gift. Through this change in family, Gordimer depicts the political transformation of her world in the most emphatic terms. July, the former "boy," becomes the father, the Smales children part of his African house.

The children are more likely to flourish in July's house than in the mother's house they had known. In *The Black Interpreters*, her critical study of African fiction and black South African poetry, Gordimer contrasts the unhealthy Western mother-son relationship, as seen in the fiction of the "mother-fixated" Proust and the "terrible burden" of a mother's love in *Sons and Lovers*, with the relationship depicted in African fiction, in which "there is never any suggestion that mother love can be warping."[25] The Smales children, all younger than the age when Gordimer's development was fundamentally warped by her mother's terrible burden, are suddenly offered an inspiring alternative life. This inspiration is the harvest of Gordimer's long apprenticeship in the liberation of children.

III

Gordimer's "individual vision, privately pursued" was profoundly influenced, indeed for a time "conditioned," by her situation.

25 Nadine Gordimer, *The Black Interpreters: Notes on African Writing* (Johannesburg, 1973), 12. See Gordimer, "The Child Is the Man," 2–6.

She has acknowledged this influence with alacrity. She opens *The Black Interpreters* by emphasizing that African writers must treat certain themes, "the statements or questions arising from the nature of the society in which the writer finds himself immersed." Indeed, she continues, their choices are even more circumscribed, for "their themes chose *them*." In 1981 she applied this view to other post-colonial writers at the more fundamental level of subject when she commented that certain of V. S. Naipaul's novels struck her as unappealing because "I feel he 'chose' the subjects, whereas with *A House for Mr. Biswas*—a marvellous novel—and *A Bend in the River*, his subjects chose him."[26]

This preoccupation with the demands of the situation is not surprising, considering how intractable it has proved for her countrymen. Gordimer's predecessors and contemporaries had, even more recurrently than colonial writers elsewhere, forsaken the attempt to treat their situation by identifying with the metropolitan tradition. Usually they expatriated; "England at last!" wrote Olive Schreiner on arrival in England in 1888, and that journal entry would serve as an apt epigraph for a history of the South African novel for over a quarter century. Three of the four major novelists between 1920 and World War II—William Plomer, Laurens van der Post, and Pauline Smith—expatriated early in their careers. The output of this generation of writers had been small, a single novel of merit with a South African setting for Schreiner, Plomer, and Smith. The sole exception was Sarah Gertrude Millin, whose novels had been based on *herrenvolk* views throughout her long career.

Gordimer's task was even more difficult than her predecessors' for a number of reasons. Most obvious were the special problems caused by the political situation during which the "first birth" began. The swift application of apartheid by the Nationalist government after 1948 coincided with contrary trends—massive urbanization and decidedly more energetic activity by the African National Congress—which seemed to presage the development of a more egalitarian society. The clash of these forces prompted what was, surprisingly, the first large-scale treatment of race by South African writers. This subject "chose" most of the more adept postwar writers. Liberal whites like Paton, Jack Cope, Jacobson, and Gordimer found the situation attracting them to a

26 Gordimer, *The Black Interpreters*, 11; Riis, "Nadine Gordimer," 25.

particular theme as well, what Paton called "bridge building" between the disaffected whites and blacks. Partly because this theme was new, but even more because the Nationalists had substantially curtailed possibilities for building bridges by the mid-fifties, these writers found it difficult to infuse their works with a historical sense. As Plomer noted in 1956 during his return to South Africa for the Witwatersrand Conference, the nation was "rushing headlong into a future that won't be much like its past." In this atmosphere the novelists too often sim- ply reacted to discrete events of their situation. It was characteristic that the activities of a small group of white radical saboteurs in the mid-sixties prompted four novels from a small writing community: Gordimer's *The Late Bourgeois World* (1966), Mary Benson's *At the Still Point* (1969), C. J. Driver's *Elegy for a Revolutionary* (1970), and Jack Cope's *The Dawn Comes Twice* (1971). Plomer's complaint in 1956 that South African novels were "too documentary, too much like newspaper reports" clearly remained apposite over a decade later.[27]

The cause of the condition Plomer described was a source of consid- erable discussion by South African critics. To Arnold Abramowitz, also writing in 1956, it was "the paucity of prophets with a rational and coherent message relevant to the historical context of our times." In 1960, H. K. Girling noted the absence of an underlying vision in the works of Gordimer and Jacobson in particular. Gordimer's work, he found, demonstrated "a single truth about our lives in this country; that we go on observing and accumulating information, but never reach the stage of understanding what we have assembled." His earlier comments on Jacobson apply to Gordimer as well: "He observes and he records with an honesty almost frighteningly detached. Here is a mind without a contemplative apparatus. . . . When he decides that the con- clusions inherent in his observations have to be assimilated into the constructions of his novels, he will be faced with an aesthetic problem that he may take years to solve."[28]

27 William Plomer, "Several Revolutions," *Twentieth Century*, CLXV (1959), 396; Plomer, "South African Writers and English Readers," in Partridge (ed.), *Pro- ceedings of a Conference*, 67.

28 Arnold Abramowitz, "Nadine Gordimer and the Impertinent Reader," *Purple Renoster*, I (September, 1956), 14; H. K. Girling, "Provincial and Continental: Writers in South Africa," *English Studies in Africa*, III (September, 1960), 115; H. K. Girling, "Compassion and Detachment in the Novels of Dan Jacobson," *Purple Renoster*, II (Spring, 1957), 23.

The most penetrating assessment of South African literature through the mid-sixties came in a review of Jillian Becker's *The Keep* (1967). The reviewer concluded, "Up to the present, the serious fiction of South Africa has been overwhelmingly the fiction of fact. Its great tasks have been to represent the social and physical facts of this country, to record the 'feel' of life with these facts, and to illuminate the implications of our particular circumstances."[29] As Girling noted of Jacobson and Gordimer, the recording of the facts was often striking, yet the multitude of problems confronting the novelist made the integration of them into a unified vision difficult. Achieving such a vision, Bernard Bergonzi observed in a 1966 review of Jacobson's *The Beginners*, would show that being a South African, even more than an American, was a complex fate.

Gordimer has described this complex fate in terms of the two aspects of the South African situation which "chose" her. The more pervasive influence was what she succinctly termed "the politics of race." But the other, the relatively unexamined nature of her colonial society, influenced her more at the outset of her career. She has recalled that "Katherine Mansfield and Pauline Smith, although one was a New Zealander, confirmed for me that my own 'colonial' background had scarcely been looked at, let alone thought about, except as a source of adventure stories." This condition, Gordimer has argued, required a distinctive type of literature. The European may be "too stuffed with facts about himself," she wrote in 1961, but in South Africa "we are still at the stage of trying to read ourselves by outward signs." Her first two novels provide that reading for Johannesburg and its surrounding mining communities. In *The Lying Days* Helen Shaw emerges from the sheltered mine compound to describe "the sixty miles of Witwatersrand veld that was our Africa." In *A World of Strangers* Gordimer uses the perspective of the Englishman Toby Hood to juxtapose the privileged white world of the High House with the lively but impoverished African locations in Johannesburg.[30]

---

29 Libra [pseud.], "Beyond the Fiction of Fact," *Purple Renoster*, VII (Winter, 1967), 30.

30 Ravenscroft, "A Writer in South Africa: Nadine Gordimer," 23; Nadine Gordimer, "The Novel and the Nation in South Africa," *TLS*, August 11, 1961, p. 521.

While much admired, Gordimer's pictures of these worlds do not co-alesce into a coherent view of her society. As one South African critic complained in 1960, "To take High House and the location in contrast is eminently valuable. But it is not permissible merely to lay them side by side and say, 'There, look.'" Gordimer was criticized, in short, for providing only "the fiction of fact," slices of Johannesburg life which were not informed by a sense of a coherent society or a continuing history. It was not just that her worlds lacked shape; the depiction of them was so overriding a concern that her narratives were unacceptably attenuated. One commentator anticipated Es'kia Mphahlele's broad criticism in *The African Image* (1962) that character counted "for little or nothing" in the postwar South African novel when he complained that Toby Hood was "not a hero, directing, acting upon life, but a spectator who is acted upon." While *A World of Strangers* is the most pronounced example in Gordimer's fiction of the primacy of recording, the tendency simply to depict "outward signs" continues through *The Late Bourgeois World*. Gordimer's concern too often remains the description of "worlds" which her characters observe well but with which they do not engage.[31]

In the fifties this condition derived less from the constraints of the racial situation than one might expect. In fact, Gordimer's perception of her society's racial development was relatively sanguine; racial barriers, she felt, were being scaled through individual contact between blacks and whites. In a 1954 essay, for instance, after discussing the recent changes in the position of Africans, she concludes: "And here, too, are the whites in all stages of understanding this inevitable historical process—some afraid and resentful, some pretending it is not happening, a few trying to help it along less painfully. A sad, and confusing part of the world to grow up and live in. And yet exciting."[32] *The Lying Days* and *A World of Strangers* are predicated as much on the excitement as the sadness. Gordimer's belief in the power of what she called the "strange partnership" of blacks and whites underlies both of her novels in the fifties.

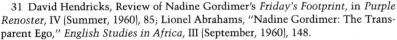

31 David Hendricks, Review of Nadine Gordimer's *Friday's Footprint*, in *Purple Renoster*, IV (Summer, 1960), 85; Lionel Abrahams, "Nadine Gordimer: The Transparent Ego," *English Studies in Africa*, III (September, 1960), 148.

32 Nadine Gordimer, "A South African Childhood: Allusions in a Landscape," *New Yorker*, October 16, 1954, p. 143.

The 1960 Sharpeville massacre, the prohibition of the right to even peaceful protest by blacks, and the banning of the most promising black writers were but some of the signs in the early sixties that the "historical process" Gordimer had foreseen was not "inevitable" after all. No alternative view of South African history emerges in the following two novels. In *Occasion for Loving* Jessie Stilwell's ironic surname epitomizes the change from the hopeful earlier novels. She is far from well, for she fails to discern a new code to replace her initial belief in personal relationships across the color bar. After witnessing the undermining of an interracial love affair by political restraints, Jessie concludes that "so long as the law remained unchanged, nothing could bring integrity to personal relationships." She ends silent and impotent, her white privilege imaged as "a silver spoon clamped between your jaws." *The Late Bourgeois World* raises the prospect that Liz Van Den Sandt will align herself with a new historical force, the illegal Pan African Congress. But that prospect is slight; most assessments (including, recently, Gordimer's own) are that Liz will remain within the dead white world. The liberal code that informed Gordimer's earlier work may be "late," but no alternative to it exists in her novels of the sixties.

The special conditions of her colonial society and the political situation left Gordimer at an impass by the mid-sixties. She had detailed her country's "outward signs" and provided the most trenchant analysis of the decline of liberalism in South African fiction. But she had been unable to show her characters engaging with the situation they confront; they record and they witness, but they do not act. Indeed, in her novels this inability to act was the major symptom of her society's diseased state. As Margaret Atwood has suggested, societies have their own peculiar psychological disorders; a voyeurism extending beyond sexual objects to the entire social world is the disorder Gordimer emphasizes in hers. As I shall discuss in Chapter Three, Gordimer's fiction centers increasingly on the ways her countrymen keep their fellows at bay by turning them into observed objects. This has remained her concern through to the present. Voyeurism is the primary theme in her 1984 collection *Something Out There*, as the title's reference to the photographer (the very model of the modern voyeur) capturing a world "out there" implies. By the mid-sixties, this separation of character from situation observed was the clearest reflection of the frustration of the novelist as humanist that Martin Staniland observed in *Occasion for Loving*.

Gordimer would overcome this frustration in *A Guest of Honour* and the novels that followed it through a threefold process. She found a comprehensive cultural view to replace the Forsterian "only connect," a means of reflecting this view in her novels, and a method of showing her characters acting in accord with it. She effected all three changes through her use of landscape, the most concrete embodiment of the South African situation. That the landscape should be the locus of this major change in her work seems almost inevitable in retrospect. Throughout her career Gordimer has referred repeatedly to her "strong sense of place." Indeed, her only substantial autobiographical fragment, published in 1954, is "A South African Childhood: Allusions in a Landscape." While the subtitle shows her preoccupation, it implies more perception of meaning in the landscape than was present in the early novels. In the fifties Gordimer functioned as a surveyor of the Witwatersrand and its garish metropolis of Johannesburg, a difficult undertaking in its own right since this locale was then almost uncharted in South African fiction. Although she was justly praised for her observation, the pictures of her world coalesce into no clear allusive pattern. As late as 1961, Gordimer herself acknowledged this condition in another allusion to her landscape. "It is unlikely," she wrote, "that while you are within the stockade thrown up around your mind by the situation about which you are reading, you will be aware that a common ground runs beneath your feet to beneath the stockade of another particular situation, and another."[33] There were, in short, only "particular situations" lacking connection in her world.

Only in the early seventies did Gordimer's landscapes come to reflect a coherent allusive pattern when she adopted an African view of her culture. It provided a cultural construct missing in her work since the Forsterian "only connect" proved inapplicable in the late fifties. Gordimer's essays in the sixties reveal a growing interest in African

33 Gordimer, "The Novel and the Nation in South Africa," 523. For two references to her "strong sense of place," see Stephen Gray, "Writing in South Africa: Nadine Gordimer Interviewed," *New Nation*, September, 1972, p. 2; and Hurwitt, "The Art of Fiction LXXVII," 85.

culture. By 1972 she could write that "It's a curious and essentially artificial combination of circumstances that have somehow made us skip the rest of Africa and link with Europe"; the following year in *The Black Interpreters* she claimed an "African-centered consciousness."[34]

This change in Gordimer's cultural views was reflected in a change of locale in her novels from the European city of Johannesburg to the veld, which had always remained African land informed by an African history. During the fifties Gordimer had seen a new society being molded in Johannesburg. As she wrote in 1955, "The push of something cruel as the push of birth is carrying the people of Africa toward Johannesburg." Only in 1965 did she begin to muse about the possibility of a novel centered on the veld, an area which had figured only peripherally in her early novels. Indeed, three of the four beginning with *A Guest of Honour* would take it as their primary setting. In these novels she emphasizes the "common ground," not the stockades, by viewing South Africa in the context of the larger developments affecting Africa. By the early seventies she could assert that "it's the superstructures that are different, but the underpinnings, the earth is the same."[35]

This African setting, affording a sense of a continuous history, allowed Gordimer for the first time to portray characters who are not merely observers. The impotence of Jessie Stilwell with the silver spoon clamped between her jaws yields to the commitment to action of James Bray in *A Guest of Honour*. Indeed, the interview in which Gordimer identifies this novel as the first with which she was satisfied ends with her assertion that Bray is most notable because "he had taken the risk, moral and physical, of *action*. Become radicalized, if you like. To risk, I think, is to live."[36]

The means by which Bray comes to act shows that Gordimer had conceived of a markedly different relationship of character and landscape than in the preceding novels. In a 1981 interview, she recalls driving in the family car as a child and "somehow *learning* the land-

---

34 Gray, "Writing in South Africa," 2; Gordimer, *The Black Interpreters*, 5.
35 Nadine Gordimer, "Johannesburg," 50; Gray, "Writing in South Africa," 2.
36 Stephen Gray, "Landmark in Fiction," 81.

scape around us."[37] Her following comment, "I could reproduce every detail of it," describes well the relationship of character and landscape in the novels before *A Guest of Honour*. In them, her characters observe the "outward signs" in a discrete landscape. Simply observing these signs, even in the African veld, finally proves insufficient by itself to provoke the kind of engagement Bray achieves. Jessie Stilwell can perceive "a continuity" which seemed to grow from "a legendary past" in the African kraals in the veld near the close of *Occasion for Loving*, but she still cannot act. Only when characters are able to "learn" the landscape through a radical identification with it can they overcome the frustrations of their situation and act. A succinct expression of this identification is the epigraph to *Burger's Daughter*: "I am a place in which something has occurred." As it implies, in the later novels the situation is no longer something "out there" in which cultural signs can be read, but rather a presence which permeates the characters. All of them are, in the phrase applied to Mehring in *The Conservationist*, defined by their "topography of activity." Whether they accept the coincidence of their actions and their topography, like Bray, or refuse to, like Mehring and Maureen Smales, their complex fates are fundamentally tied to the landscapes they inhabit. Their landscapes, concrete embodiments of their cultural situations, choose them.

IV

The resolution of Gordimer's private and public loyalties finds broader expression in another double process, which she described in the introduction to her *Selected Stories* in 1976: "Powers of observation heightened beyond the normal imply extraordinary disinvolvement; or rather the double process, excessive preoccupation and identification with the lives of others, and at the same time a monstrous detachment. . . . The tension between standing apart and being fully involved; that is what makes a writer." The passage reveals the un-

---

37 Edmund Morris, "A Visit with Nadine Gordimer," *New York Times Book Review*, June 7, 1981, p. 26.

usual strength of these forces within Gordimer; the detachment is "extraordinary," even "monstrous," the identification "excessive." But detachment has been the far more pervasive tendency in her approach to her world. Even when she makes the uncharacteristic gesture of discussing her own personal response to the South African situation in the 1982 lecture "Living in the Interregnum," she "stands apart." "I have to offer you myself," she writes, "as my most closely observed specimen from the interregnum." Gordimer's case may be particularly pronounced, but identification with the South African world, as she has noted, is difficult for all her countrymen. In a 1984 review she said she could fully understand J. M. Coetzee's "desire to hold himself clear of events and their daily, grubby, tragic consequences in which, like everyone else living in South Africa, he is up to the neck." That the impulse to "stand apart," to "hold clear," is so strong for the South African artist explains why Gordimer has emphasized the need for identification so often in recent years. Indeed, her favorite framework for describing artistic creation has become Proust's dictum that "style is the moment of identification between the writer and his subject."[38]

Often, as Gordimer has stated, this identification did not occur in her early work. Both public and private factors explain this failure as well as her increased capacity for identification with her subjects after 1970. The public aspect is easier to specify, and probably more significant. When the Forsterian "only connect" proved unworkable, Gordimer was forced to stand apart from a society with which she found no way of connecting. Only by claiming an African tradition as her own in the early seventies did she find a new code and a means for herself to identify with her world. The private aspect is necessarily more obscure. I suggest—and this must be a guess—that Gordimer's early detachment was caused in part by her "strange childhood" during which, she says in the *Paris Review* interview, she "retreated into" herself. The three novels about mothers and daughters through the

38 Gordimer, *Selected Stories*, 11; Nadine Gordimer, "Living in the Interregnum," *New York Review of Books*, January 20, 1983, p. 21; Nadine Gordimer, "The Idea of Gardening," *New York Review of Books*, January 2, 1984, p. 3. For references to Proust's dictum, see Riis, "Nadine Gordimer," 20; Nadine Gordimer, "Death, Love, and the Fruit Basket on Carmen Miranda's Head," *London Magazine*, XX (June, 1980), 93; Hurwitt, "The Art of Fiction LXXVII," 111.

mid-sixties were therapeutic; through them she reemerged by confronting the feelings of loneliness and resentment her mother's actions provoked. As Gordimer said in the interview, "At ten, you know, you don't argue with your mother—she tells you you're sick, you believe her." In these three novels Gordimer does argue, and in doing so she could, to overstate the case, "change her whole character" as her mother had done once before. Through these two transformations, the "cold and clinical" quality Paton noted in her early work is leavened by a sense of the novelist's greater engagement with her world. This increased identification allows Gordimer's later novels, beginning with *A Guest of Honour*, to be informed by the tension which makes the writer.

Gordimer's pronounced detachment from her world by the late fifties is especially striking because of the "excessive" identification with it at the very outset of her career when she still had faith in a Forsterian world. *The Lying Days* is notable, indeed has been criticized, for the closeness of the first-person narrator Helen Shaw to her world. Raymond Sands, for instance, finds the novel muddied by a "lyrical diffuseness," which is not grounded in an adequate depiction of the social order. Yet the major strength of the novel is the often tactile sense of a writer immersed in her world. In reference to "the great Lawrence bender" she went on early in her career, Gordimer recalls that "his sensuousness dilated my senses and brought up close to me rocks, petals, and the fur of animals around me." The feel of a world seen "up close" animates *The Lying Days* in a way Gordimer would not match again until *A Guest of Honour*.[39]

By the late fifties the countervailing tendency toward detachment had become not just the dominant but the single process in Gordimer's art. This development was first discussed in depth by Lionel Abrahams in his 1960 essay, "Nadine Gordimer: The Transparent Ego," still the most cogent analysis of her early fiction. After noting Gordimer's involvement with her world in the early fifties, he found that in *A World of Strangers*, "hers is essentially an illuminating intelligence: its central function is to render visible, or be rendered visible by, the physical,

39 Raymond Sands, "The South African Novel: Some Observations," *English Studies in Africa*, XIII (March, 1970), 98; Nadine Gordimer, "Notes of an Expropriator," *TLS*, June 4, 1964, p. 484.

social and emotional phenomena of experience. That, and not to impress upon the world the shape or even the lantern-slide shadow of the self." In his view, Gordimer's work in this period reveals the dominance of the situation ("the phenomena of experience"), the attenuation of the writer's self, which is a mere "transparent ego."[40]

Abrahams' is a sympathetic account which ends with his hope that Gordimer would find a means of integrating the tendencies toward involvement and detachment expressed separately at the beginning and the end of the fifties. Others, less charitable, employed mechanistic metaphors to convey the coldness of an author who stands too much apart from her world. While admiring the pictures of "the writer with the eye of the camera," as Gordimer was called on more than one occasion, these critics went on to complain that she simply recorded. In a 1970 retrospective of her work, for example, Don Maclennan found that a Gordimer narrator was a "highly sensitive transmitter/receiver" serving as "a frame of reference for her voracious observation of details." The most trenchant criticism in this line was Dennis Brutus' in an appraisal of *The Late Bourgeois World*, the novel in which Gordimer's detachment is most pronounced. He found that

> there is in her the kind of impersonality you find in a microscope. She does not herself react to feeling. In her books even the emotional relationships are forced, are conjured up, are synthetic. Though Nadine Gordimer would say that she is condemning South African society for being dehumanized, I would say that Nadine Gordimer, who is one of our most sensitive writers, is also the standing, the living example of how dehumanized South African society has become—that an artist like this lacks warmth, lacks feeling, but can observe with a detachment, with the coldness of a machine.

Maclennan and Brutus sense the writer's capacity for involvement when they note her "highly sensitive" narrators and label her "one of our most sensitive writers." But both find her even more "frighteningly detached" than H. K. Girling had a decade earlier.[41]

40 Abrahams, "Nadine Gordimer: The Transparent Ego," 148.

41 Don Maclennan, "The South African Short Story," *English Studies in Africa*, XIII (March, 1970), 115; Dennis Brutus, "Protest Against Apartheid," in Cosmo Pieterse and Donald Munro (eds.), *Protest and Conflict in African Literature* (London, 1969), 97.

Overstated as they may be, Brutus' comments remind us that Gordimer's detachment in the sixties had an emotional as well as an intellectual basis. In the fifties Forsterian liberalism had provided her with not just an historical vision but a rationale for personal engagement. In the comment I quoted at the beginning of this chapter, Gordimer said that she was drawn to the Forsterian code because it held "the possibility that in changed circumstances blacks would view us as fellow human beings." By the late fifties the circumstances changed in a way she had not foreseen. The multiracial writing community of whites and blacks in which she participated was dying as the townships like Sophiatown which nourished it were designated "white areas"; the multiracial African National Congress was banned. The government was intent on showing blacks that they didn't fit in. Gordimer drew a different conclusion: If blacks and whites were forced into separate worlds, it would be the whites who would be alienated. To the question posed by the title in her 1959 essay "Where Do Whites Fit In?" Gordimer answered, only as observers, who if they are to fit in at all must do so in accordance with decisions made by Africans. Gordimer asserts here that African history is primary, but she cannot explain what role a white like herself can play in it. For over a decade she would search for this role. Her discussion of Yeats in a 1964 essay is but one of many in the sixties which show her emphasizing the benefits of the unified historical and personal vision she sought: "More than any poet I have read, he has been able to use in the intensely private and personal terms of his poetic vision, the (from the poet's point of view) curiously abstract historical events of which he was a part, and even the personalities involved—the stuff of newspapers and political platforms taken into poetry."[42] Yeats was able to incorporate "the stuff of newspapers and political platforms" into his poetry because he had an almost perversely detailed vision of an historical pattern corresponding to his conception of personality. Not surprisingly, it took Gordimer nearly a decade to identify with a new historical vision antithetical to her early perception of South African history and based on a culture not her own.

Two developments, in particular, fostered her search for a place in an African culture. On the one hand, the silencing of the black writing

42 Gordimer, "Notes of an Expropriator," 484.

community in the early sixties through banning orders led her to cease thinking in terms of a national literature, as she was still doing, for example, in the 1961 essay "The Novel and the Nation in South Africa." On the other, she discovered—and quickly became conversant with—the growing body of African literature in English and French. Reviewing Claude Wauthier's *The Literature and Thought of Modern Africa* in 1967, she found that the work filled "the gaps in our ignorance," and in the following years her essays indicate a particular interest in the works of the Afro-Caribbean intellectuals Frantz Fanon and Aimé Césaire, who had reformulated the colonial experience in a black perspective. In "Censorship and the Primary Homeland" (1970), Gordimer links these two developments affecting her thought:

> The success of censorship must be seen in the completeness with which we are cut off not just from the few books dealing with our own ingrown society but also from the books which formulate the thinking that is going on all around us, in particular on this continent to which we stake our lives on belonging. From Fanon to Mazrui—yes, you may well ask who they are—important writers are merely names to us.

Through such considerations Gordimer came to claim a tradition defined in African rather than South African or European terms. By 1966 she was lecturing on African fiction and, somewhat later, on the "new black poetry" of South Africa, both of which she discussed with authority in a series of articles subsequently collected in *The Black Interpreters*. At the outset of this study she speaks of the importance of an "African-centered consciousness" and provides an unorthodox definition of African literature which encompasses work, including her own, by those "of whatever skin color who share with Africans the experience of having been shaped, mentally and spiritually, by Africa rather than anywhere else in the world." Certainly her own later work is shaped by her African experience. The obvious affinity of *A Guest of Honour* is with the group of works centering on tensions in postcolonial Africa, such as Chinua Achebe's *A Man of the People* and Ayi Kwei Armah's *The Beautyful Ones Are Not Yet Born*, rather than with contemporary South African or European novels. *The Conservationist* is, in effect, two works, excerpts from Zulu religious rituals counterpointing the European-style narrative. The caricaturist David Levine provided an apt image of Gordimer's stance in her later novels as a whole when he portrayed her as an African prophetess in a *doek* for the review of *July's People* in the *New York Review of Books*. Gordimer had indeed claimed an African perspective which had brought her back into her world. She had found her way to fit in.[43]

The change that this development produced in Gordimer's fiction is put in the simplest terms by Alan Paton in his 1981 review of *July's People*: "Miss Gordimer has acquired a massive reputation for her powers of observation of the human species. But her sterner critics have said that her observation is too cold and clinical. I have thought so myself. But I do not think that of *July's People*." He finds it and *Burger's Daughter* her novels with the "greatest warmth" and therefore her best. So pronounced is Gordimer's change in attitude, which Paton impressionistically describes, that it is reflected in ways extending from titles, epigraphs, and point of view to treatment of characters and groups, structure, and endings. These are but some of the means by which two different senses of Gordimer's relation to her fictive world emerge: in the early novels, of a writer not only coolly observing but imposing meaning and form from without; in the later, of her much more often depicting the flux of her world from the perspective of one immersed in it. Gordimer herself described this transformation well in the 1968 *Kenyon Review* "Short Story Symposium" when she rejected the French "laboratory novel" for the impulse she found dominant in Germany and America, "a splendid abandon in making a virtue of the vice of the novel's inherent clumsiness by stuffing it not with nineteenth-century horsehair narrative but twentieth-century anecdotal-analytic foam." Gordimer's own development reveals the reduction of a detached, even clinical treatment of her material and the growth of a "splendid abandon" in novels with her own stuffing, "the stuff of newspapers and political platforms."[44]

Gordimer's growing identification with her fictive world is most broadly revealed in the structure of the novels. *The Lying Days* and

43 Nadine Gordimer, "Censorship and the Primary Homeland," *Reality*, I (1970), 82; Gordimer, *The Black Interpreters*, 4.

44 Alan Paton, "Gordimer's South Africa," *Saturday Review*, May, 1981, p. 67; Nadine Gordimer, "The International Symposium on the Short Story: South Africa," *Kenyon Review*, XXX (1968), 458.

A World of Strangers are novels of education in which the protagonists progress through discrete stages, often summarized by authorial spokesmen, to greater understanding of their worlds. Indeed, Gordimer's favorite metaphors in the fifties centered on emergence from a sheltered, uninformed existence to successively higher levels of perception. She told Lionel Abrahams in the late fifties that "someone growing up in a country like this had a whole series of cocoons to break out of," and she elsewhere described her early life as "my clumsy battle to chip my way out of shell after shell of ready-made concept."[45] Such battles seem "clumsy" only at the outset of the early novels; as they develop, there is a progressively greater sense of order until they end, all ambiguity spent, in a summary of themes. Helen Shaw assesses her education from the detached perspective of a Durban balcony; Toby Hood neatly objectifies the alternatives of the two worlds of strangers in newspaper clippings from the morning paper. A similar effect is created by the novels of the sixties. Reviewers referred with regularity, and with justification, to the "silver spoon" passage in *Occasion for Loving* as the summary of the novel's theme. Even the attempt at an open-ended conclusion to *The Late Bourgeois World* creates the same effect. Liz Van Den Sandt lies in bed, her heart ticking "afraid, alive, afraid, alive" as she thinks of the prospect of aiding the illegal Pan African Congress. The stark contrast of choices is not only foregrounded but the answer clear, for Liz has been throughout a creature of her "late" world.

Both of these novels attempt, unsuccessfully, to create the sense of a disjunct world. Each ends in "a gap" filled with "silence," favorite Gordimer terms for describing the discontinuities of her society in the seventies. In the sixties, they are very orderly gaps and very self-conscious silences, as is Bray's final thought, "I've been interrupted, then—," at his death in *A Guest of Honour*. Only with *The Conservationist* do the novels create a sense of immersion in the South African world through mirroring its discontinuities, rather than stating or displaying them in a highly formal way. Both *The Conservationist* and *July's People* are composed of about forty fragments, between which transitions are almost always lacking. As Gordimer said of the conser-

45 Abrahams, "Nadine Gordimer: The Transparent Ego," 150; Gordimer, "Leaving School—II," 64.

vationist Mehring in a 1980 interview, "it was absolutely necessary to let him reveal himself, through the gaps, through the slightest allusions."[46] And instead of trying to define the pervasive alienation of her society through discussion of its codes, she allows her characters to confront the pervasive silence—they find nothing on the other end of telephones, no broadcasts on radios—which typifies her world. The most marked example of Gordimer's identification with her world comes in *Burger's Daughter*, which, as she has commented, was "interrupted" by the 1976 Soweto student revolt. It interrupts the novel abruptly, in the form of a handbill actually used by the revolting students, which is inserted without comment into the narrative. This is the stuff of newspapers taken, very concretely, into fiction.

The changes in the perspectives employed in the later novels are various, but two best reveal Gordimer's increased identification with her world. First, using a multiple-perspective third-person narration in all the novels from *A Guest of Honour* on, she develops a broader range of viewpoints. Most notable is the authority with which she portrays a more diverse black society—Africans and Indians in *The Conservationist*, rural Africans in *A Guest of Honour* and *July's People*. She also reveals no less of an ability to identify with a pig-iron merchant like Mehring in *The Conservationist* than with a man like Bray in the process of committing himself, at the risk of his life, to social change. A second sign of Gordimer's identification with her subjects is the vitality of the central figures whose perspectives are most often used. Bray, a huge man with an abundance of energy, perception, and courage, can aptly be described as Gordimer's first hero. Mehring manifests a comparable vitality. Much of it is sexual, but he also has remarkable professional abilities and a true sensitivity to the land he tries to conserve. Like their male counterparts in the later novels, the Communist Rosa Burger and the bourgeois Maureen Smales are intense and active, by contrast with the detached, cerebral, and finally enervated Toby Hood, Jessie Stilwell, and Liz Van Den Sandt. Gordimer's later protagonists move within their own orbits; they tell their own stories, rather than observe those of others. *Burger's Daughter*, for instance, is structured around Rosa's telling of her story to others—a lover, her par-

---

46 Gray, "An Interview with Nadine Gordimer," 266.

ents, her father's first wife. Even Rosa, so timid at the novel's outset, is concerned with *her* story, not those of others as are Jessie Stilwell and Liz Van Den Sandt.

More detailed treatment is warranted for the restraints to identification posed by the racial situation which makes South African writing its own category. Throughout her career Gordimer has acknowledged what she terms the "unscalable barriers" presented by her "deeply and calculatedly compartmentalized society." As she said in 1962, after a consideration of the major South African novels focusing on the country's racial barriers, "it still is *the* question." It was not until a decade later that Gordimer would find the answer by ceasing to seek a connection between those two separate societies, but rather by identifying with a resurgent African culture. As reviewers of *July's People* noted, Gordimer still steps back to comment on her society in the later novels, but this impulse is easily balanced by her identification with the African culture she has claimed as her own. *A Guest of Honour* and the novels that follow illustrate well Georg Lukács' statement that great writing depends on "an objective and, at the same time, living involvement with the major tendencies of social development."[47]

Most basically, Gordimer's radically divided society posed the problem of portraying the world of the over three-fourths of her countrymen whose lives were largely inaccessible to her. In the first two decades of her career she made little progress in doing so. The novels through *The Late Bourgeois World* have a limited range of African characters—all are urban Africans who have had unusually broad contact with the white world—and they are almost always seen moving in white society. There are only occasional glimpses of the world of shebeens (location houses where parties are held and illicit liquor served), even fewer of African political discussions. Moreover, those few African characters—only five have more than cameo roles in the early novels—are almost always viewed from the perspective of the white protagonists. As Gordimer stated in 1961, white South African writers had "created our own sense of sin and our own form of tragedy."[48] In the early novels not only the sin but the tragedy is white. We mourn for

47 Gordimer, "The Novel and the Nation in South Africa," 521; Georg Lukács, *The Historical Novel*, trans. Hannah and Stanley Mitchell (Boston, 1962), 275.
48 Gordimer, "The Novel and the Nation in South Africa," 521.

Toby Hood's loss of an African friend and for Jessie Stilwell's frustration at not being able to maintain her bond with Gideon Shibalo because of the country's racial codes. These tragedies are connected with Africans; they are real and they do count. But they are white tragedies which do little to illuminate that other, African world.

Gordimer's greater involvement with this world is immediately apparent in the novels beginning with *A Guest of Honour*. Indeed, so strongly is the focus shifted to Africans that this novel almost seems to be Gordimer's demonstration of her ability to present a various African world. In an African state newly freed from British rule, she portrays easily a score of well-developed African characters, most of whom are from the rural African society which had not figured in her earlier works. James Bray may be the protagonist of the novel, but as his title "guest of honour" indicates, he inhabits an African world. This novel is, of course, a special case, for it does not have a South African setting; it is a world freed from the "unscalable limitations" of Gordimer's separated society. No such qualification is required for the following three novels. Most notably in *The Conservationist* and *July's People*, Gordimer creates the sense of a various African world by treating African society in separate sections from those centering on the white protagonists. Through accepting that African society is separate—by accepting those "unscalable limitations"—she brings it into the world of her novels for the first time. It is as if she could finally portray in her work the widely quoted dictum from Plomer's *Turbott Wolfe*—that the "African problem" is not a problem but a solution.

Gordimer's achievement in these later novels was made possible by a quality which Paul Bailey described well in a 1976 retrospective review of her work: "She has fought her way into the front rank of contemporary writers by taking risks, and the flaws in her early fiction were a necessary factor in that daunting development."[49] Nowhere are the risks more apparent, the results more striking, than in Gordimer's portrayal of Africans. One risk was the radical change in the social world of her novels that a broader picture of Africans mandated. Until the mid-sixties Gordimer's world had been a rather narrow segment of Johannesburg society. As late as 1965, she had claimed not to know

49 Paul Bailey, "Unquiet Graves," *TLS*, July 9, 1976, p. 841.

enough about "country people" to portray them, but from *A Guest of Honour* on, their culture—the repository of traditional African values—became the primary one in her work. Moreover, the desire to present an African culture in the following South African novels required Gordimer's renunciation of her traditional narrative style for the "splendid abandon" which was manifested so abruptly in *The Conservationist*.

Indeed, Gordimer's risk in portraying a fuller African world prompted the most pervasive change in her later novels, her movement from a satiric to an inspirational approach to her material. Commentators on Gordimer's early fiction like Anthony Woodward and Robert F. Haugh recurrently describe her as a satirist who observes the foibles of her society with a cool, dispassionate eye. Others, like David Hendricks, imply the same detachment when they see irony as her major tool. Satire and irony, Gordimer herself has noted, were essential in her early work, but she has recently questioned their usefulness in the current conditions of South African society. In the 1980 "New Forms of Strategy—No Change of Heart," she asserted that "so effective a weapon though satire may be, as a social probe in certain historical circumstances or stages," it cannot serve in her world. She indicated what can when she added, "There is no ignoring the fact that the inspirational is a dynamic of our literature at present." The clearest indication of the role of inspiration and irony in Gordimer's later fiction is the description of *Burger's Daughter* she gave to Susan Gardner in 1980:

> My method has so often been irony. I find irony very attractive in other writers, and I find life full of irony, my own life and everybody else's; somehow one of the secret locks of the personality lies in what is ironic in us. In *Burger's Daughter* irony is like a kind of corrective, a rein. It comes from Rosa, she has that in her confrontation with Clare (a contemporary of hers, also the daughter of Communist parents), but very often the inspirational took over. Because there are things—it comes from what is here, if you look at what happened in Soweto in '76 and what has happened again now (school and meat workers' boycotts; municipal workers' strikes in Johannesburg), there's so much inspiration in it: a reaching out, a bursting forth . . . the very recklessness comes from that.

The ironic impulse continues, but only as a "corrective, a rein," to that inspirational impulse which "took over" in Gordimer's fiction in the seventies. This impulse is reflected in a more exuberant style, such as Gordimer's own "bursting forth" at the end of this passage.[50]

The inspirational impulse prompted by Gordimer's identification with a resurgent African culture has rarely been apprehended. To the contrary, "bleak vision" is a term applied to her later fiction as often as it is to V. S. Naipaul's. A typical response is Jane Kramer's in a December 1982 *New York Review of Books* article on recent novels by André Brink and J. M. Coetzee. Kramer finds that contemporary white South African fiction is

> about decoding the future—as if "black" were a secret text that might explain to the white man the annihilation of his identity and give that annihilation meaning. "It's about suffering. How to send suffering. And it ends in suffering," Rosa Burger says in Nadine Gordimer's *Burger's Daughter*. The Afrikaner Mehring, in Gordimer's *The Conservationist*, runs to an unknown ending on a Johannesburg mine dump. Maureen Smales, the white housewife in *July's People*, runs toward the noise of an unseen helicopter. The endings in Gordimer's novels seem to say that there can be no "ending" to a South African story anymore, no meaning, no decoding, no relief for ordinary liberal people like Maureen Smales— only flight and defection.[51]

This approach goes wrong from the opening assumption: "decoding," whether in its traditional or contemporary critical sense, assumes a detachment from one's subject. What she and others who find Gordimer's later novels so bleak miss is that Gordimer's identification is not only—or even primarily—with the white protagonists (although

---

50 Haugh, *Nadine Gordimer*, 44; Anthony Woodward, "Nadine Gordimer," *Theoria*, XVI (1961), 5; Hendricks, Review of *Friday's Footprint*, 85–87; Nadine Gordimer, "New Forms of Strategy—No Change of Heart," *Critical Arts*, I (June, 1980), 32; Gardner, "'A Story for This Place and Time,'" 110.

51 Jane Kramer, "In the Garrison," *New York Review of Books*, December 2, 1982, p. 10. Kramer's view is widely held. Cf. Rowland Smith, "Living for the Future: Nadine Gordimer's *Burger's Daughter*," *World Literature Written in English*, XIX (1980), 172; Tamar Jacoby, "Harsh and Unforgiving Vision," *Nation*, June 6, 1981, p. 706.

even Rosa's story and the adaptation of the Smales children to July's world reveal that annihilation isn't a prospect for whites in general). For "black" is not "a secret text" which can't be decoded; it is an answer revealed in the novels, most clearly in the very endings Kramer cites: in Mehring's renunciation of his farm, the African laborers' claiming of it at the close; in Rosa's identification with the struggle of which those laborers are a part; in the continuing vitality of July's village during the interregnum. For Gordimer, these black actions do count. Indeed, her own 1984 review of Coetzee's *The Life and Times of Michael K* reads like a reply to Kramer's claims. Gordimer's major criticism is that Coetzee's novel "denies the energy of will to resist evil. That *this* superb energy exists with indefatigable and undefeatable persistence among the black people of South Africa—Michael K's people— is made evident, yes, heroically, every grinding day. It is not present in the novel."[52] It is "*this* superb energy" which makes "black" an answer in Gordimer's novels. There is as yet "no ending," but the "indefatigable and undefeatable persistence" of blacks suggests what the ending will be. And Gordimer clearly assumes that ending will come; the "interregnum," her term for the period in which her later novels are set, is defined by a future as well as a past order. The sense of a continuing history is, in fact, the most striking achievement of these later novels. It was widely acknowledged in *A Guest of Honour*, which was variously described as "the novel as history" or occurring at "the point where fiction and history overlap." That Gordimer has continued to pursue this history in her fiction is most succinctly indicated by her claiming of the tradition of "critical realism," which she defined in 1973 as literature in which "the human condition is understood dynamically, in an historical perspective."[53] In her later novels, Gordimer does not prophesy "annihilation"; she envisions the dynamic process of a continuing African history from within its current interregnum.

This historical sense is the product of Gordimer's search over three decades for the meeting of writer and situation of which Proust spoke. At the outset of her career, she attempted to impose order on her world through the application of a foreign value system, the Forsterian "only

52 Gordimer, "The Idea of Gardening," 3.
53 Gordimer, *The Black Interpreters*, 32. She paraphrases Georg Lukács' formulation.

connect." With the failure of black and white to connect, Gordimer, increasingly through *The Late Bourgeois World*, removed herself from her situation, using formal ordering devices to give her world shape in the absence of a vision. She became, in fact, very much what her severest critics perceived her to be: a disaffected lady overlooking Johannesburg from the Olympian detachment of her Parktown home. She came down into her world in the late sixties after fashioning an "African-centered consciousness" which allowed her to "fit in." If this provided her with a sense of history which has been so lacking in South African literature, it was a different kind than her Forsterian construct. It was, in short, a new consciousness, not a specific idea of how her world would develop. Gordimer has lived too long in South Africa to expect her world to change in an orderly or easily predictable way. She has become, finally, not so much Levine's African prophetess as an African writer who envisions a new order during an interregnum, a world in flux. In 1981, speaking of the failure of black and white to connect, Gordimer acknowledged that a coherent world cannot yet be created by the South African artist:

> It is the artist's nature to want to transform the world. The revolutionary sense, in artistic terms, is the sense of totality, the conception of a "whole" world, where theory and action meet in the imagination. Whether this "whole" world is in the place where black and white culture might become something other, wanted by both black and white, is a question neither I, nor anyone else in South Africa, can answer; only pursue.[54]

The "revolutionary sense," the desire "to transform the world," remains, but the writer has accepted the uncertainties of a situation in which black and white cultures only "might become something other" than the separated entities they now are. These uncertainties are reflected in the "splendid abandon" of Gordimer's mature style. From attempting to impose order on the South African situation from without to envisioning through its glass darkly—from "only connect" to "only pursue": in this transformation lies the best explanation of why there is still no epitaph in sight.

54 Nadine Gordimer, "Apprentices of Freedom," *In These Times,* January 27–February 2, 1982, p. 22.

2

Leaving the Mother's House: *The Lying Days, Occasion for Loving,* and *Burger's Daughter*

I

In the 1972 review "A Private Apprenticeship," Gordimer focused on Carson McCullers' obsessive concern with adolescence in her journals and novels. Gordimer's own "private apprenticeship" shows a preoccupation as great as her subject's; Gordimer can accurately be termed, to vary a phrase she applied to McCullers, "the high priestess of childhood." As Gordimer told Lionel Abrahams in the late fifties, "the ways of seeing we acquire in our youth remain with us always."[1] In her fiction those ways of seeing are determined, above all else, by unusually possessive mothers. Gordimer's "strange childhood" provides a clear motivation for this focus, yet her novels by themselves reveal her obsessive concern with domineering mothers, the resulting resentment and sense of powerlessness of their children. Gordimer deals with such relationships most concertedly in *The Lying Days, Occasion for Loving,* and *Burger's Daughter,* which form an extended *Bildungsroman* centering on the attempts of daughters to break free of the mother's power and establish lives of their own.[2] But with the exception of *A World of Strangers,* whose protagonist can scarcely be

---

1 Abrahams, "Nadine Gordimer: The Transparent Ego," 150.
2 *The Lying Days* (1953; rpr. London, 1978); *Occasion for Loving* (1963; rpr. London, 1978); *Burger's Daughter* (New York, 1979). Subsequent references in the text are to the editions from the 1970s.

said to have a private life, all of Gordimer's novels show her returning, again and again, to such strange childhoods as her own.

Mothers in Gordimer's novels respond with remarkable persistence in one of two ways to their children: by attempting to prolong the child's dependence or, conversely, if they acknowledge this desire in themselves, by renouncing the care of the child. The mother most conscious of this dynamic is Liz Van Den Sandt in *The Late Bourgeois World*. She decides to bring her son Bobo a treat when visiting his school at the novel's outset, for she knows that

> It is my way of trying to make up for sending him to that place— the school. And yet I had to do it; I have to cover up my reasons by letting it be taken for granted that I want him out of the way. For the truth is that I would hold on to Bobo, if I let myself. I could keep him clamped to my belly like one of those female baboons who carry their young clinging beneath their bodies. And I would never let go.[3]

This is not just a chance metaphor, provoked by the strain of her ex-husband's suicide the previous day, for later in the novel Liz busies herself with an icon of her powerful possessive urge—"the head of the baboon mascot I brought back for Bobo from Livingston" (p. 92). Liz does resist the desire to clamp on to her son, but only through exiling him to a school she describes as being "like a prison."

Both the urge to possess and its sublimated reflection to reject completely are manifested again and again by mothers in Gordimer's novels. In *The Lying Days* Mrs. Shaw's success in maintaining control over her daughter Helen is reflected in the action which gives the narrative its shape, Helen's compulsion to return repeatedly to her mother's house. In *Occasion for Loving*, Jessie Stilwell struggles to keep from acting like "her mother [who] had sucked from her the delicious nectar she had never known she had" by using the pretext of a heart condition to prolong Jessie's dependence (p.45). Mrs. Burger usurps Rosa's early years by using her relentlessly in the service of her political goals; Rosa is even persuaded to feign engagement to a political pris-

---

3 *The Late Bourgeois World* (New York, 1966), 11. Subsequent references in the text are to this edition.

oner in order to smuggle messages into prison. The reverse process, denial of the child, figures recurrently as well. Like Liz Van Den Sandt, Jessie Stilwell attempts to escape her son Morgan through shunting him off to a boarding school, and during his vacations she eagerly awaits the day of his return there. Rebecca Edwards, James Bray's lover in *A Guest of Honour*, has left her children in the care of her husband; and when Maureen Smales in *July's People* is confined in the same hut with her children, it is striking how little they figure in her thoughts.

Over the course of Gordimer's career, the mothers do reveal—as Liz's very awareness of the problem indicates—an increasing desire to overcome this possessiveness. Jessie Stilwell will finally show the impulse to accept Morgan's nascent manhood; Liz wants to free Bobo from her suburban world, which she knows is destructive. When Rebecca Edwards journeys alone to London after Bray's death, she fleetingly conceives of a new life for herself through taking her children back. But these are impulses which find no expression in action. It is finally outside the family that a kind of restitution is actually made for the wounds inflicted by mothers on children. Rosa Burger, the only Gordimer heroine except for the young Helen Shaw who chooses not to become a mother, exhibits the most selfless motherly instinct of all Gordimer's characters by working in a hospital for children. Her treating children, "whom it was her work to put together again if that were possible," is a telling contrast with Liz's putting together of the image of her desire for Bobo's continued dependence (p. 345).

In the world of Gordimer's later novels it is possible, as Rosa hopes, to put children back together. Indeed, only children, whose "ways of seeing" are still being formed, are capable of regeneration. By *Burger's Daughter*, this hope lies in identification with an African world in which children are granted a life of their own through the African family, in which, as Gordimer wrote in *The Black Interpreters*, "there is never any suggestion that mother love can become warping." The regeneration of the white children with whom Gordimer is concerned occurs through a double process over the course of her career. One of its parts is the gradual loss of importance, and finally the eradication, of the white house in which the mother's power was supreme. Where the white house serves as the focal point in *The Lying Days* and *Occasion for Loving*, by *The Late Bourgeois World* it has diminished to an apartment. In the following novels it is absent: Rebecca Edwards has a house in Kenya, but it is never seen in the novel; the Burger house has been sold before *Burger's Daughter* begins; the Smales house has been abandoned in a war-torn Johannesburg before the start of *July's People*. Only in the later novels, however, is there any replacement for this white house. It is prefigured in such small ways as the maternal feeling of the African nurse Edna Tlume in *A Guest of Honour*, who expresses a purer grief for the departure of the Edwards children than does their own mother, and in the greater rapport of the conservationist's son Terry with the African farm laborers than with his own father. It is claimed by Rosa Burger through her identification with the 1976 black children's revolt, which leads to her "sense of sorority" in a multiracial prison. It is manifested, unmistakably, in the integration of the Smales children into July's house.

Gordimer's later novels finally reveal a complete unification of her private theme of children gaining freedom from possessive mothers and her public theme of Africans taking control of the South African house. In her earlier novels she had conceived of these processes as separate, as she expressed it to John Barkham in 1963: "First, you know, you leave your mother's house, and later you leave the house of the white race."[4] In the later novels these developments merge. For Rosa Burger and the Smales children, these two leave takings are one.

II

The emotional center of *The Lying Days* is a child's desire but inability to leave home. Helen Shaw's first-person account details her forays away from her parents' home on the Atherton Mine outside Johannesburg, each one introducing her to broader worlds of sexual and political experience than the regimented colonial society of the mine affords. She spends a summer vacation on the East Coast near Durban with some family friends, Mrs. Koch and her son Ludi; she moves to Johannesburg where she lives with a liberal couple, the Mar-

4 John Barkham, "South Africa: Perplexities, Brutalities, Absurdities," *Saturday Review*, January 12, 1963, p. 63.

cuses; and she finally has a long affair with Paul Clark, a radical social worker in the Johannesburg locations. But despite the convincingly dreary portraits of the mine life she wishes to reject, Helen is never quite able to forsake her childhood home. She feels compelled to return periodically to appraise her mother of her unorthodox sexual behavior and political beliefs, and when her mother finally banishes Helen from the house, she is left paralyzed, unable to envision a life of her own. The twenty-four-year-old Helen we see about to embark for England at the novel's close remains as much in her mother's thrall as the nine-year-old girl at the novel's outset.

The heroine herself would disagree quite emphatically with this account of her story, for she ends by making a cheery declaration of freedom from her parents and their colonial world as she waits for the boat to England. In what can accurately be termed a summation of her experience in the novel, she claims not to be running away any more—from her mother, from the South African world, from the responsibilities of adulthood. With few exceptions, critics of the novel have accepted her claim to independence and maturity. Michael Wade finds that "Helen realizes, at last, the three things that separate mature from immature perception of reality"; Robert F. Haugh concludes that the song of African children she hears at the close is an "image of promise and hope"; and Kolawole Ogungbesan and Abdul R. JanMohamed take Helen's summation as their own conclusion.[5] All of them see *The Lying Days* as the most affirmative novel that Gordimer would write until *A Guest of Honour*. In fact, it is one of her bleakest, Gordimer's only novel in which private and public responsibilities are avoided and nothing learned.

There are, to be sure, aspects of the novel which lend credence to the matured understanding Helen claims at the close. One is her acceptance of the criticism of her behavior by Joel Aaron, her friend and ofttime mentor, as they wait to take separate boats abroad. Another is the two converging perspectives employed in the narrative: the young Helen's as she experiences her life during the 1935–1950 period in

5 Michael Wade, *Nadine Gordimer* (London, 1978), 37; Haugh, *Nadine Gordimer*, 105; Kolawole Ogungbesan, "The Way Out of South Africa: Nadine Gordimer's *The Lying Days*," *Ba Shiru*, IX (1978), 62; JanMohamed, *Manichean Aesthetics*, 95–96.

which the novel is set; and that of an older Helen, who identifies herself as the writer in the novel's closing pages, looking back on these years. While the observing narrator is used mainly to depict the "outward signs" of a world that the experiencing narrator is too immersed in to view, the convergence of perspectives gives the impression of Helen's developing maturity.

Readers have given insufficient weight to Helen's continuing dependence on her mother largely because it is obscured in a fundamental way: the world of the novel provides no motivation for Helen's dependence and the resentment it produces. Mrs. Shaw does attempt to direct Helen's life, but no more so than one would expect of a mother with an only child. Indeed, Mrs. Shaw not only manifests a broader and more tolerant view of the South African world than her contemporaries but also introduces Helen to it. She allows Helen to read her books from the lending library even when, as with the proletarian novels of the thirties, she is uncertain about their effect on a developing child. Mrs. Shaw will confide in her housegirl Anna and talk freely with the African gardener, asserting to others that "he's a lot more sensible than a lot of white people" (p. 34). Indeed, no one in the novel can fathom Helen's resentment toward her mother; no one else suffers from her problem. Mrs. Aaron's offhand response to Helen's complaints about her parents is characteristic: "So? It's your home, we all got to like our home" (p. 117). We don't, of course, but in a novel in which everyone else has either chosen to like her home or chosen not to with little difficulty, Helen's deep and unresolved animus toward her mother is not explainable. There is, in short, no objective correlative in the world of the novel for Helen's feelings about her mother. It is for this reason that critics have seen the racial problems which become more pronounced near the novel's close as the cause of Helen's malaise.

The absence of motivation for the novel's moving force, Helen's resentment of her mother, lies in Gordimer's reluctance to fully confront the relationship with her own mother. This reluctance is revealed most clearly by the fact that the novel follows the outlines of Gordimer's own life in all essential aspects except one, the "strange childhood." Not only is Mrs. Shaw presented as relatively unpossessive, but the narrative skips the years from about nine through fifteen when Gordimer was kept at home. The other major characters and the narrative, by contrast, have clear correspondences with Gordimer's own life. The original for the enervated Mr. Shaw, for instance, is Gordimer's own father, whom she has described as "burned-out," even as an "arrested" personality.[6] And the model for much of Helen's story is Gordimer's life. Helen's vacation on the East Coast with the Kochs has the same idyllic quality as the summer vacations there that Gordimer describes in "A South African Childhood." Helen, like the author, lives at home when first attending the university in Johannesburg, then in the city. Numerous other details from Gordimer's life, such as the fear instilled in young Nadine of sexual advances by the "mine boys," find their way into the novel. What doesn't is the "strange childhood" and the possessive mother responsible for it.

It is not simply the obscuring of the mother's role in the novel which has led critics to accept Helen's assessment of her own story, for Gordimer has set the novel in the context of an almost idyllic view of childhood. The epigraph suggests that the novel is to be about an expansive childhood which ends with the sobering responsibilities of adulthood:

> Though leaves are many, the root is one;
> Through all the lying days of my youth
> I swayed my leaves and flowers in the sun;
> Now I may wither into the truth.

The epigraph, which is alluded to frequently in the novel, depicts a childhood which is the antithesis of Gordimer's own. *The Lying Days* appears to be a kind of alternative childhood, perhaps Gordimer's bequeathing of a freer childhood than her own to her first daughter, to whom the novel is dedicated.

Only in the later novels, which do not have such a clear autobiographical focus, would possessive mothers, and the resulting "strange childhoods" and filial resentment, cease to be masked. Here the mother-daughter relationship emerges, in a phrase Gordimer has applied to many of her narrators, as "an unconscious self-revelation." This revelation is most obviously reflected in Helen's obsessive references to her

---

6 Gordimer has noted the novel's autobiographical basis (Gardner, "'A Story for This Place and Time,'" 102–103.) The depiction of her father is from Hurwitt, "The Art of Fiction LXXVII," 87–88.

own childish behavior; there are easily three score similes to this effect. But two indications of the mother's dominance and Helen's protracted childhood are most telling. One is her sense that not only her mother but nearly all the other women in her world possess a power that she does not. The other is the construction of the narrative around Helen's compulsion to return to her mother's house. In these covert but essential ways, the "strange childhood" shapes *The Lying Days*. While submerged, the animus of the daughter toward the repressive mother is still there, which explains Gordimer's expression of concern, on more than one occasion, about her mother's response to the novel.

Mrs. Shaw is the novel's dominant personality. She rules the home, only feigning deference to Helen's unassuming, "arrested" father. Seen infrequently, Mr. Shaw is glimpsed reading books on dietary fads or ineffectually protesting his wife's discarding his old golf umbrella during one of her frequent house cleanings. Young Helen learns early that "He had little authority over me" (p. 14). In every other family in the novel, fathers are weak or absent, and mothers dominate. Ludi's father is dead and Mrs. Koch easily runs the household despite her son's lack of assistance. A more developed case is the Aarons, the family of Helen's university classmate Joel. On entering their house, Helen's sight is first attracted by two pictures:

> A pair of stern, stupid eyes looked out from the smoky beard of an old photograph; the face of a foolish man in the guise of a patriarch. But next to him the high bosom, the high nose that seemed to tighten the whole face, slant the black eyes, came with real presence through a print that seemed to have evaporated from the paper: a woman presided over the room. (p. 113)

Helen soon learns that a woman continues to preside. While she first perceives Mrs. Aaron as a rather disheveled Jewish mother with a "swollen doll's body" and smiles "as if to excuse her to herself," Helen is soon eating a biscuit "like a child who is anxiously being fattened" (pp. 115, 117).

Helen's experience with young men is wide and, she claims, intense, but all of them are of only passing significance. Of an early beau she refuses to sleep with, she observes, "He was probably disgusted with me. In any case it did not matter; there were others. The important thing was the knowledge of being desired that brought me a consciousness of myself as a woman among the women I knew" (p. 183). Helen's strong feelings are reserved for other women, and she is often motivated by the reactions they provoke in her. Indeed, it is the assessment of Helen as "a giver" by Isa Welch, a strong, sharp-tongued woman in Helen's Johannesburg circle, that arouses her desire for Paul Clark. "Isa's idea of me excited me," Helen thinks, a good example of her tendency to put power in the hands of other women (p. 231). But it is probably the example of a young girl present at a bohemian party one evening which influences Helen more to take Paul Clark. She is "a girl in a taffeta dress with a string of pearls round her neck of the graded kind that small girls are given on their ninth or tenth birthday, along with their first bottle of scent, and a lace-bordered handkerchief which she kept clutched in her hand all through dinner" (p. 220). Helen's animosity to this harmless creature derives from her disconcerting embodiment of what Helen is trying to escape. Dressed in the "mine style" young Helen had worn (at the very age when Gordimer's "heart ailment" forced her seclusion), the girl is depicted in scathing terms as a completely unformed creature. When asked to leave a piece of her jewelry as a donation, the girl "froze as if it had been suggested that she leave her virginity at the door" (p. 223). Helen has yet to lose her own virginity, but given this girl—another "idea of me"—she soon makes love with Paul Clark. Throughout the novel, power over Helen lies in the hands of other women, whether through positive or negative example, as it lies in the hands of a child's mother.

Indeed, when Helen leaves home, ostensibly to gain freedom from her parents, she adopts the role of a child in her new setting. When Helen is first introduced to the Marcuses, she finds Jenny nursing on the divan "with her bare breasts white and heavy and startling" (p. 197). Others, like Isa Welch, see Helen as "a keen little scout," and as Helen's account of awakening in the mornings indicates, such appraisals are apt:

> I used to wake up for the first time very early at the baby's one strange sad cry for food. . . . In the next room, the soft dull sounds of Jenny moving about. Round the curtains that did not fit well, white edges of light; and quietly, deathly still, the books came out

round me on the walls, a silent arpeggio of a gleam ran across the case of the piano. Somebody's coat rose on a chair. A beer bottle answered from a corner. (p. 207)

The sounds of the mother in the next room and the motion of objects in the dark are a child's waking desires and fantasies. Indeed, Helen could find in Jenny Marcus, who exercises control over her child through submitting it to the current fads in child rearing—from the rigid schedule to "the natural young animal" approach—a parallel to her mother's desire that she conform to other conventional strictures, the colonial code of the mine.

The narrative is given shape by Helen's recurrently returning to the world of the mine. The novel's opening scene, in which Helen desires to escape the mine but returns to the shelter it offers, is a paradigm of her behavior throughout the novel. Young Helen—her age is not given but she seems to be about nine or ten—attempts to establish her independence from her mother by staying home alone when her parents go to play tennis one Saturday. Ignoring her mother's warning that "native boys" might be about, Helen ventures out of the mine enclave to visit the concession stores a short distance across the veld. She finds there a world too powerful and disordered for her to apprehend. Gordimer captures her disorientation through lavish use of synesthesia—"a crescendo of heavy, sweet nauseating blood smell, the clamor of entrails stewing richly, assailed me like a sudden startling noise" (p. 19)—and through the accretion of objects:

> Fowls with the quick necks of scavengers darted about between my trembling legs; the smeary windows of the shops were deep and mysterious with jumble that, as I stopped to look, resolved into shirts and shoes and braces and beads, yellow pomade in bottles, mirrors and mauve socks and watch chains, complicated as a mosaic, undisturbed, and always added to. (p. 19)

Helen wants to "resolve" this ever-growing mosaic behind "smeary windows," but what she finds are eyes, first a chameleon's then a snake's, which is "like the eye of a crocodile that waited looking like a harmless dry log" (p. 21). Her experience here is unfathomable—a chameleon can transform itself, a snake looks like a crocodile—and Helen is finally overwhelmed by this rich jumble: "I suddenly felt that I wanted to bat at my clothes and brush myself down and feel over my hair in case something had settled on me—some horrible dirt, something alive, perhaps" (p. 23). Helen had thought upon leaving the mine that to stay was to go "nowhere," to leave to go "somewhere," but this somewhere, while alive, contains too much life she cannot fathom. She runs back home where life suddenly comes into a clean, sharp focus:

> Round the dark hedge in the clear sun I saw them suddenly as a picture, the white figures with turning pink faces running on the courts, the striped blazers lying on the pale grass, the bare pink legs and white sand shoes sitting in the log house. (p. 24)

Among these clear shapes she seeks out her mother, whose "hand felt over my damp forehead, lifting the hair back" (p. 25). Both are reassured, the mother because of the "loneliness that had sent me tailing after her, after all," and Helen by the soothing hand lifting back the hair to remove, perhaps, "something alive" that might remain. Of this world, comfortable and clean if nowhere, Helen thinks later, "It was this to which the road brought me back always" (p. 29).

Set against a "somewhere" too powerful and foreign to apprehend is the "nowhere" of the mine; through Helen's attempt to reject its culture, the novel's public themes develop. The mine culture's distinguishing feature is narcissism. We first see Mrs. Shaw "looking straight back at herself in the mirror," and Helen, her mother's daughter, gazes at her own image in the mirror before leaving for the concessions (p. 13). This quality is generalized to the entire mine world at the close of the novel's first section when Helen sees "the whole world repeated, upside down" in the water hole of the golf course (p. 44). The basis of the self-love of the mine people is their Englishness: they read English books, dress in "the Mine style: the flower-patterned, unobtrusive blues and pinks of English royalty," and make the ritualistic trip to England with all the fervor of Muslims making the *hajj* (p. 120). As Helen reflects, colonialism is "the identification of the unattainable distant with the beautiful," and the surrounding veld, being neither distant nor beautiful, is ignored. "Mostly there was no focus of attention" between the town of Atherton and the mine, Helen notes during her description of the weekly visit with her mother to the Atherton stores, where their ritualized procedures are a marked contrast with Helen's disconcerting visit to the concessions.

Helen is a product of this environment, in the central metaphor of the novel, of the house in which she has been reared. Of Atherton, she observes, "There our house was; and I lived in it as I lived in my body" (p. 27). Helen views this house as her mother's; she characteristically describes it as being "like a woman with bad features and a poor complexion who seeks to distract with curls and paint, had [its] defects smothered in lace curtains" (p. 126). As Helen's initial transgression of mine codes by visiting the concessions indicates, she has the desire for a world broader than the mine affords. But throughout the novel she can conceive of expanding her world only by taking parts of it into her mother's house.

She first attempts to do so by proposing that Mary Seswayo, one of the few African students at the university, be allowed to stay at the Shaw home to study for examinations. Helen plans to mollify her mother by proposing that Mary stay in "the cooler," which is "neither inside the house, nor out in the yard with Anna, but something in between" (p. 187). What Helen desires is some sign of continuity between the worlds of her parents and Anna, the Shaw house servant—in other words, an "in between" linking the mine and the Africans outside. Helen's audience with her mother is constructed to show how impossible this desire is. At its outset Mrs. Shaw mistakes Helen for Anna, and even before Helen broaches the subject, she feels "almost as if I were making a charity appeal" to the mine charity committee of which her mother is secretary (p. 188). Helen senses that her mother will find her proposal absurd—as within the mine community it certainly is— and that there is no "in between"; if she is not allied with her mother, then she must be allied with Mary, with Anna, with the frightening, if alive, world outside the mine compound. When her request is denied, Helen feels as if her mother had said, "Have I really got a child? Is she *there*? And in the end, no authority could speak above hers" (p. 191).

That Helen cannot live with this rejection and can conceive of no other authority is demonstrated by her choice of the Atherton Tea Room, her mother's preserve, to discuss the fight with Joel Aaron. There she finds an image of her own dilemma: a mother with a little girl who rejects the mother's entreaties to give the expected greetings to her friends. Helen also resists her mother's authority but, having no voice of her own, is immobilized. The tea room scene makes her feel caught "in between" once again:

> In between I sat in a kind of listless daze, as if I were not there at all. I kept thinking: I want to go away. But there was no indignation, no strength in the idea any more. I did not want to be at home, but there was nowhere else I wanted to be, either. (p. 195)

With nowhere to go away to, Helen remains under her mother's authority here, in effect responding to her question, "Is she *there*?" that she's "not there at all." When they meet later, Mary Seswayo implies how Helen can be somewhere, be someone: "'If it had been your own house,' she said, 'but you can't expect to do it with the house of your mother'" (p. 204).

But Helen can conceive of no house of her own. She remains a child in the Marcuses' home, and when she fleetingly creates a home with Paul Clark, she feels the need to bring this experience into her mother's house by apprising her mother of it. On learning that Helen is sleeping with a man to whom she is not married, Mrs. Shaw tells her, "I don't want you in this house again" (p. 274). On her way back to Johannesburg, Helen observes a scene which confirms once again that there is no escaping her mother: "Opposite me in the carriage was a very young Afrikaans girl with a daughter four or five years old, curled and hatted, and hung with trinkets, like her mother. Like her mother she was . . ." (p. 275).

Like her mother but banished from her house, Helen feels homeless everywhere. She retreats to the balcony of the apartment she shares with Paul, for their room "was Paul's room, these were Paul's things among which I had been living. . . . I had made no mark, no claim on this room" (p. 315). Denied the opportunity to define herself in the only way she knows, by trying to integrate her own life into her mother's world, Helen feels disconnected from life around her. While she attributes this condition to "a kind of interim period" created by the Nationalist rule of the past two years, the cause lies in her mother's house. Helen had sensed this once when she observed that "we were presented to visitors in our own home as creatures without continuity, without a life put down and ready to take up again, like actors on a stage set" (p. 180). But she doesn't pursue how this condition arose or how she can avoid being such a creature. She can confront this lack of continuity only at a distance, as a quality not of her own but of Paul's life:

> Paul throws himself more and more violently into a job in which he believes less and less. So where does that lead? Where does that find a future? It has only a now; it cancels itself out.
> It cancels itself out!—I was afraid of this thought I had stumbled on. I was appalled at the frame of it in words. (p. 288)

Helen has "stumbled" on the appalling thought of life without a future, but her alienation is more severe than she apprehends; having made no claim on "Paul's room," she lacks even "a now." Not only her expressions of fear but her articulation—"that" and "it" have no clear antecedents—shows her inability to confront her problem: without a sense of her own past, she lacks not just a future but a present. Those actors on a stage set in her mother's house look almost appealing compared to the fly "paralyzed but not killed by a spider" she pictures herself as now (p. 291).

The lack of continuity in Helen's life is reflected in her choppy child's phrasing even as she grasps at a solution to her malaise: "It came to me quite simply, as if it had been there, all the time: I'll go to Europe. That's what I want. I'll go away" (p. 333). This thought has indeed "been there all the time" in Helen's life. She wanted to go away to the concessions; she wanted to go away after the fight over Mary Seswayo; she wanted to go away with Paul. Each time she had returned to her mother's house, and so she does again at the close by going, as her parents had recently, to Europe, which provides the standards for mine society. Like her mother, Helen has been attracted to England, the mother country, throughout the novel. She had envied Jenny Marcus' English background, and she had idealized Paul's upbringing in Natal, the most English of South Africa's provinces, because "his life as a child included his parents' odd English tradition of courtesy towards any difference that became evident, as he grew up, between their ideas and his" (pp. 211, 216). The English, it seems, have the secret even to alleviating the family conflicts Helen has been unable to reconcile.

Helen's desire to go to Europe is thus a final symbolic return to her mother's house, even though at the novel's close in Durban Helen claims otherwise. While waiting for her boat, she meets Joel Aaron, her admirer throughout the novel, and sees that he has matured in large part because "unlike me, he loved his parents enough to accept their deep differences from him" (p. 366). From her talk with Joel, Helen claims to have "accepted disillusion as a beginning rather than an end" (p. 367). The self-absorbed, depressed young woman she has been for the past year in Johannesburg has been transformed, Helen avers, into one who accepts the harsh reality of her situation and is ready to begin anew. Transformations do happen, but this one asks us to accept the road to Durban as Helen's road to Damascus. She reaffirms this new-found maturity after Joel's ship leaves. As the novel closes, Helen stands alone on another balcony, a setting which recalls the Johannesburg balcony to which she withdrew when her affair with Paul soured. She hears a sound which she thinks is "the ringing of my ears," suggesting that the "small sad voices" below in the street that this sound becomes are a reflection of her inner condition:

> I saw in the street below the huddled figures of some little native minstrels, singing as they padded along in the rain. The song was a popular dance tune of a few years before, "Paper Doll", but they made it infinitely mournful, infinitely longing. I stood there quite still, for a minute or more. I shall never forget how I felt. A feeling of extraordinary calm possessed me; I felt I could stand there in full possession of this great calmness for ever. It did not seem to me that it would ever go. (p. 367)

The passage is a second, more emphatic assertion that she has achieved a state of peace, that the conflicts which have obsessed her are resolved. And her phrasing suggests that she has not just passively accepted but actively claimed this new condition in the movement from the "extraordinary calm possessed me" to her standing "in full possession of this great calmness." But the details of this inner landscape make a contrary statement—that she remains the passive, depressed, and withdrawn Helen we have previously known. Not only the little figures "huddled" in the rain, but the song they sing indicates that Helen has not been transformed. J. S. Black's "Paper Doll" tells of a jilted lover who gives up the "dollies that are real" for a paper doll:

> When I come home at night she will be waiting
> She'll be the truest doll in all this world.

I'd rather have a paper doll to call my own
Than have a fickle-minded real live girl.

The song shows that Helen is still withdrawn from the "real live" world. She yearns to be a child playing with dolls. Later Gordimer heroines will show the same impulse; Jessie Stilwell in *Occasion for Loving* and Liz Van Den Sandt in *The Late Bourgeois World* will cuddle dolls. But while they use the experience to refashion their experiences both as children and as mothers, Helen does not. The "infinitely mournful, infinitely longing" song of the children suggests that she is at best beginning to mourn for the childhood she was denied, at worst longing to withdraw into a childish state. These sad children's voices speak well for Helen; these voices, too, had "been there all the time."

More than any of Gordimer's other novels, *The Lying Days* focuses on a private identity as the key to a good life. Those small, sad voices mainly mourn the loss of a childhood, not the postponement of Lorca's "reign of the ear of corn." But these voices mourn as well for a society which, the novel shows, fails to provide roots not only for Helen but for the rest of her generation as well. The use of the black children's song to objectify Helen's longings would have been understood by her liberal-bohemian friends; indeed, her depiction of the black children as minstrels, white comedians made up as blacks, indicates the kind of identification Helen's friends had tried to make. The minstrel mask had not remained in place for any of them. Helen had described their conflict as being "tethered to a thin line of culture from Europe on one side, dragged down toward an enormous, weighty racial tangle on the other" (p. 159). These racial problems prove too weighty; unlike Gordimer's later protagonists, Helen and her friends run from them. Paul Clark loses hope in his work, the Marcuses settle into a comfortable suburban house, Joel Aaron seeks a place in Israel, and Isa Welsh will turn to "writing intensely indigenous South African books from the self-imposed exile of England, America or Italy" (p. 161). None of them, in short, continue in their attempts to forge a new South African society. Joel Aaron will find his struggle in Israel; the rest in various ways retreat to that "thin line of culture from Europe." Colonial enclaves like the mine at the novel's opening become the only inhabitable territory for Helen and her friends.

In the novel's closing paragraphs, Helen claims yet a third time that she has changed. She is leaving for England, she says, but vows to return. The narrative itself makes this claim seem unconvincing; Gordimer's own perception of her cultural roots at the time the novel was written makes it even more so. Like her heroine, Gordimer had not yet been to England. She discusses the impact of the 1953 trip she made there in the *Paris Review* interview. Before the trip, she writes, "I didn't know I was a colonial, but then I had to realize that I was. Even though my mother was only six when she came to South Africa from England, she still would talk about people 'going home.' But after my first trip out, I realized that 'home' was certainly and exclusively—Africa. It could never be anywhere else."[7] The writer of *The Lying Days*, in short, still suspected that England might be "home." This feeling is reflected in the final claim of her heroine as the novel closes:

> I'm not running away. Whatever it was I was running away from—the risk of love? the guilt of being white? the danger of putting ideals into practice?—I'm not running away from now because I know I'm coming back here. (p. 367)

Helen protests too much. She ends a solitary figure without a cultural role, running in search of a land her own mother has so often described as "home." In fact, Helen calls to mind that little girl who ran from the African concessions to her mother's house at the novel's outset. Helen hasn't changed enough to convince us she's not running there still.

III

Near the close of *The Lying Days*, Helen tells Paul Clark that their problems are "inside ourselves in the—what's the word I want—the non-political, the individual consciousness of ourselves in possession of our personal destiny" (p. 291). A nonpolitical consciousness is impossible in *Occasion for Loving*, published in 1963 after the implementation of apartheid, after the Sharpeville massacre, after the banning of peaceful protest by Africans, after the Nationalist government's

7 Hurwitt, "The Art of Fiction LXXVII," 87.

rejection of "the winds of change" that Macmillian had correctly predicted would come from the North. Lewis Nkosi wrote after the novel's publication that while Gordimer's "enquiry was always conducted from the centre of a very private self," as "the South African situation grows progressively worse, Gordimer has moved further outward to the public area where the noise is."[8] His view is confirmed early in *Occasion for Loving* when the thirty-eight-year-old Jessie Stilwell responds to just such an assertion as Helen's. To the claim of her guest Boaz Davis that he is "dead off politics," she rejoins, "Oh, yes, but they blow in under the door" (p. 15). The directness of this statement, in contrast to the searching for expression in Helen's, reveals a more discerning personality molded by conditions in which the weather is stormy outside as well as within her house.

Yet Jessie's response to Boaz is too pat. She knows the winds blow, but they have yet to come in under her door. Ironically, it is Boaz' wife Ann who brings them in through her affair with an African painter, Gideon Shibalo. At the novel's outset Jessie doesn't want the Davises or anyone else in her house, for she is in an almost pathological depression engendered by her personal past. It is only through the process of resolving this past, the novel shows, that she will achieve a deep feeling for the public noise the Davises introduce. As in *The Lying Days*, a very private self lies at the novel's center.

Jessie's story is in very specific ways a continuation of Helen's. Indeed, the novel begins with the same metaphor with which *The Lying Days* closed:

> Jessie Stilwell had purposefully lost her way home, but sometimes she found herself there, innocent of the fact that she had taken to her heels and was still running. Still running and the breathlessness and the drumming of her feet created an illusion of silence and motionlessness—the stillness we can feel while the earth turns—in which she had never left her mother's house. (p. 9)

The mothers from whose houses Jessie and Helen run but cannot leave are from the same mold. Jessie's mother, Mrs. Fuecht, is like Mrs. Shaw concerned above all with proper appearances; Jessie's husband Tom had never seen her without a hat, and even in her own house she

8 Nkosi, "Les Grandes Dames," 163.

was always dressed like a visitor. This excessive concern with appearance reveals her rootlessness—she is not at home at home—and the lack of continuity, a sense of a past extending into the future, in her life. "As time goes by," she will say, "there seem to be more of them—other people. And then, all of a sudden, you're one of them" (p. 104). This feeling of disconnection has been passed on to "her cherished only child" Jessie, who, in the midst of a bustling house, is as withdrawn as Helen became on her balcony. Like Helen, Jessie professes a loathing for her mother—she refers to her only as Mrs. Fuecht—but still finds herself silent and motionless, in short, powerless in her mother's house. But Jessie is better placed to make peace with her past because she understands the reason for her deep animus: "She was her mother's constant companion, and this intimacy between mother and daughter became even closer when the child developed some heart ailment at the age of ten or eleven and was kept out of school. She was taught at home by a friend of her mother's, and when she grew up, during the war, she left her mother's house only to marry" (pp. 24–25). Jessie has been denied her youth, having been handed from her mother to a first husband "without ever having had the freedom that does not belong to any other time of life but extreme youth" (p. 44).

Jessie has long understood, but has not emotionally accepted, this past. She comes to do so through her own children, the essential means of her regeneration. They evoke Jessie's own childhood and allow her to relive—in some ways refashion—it through her observation of theirs. Through them, Jessie learns what Helen never did: that only by ceasing to run from her mother's house can she leave it and overcome the "silence and motionlessness" which possess her.

That Jessie is still troubled by her childhood is seen most clearly in her treatment of her four children—twelve-year-old Morgan, the son of her first marriage, and Clem, Madge, and Elizabeth, aged about five to nine, from her marriage to Tom Stilwell. Jessie fears that the children will "fasten on and suck the life out of her" as "her mother had sucked from her the delicious nectar she had never known she had" (pp. 14, 45). So she runs. The first time she hears a child, she retreats to her room, feeling a "childish triumph—she had escaped the child" (p. 11). Clearly, so long as she projects her fears of her mother's emotional domination of her onto her children, Jessie will remain "childish," locked still within her mother's house. Conversely, her behavior is often a repetition of her mother's. Against her children, Jessie "threatened and preached, saying, as she had been told in her turn, that she *would* teach them to be tidy," that is, to control the superficial details of life as her mother had admonished her to (p. 13).

What Jessie seeks most that was lacking in her mother's life is continuity. She had "known a number of different, clearly defined, immediate presents," but they lack connection. "The ribbon of her identity was always that which was being played out between her fingers; there was no coil of it continuing from the past" (p. 23). Jessie fastens on details from her past which confirm this feeling. The incident which epitomizes a Fuecht Christmas outing, for instance, is a woman "sewing without any thread in the needle. It flashed in and out of the stuff, empty, connecting nothing with nothing" (p. 44). In the present, Jessie focuses on her children's gaining a sense of time. Will they, she seems to ask herself, end up with a string of "presents" or, like her mother, find their worlds inexplicably changed "all of a sudden"? Often, her concern is manifested in small ways, the choice of a watch band for Morgan at Christmas or the conversation Elizabeth holds with her stuffed animal: "'I say it's time to wash hands for supper.' 'But what time is it?' 'The time to wash hands.' 'But what is the number of that time?'" (p. 52).

But Jessie seeks the coil from the past most consistently through Morgan, the child from that first marriage to which she had been passed from her mother's house and thereby denied her youth. Jessie has avoided Morgan; she sends him away to boarding school and counts the days until his return during his infrequent visits home. Morgan understands. He expresses himself little at home and stays in his room daydreaming and listening to his radio. When this stolid Morgan asserts his own nascent manhood by frequenting an adult dance hall, he evokes in Jessie memories of the first stirrings of her sexuality as a young girl. These memories are painful because her mother refused to accept the sexuality of a child she sought to keep in her thrall. Jessie begins to realize that she, in her turn, has stifled Morgan. Feeling compelled to visit the dance hall, she is approached there by a seedy character with eyes like those "of an animal that does not know it is born behind bars" (p. 60). This man is not only a reflection of Jessie, locked away during the period of her "heart ailment," but Morgan, whom she recalls staring "down at her on deck in silence from behind wire mesh" during a boat trip (p. 66). Jessie's awareness that through being locked away they have both become silent and motionless, each imprisoned in a mother's house, prompts her to imagine an adolescence in which they are together, communicative and expressive. She has a fantasy of their living together romantically which ends in her taking "his big, young, tender man's hand" (p. 66). It will not be until the novel's close that she actually takes his hand to express her affection and acceptance of his manhood. But she does realize how she has avoided him by shunting him off to a nursery, boarding school, his room, and she sees that by accepting him she can begin to create an image of the youthful life she was denied.

As Jessie continues to feel toward a connection with her past, she becomes involved in two political occasions, both of which are associated with her developing acceptance of Morgan. The first, her visit to a dance of the African miners, shows her discovery of a communal past as she had her private past through Morgan's dance hall escapade. The second, her participation in the love affair between Ann Davis and Gideon Shibalo, takes up the novel's central image of personal contact. As in Jessie's acknowledgment of Morgan's developing manhood, the intimacy of the lovers is instigated by their sensuous awareness of the other's hands when Ann removes a splinter from Gideon's, he a streak of paint from hers.

Jessie's visit to the mines, the scene of her upbringing, develops a parallel between her private life and the life of the Africans on the mines, both of which seem to lack a connection with the past. This parallel is introduced when Jessie reflects on the difficulty of retrieving her early experiences:

> There were signs that it was all still there; it lay in a smashed heap of rubble from which a fragment was often turned up. Her daily, definite life was built on the site of a series of ruined cities of whose history the current citizens know nothing. (p. 25)

The metaphor, echoing Freud's use in *Civilization and Its Discontents* of the Eternal City to illustrate the simultaneous existence of all psychic experience, is applicable to the discovery of ancient African kraals, ruined cities of whose history the current citizens knew nothing, on the Witwatersrand in the early 1960s.[9] This discovery undercut the often-made assertion that whites had first settled the land and thereby had rightful claim to the gold it yielded.

During a visit to one of the Sunday mine dances, Jessie makes the equation between the denial of the Africans' public past and her private past. She watches the African miners dancing on the tarmac covering an Eternal City, the kraals of past times:

> Unspeakable sadness came to Jessie, her body trembled with pain. They sang and danced and trampled the past under their feet. Gone, and one must not wish it back. But gone . . . The crazed Lear of old Africa rushed to and fro on the tarred arena, and the people clapped. (p. 37)

Jessie cries tears which "came from horror and hollowness" and "she held in her mind at once, for a moment, all that belonged to horror and hollowness, and that seemed to have foreshadowed it, flitting batlike through the last few days: the night in which she had awakened twice, once to her own sleeping house, and once to that other time and place in her mother's house" (p. 37). Jessie associates these two sets of events because she had been denied her past by the bogus heart ailment and early marriage as the Africans have their past by the myth that the land has always been a white preserve. The scene shows Jessie sensing that these buried pasts need not be inaccessible. She finds continuity between them and the present. By taking her daughter Madge's hand she feels restored to the present, and she argues that "it's the best thing" for the Africans to adapt their instruments as they enter new surroundings. Her assertion that a present can grow from the past is confirmed when, as her group leaves the mine, "the ancient instruments of Africa struck up the Colonel Bogey march" (p. 39).

9 Sigmund Freud, *Civilization and Its Discontents*, trans. James Strachey (New York, 1962), 16–18. For a good discussion of the interest generated by the discovery of the African kraals, see John Lawrence, *The Seeds of Disaster: A Guide to the Realities, Race Policies, and World-Wide Propaganda of the Republic of South Africa* (London, 1968), 298–305. The change this discovery made in Gordimer's thought is indicated by her comment in 1955 that the "part of the Transvaal which later became the Witwatersrand was not the settled home of any Bantu tribe" ("Johannesburg," 50). By the early sixties, she knew it had been.

The other occasion, the focus of the remainder of the novel, is the Ann Davis–Gideon Shibalo love affair. It has political ramifications—interracial sex is prohibited in South Africa by a series of "Immorality Acts"—as Jessie soon learns. Through the affair, politics blow under the door into Jessie's private world, for it is in her house that the Davises stay, the lovers often meet, and the Stilwells, Davises, and Gideon sometimes gather for dinner and political talk. A strange love triangle results. Boaz refuses to respond to the affair because Gideon is black, a telling illustration of how public and private lives are intertwined, and warped, in South Africa. Jessie is the first to sense the existence of the affair. She soon becomes its third member, her emotional relationship with Gideon complementing Ann's sexual bond with him. Tom Stilwell will even claim that Jessie's relationship with Gideon motivated Ann, who could take the sex seriously because Jessie "was serious about the other things" (p. 282).

Tom probably overstates the case. But Jessie does seem an integral member of the affair not simply because we most often look from her point of view but because the affair is developed in terms of the relationship of childhood to adult life with which Jessie has been concerned since the novel's outset. A scene shortly after Jessie becomes aware of Ann and Gideon's affair sets this focus in a very concrete way. In the garden one day Jessie attempts to piece together a child's doll but, even with the aid of Ann and Tom, fails to do so. Their labors are set in the context of the discovery of the affair (during them Jessie informs Tom of its existence) and the setting where it will find its most intense expression (the Fuecht beach house, which they muse about visiting). The scene therefore suggests that the stuff of childhood, piecing together of a doll, is the central issue in this affair. The different meanings the participants find in the affair depend on the extent to which each relates it to his or her childhood past and, as the affair develops, projects a future from it. The three lovers—Ann, Gideon, and Jessie—offer different childhood contexts for this occasion, for loving.

Ann, the simplest of the three, is portrayed throughout as a child, with a child's enthusiasm and liveliness and a child's sense only of the present. From the outset, she is referred to as "the girl" or Boaz' "little wife," and Gordimer quickly establishes her child's greedy desire for gratification. At the prospect of the trip to the mine, Ann responds,

"'Goody!' and the little girls took it up, Goody, Goody! 'We'll all go,' she said to Jessie. 'Shall we?'" (p. 28). Ann is unable to look beyond such immediate desires. To her, Jessie's life seems "remote as old age. She did not think of it as something that had begun somewhere different and might be becoming different. The present was the only dimension of time she knew; she woke every day to *her* freedom of it" (p. 91). Bits of sing-song appeals are the only talk we have from her in this novel filled with those—professors, African nationalists—who define themselves through converse. But Gordimer still makes Ann seem attractive, perhaps because she has aspects of an alter ego, the child dancer Gordimer had once been. Ann's element is motion; she dances as well as the best of the black women, and only occasionally pauses like "a bird balancing a moment on a telephone wire" (p. 105). Ann's love of sensual pleasure, the naturalness of her body in motion, and her joy in the present moment are caught during one of her outings with Gideon:

> Ann was seized with the desire for water and grass and willow trees, sun and birds. She swam in the brown rivers, waving to him where he lay sipping beer; she emerged seal-wet and dried off in the warm smell of water-weed rising from her skin. She picked the fragile and sparse flowers of the tough veld with enthusiasm and then let them wither, and she brought a book with her that she never read. (p. 133)

The scene also catches her dangerousness (and the author's attitude) when Ann "let" those "fragile and sparse flowers" wither. Ann's concern only with "*her* freedom" finds fuller expression in her lack of empathy for Jessie, and finally for Gideon, whom she will love only as long as the excitement lasts.

Gideon watches her on the veld "with the amusement of novelty" (p. 133). He is captivated by Ann's carefree child's existence, for like other African children—and Jessie Stilwell—Gideon has been denied a full childhood. The new subject matter of his painting after he meets Ann shows that this is the basis of her appeal. When Jessie visits an apartment Gideon has the use of, she at first finds only portraits of Ann; then Gideon puts up for her "one by one, without comment, charcoal drawings and oils of children, friezes and splashes of children, old with the life of the street" (p. 118). Gideon, who has been denied a passport to develop his art in Italy and is tiring of the long wait for African rule, wants to believe that through Ann he can claim the freedom of the present, which, as the veld scene shows, she admirably displays for him. But he makes the mistake of believing she offers a future which he had sought through his art and African politics before meeting Ann.

Jessie recurrently urges Gideon to connect with the past as she herself has begun to with Morgan and at the mine dance. In private terms, she encourages Gideon to reestablish contact with his child from an early marriage. In public terms, she argues that his acknowledging an African past is a precondition for claiming the political future he desires. For Jessie, a large part of Gideon's appeal lies in his having a public past offering a future in this society where she as a white has none. She will come to see him as one who has "the new magic" of those "who held in themselves for this one generation that dignity of the poor about to inherit their earth and the worldliness of those who had been the masters" (p. 269). Gideon refuses this public role. He characteristically argues at one of the Stilwell parties, for instance, that "when we accepted the white man's present . . . we took on his future at the same time—I mean, we began to go wherever he is going. And our past has no continuation with this. So it is lost" (p. 151). But Gideon's story is mainly about his private choice of Ann, a creature of the present alone. When Gideon finally accepts Ann, his entire outlook is reflected: her "beautiful smile rose to her face as if it existed for him and would always be there when he looked to her. Now it came to him as encouragement: not to be afraid to pronounce the future, not to be afraid to count on it" (p. 273). As the novel's conclusion will show, Gideon might well choose this future "as if" he did not have cause to be afraid.

Jessie alone of the three seeks the continuity of a past extending through the present to the future. Increasingly, her thoughts are on Morgan, to whom she writes about feeling now as she did in the Fuecht's house as a child, then of the silkworms she and Morgan have heard spinning. They were so hungry, she writes, but didn't know why, "But then they were full, and suddenly knew how to spin silk" (p. 156). They are, of course, like Jessie—and, one suspects, Morgan—"hungry" but not certain why, their fullness and knowledge the first clear sign of Jessie's regeneration. Her consciousness that it is "a grown-up's letter" she is writing Morgan is not just a statement about her perception of her son but of her own emotional state. Jessie clearly finds a connection between her past and present—the spun silk is an embodiment of the coil from the past that she seeks—and in her growing acceptance of her son, between the present and future as well.

As in *The Lying Days*, the house remains the focal point as the novel develops. The responses to the Stilwell house by Ann, Gideon, and Jessie midway through the narrative reveal, in brief, their perceptions of the occasion for loving which has developed within its bounds. For Ann,

> All the meaning of the almost-past summer gathered for her in the vision of Jessie's old house—ugly old house—as it was this evening and had been so many evenings, with the windows open like hands and a first bat fluttering without sound, wandering and rising. None of the others saw the creature; it was only the acute angle at which she had let her head fall back that let her see it. It was in the air above them all, soft, deaf, remote, steered by warnings and attractions they lacked a sense to apprehend. (pp. 160–61)

This vision is obscure enough that Gordimer feels the need for Tom Stilwell to explain later that a bat instinctively chooses, as Ann will, the path of least resistance (pp. 281–82). The details here carry the same meaning. Ann senses that the community is open to her in "the windows open like hands," but the other aspects—the ugliness of the house, its age (something ugly in itself for her), the "wandering" of this "remote" creature, and the very privateness of her vision, explicitly beyond their ken—all indicate that the union the house has fostered will be transitory for her.

Like the others, Gideon does not see this wandering creature. Of the whites in the house, he thinks, "*They* were never free now, of him. The Stilwell house was grouped invisibly round him as an empty chair at a dinner table affects the seating of those present" (p. 175). This sense of belonging is undercut by its expression in terms of his absence and by the reveling in power which informs it; Gideon, who has so long been denied his freedom, now feels that he holds power over those in the white house. Jessie, for her part, feels herself resisting the way "the Davises were drawing everyone into their own charged air" (p. 164). She withdraws with the girls—once again, she arranges for Morgan to be elsewhere—to her mother's beach house. She is running still, but as the novel's conclusion will reveal, for the last time.

At the beach house Jessie remains preoccupied with children. The first few nights she imagines that she hears "the cries of children teasing one another." But she soon feels the strains of the Stilwell house recede. In this private world of the beach, she feels special pleasure in the daily sight of porpoises, which she views "as a child watches the game of another family of children" (p. 188). When her solitude is interrupted by Ann and Gideon, seeking shelter after three weeks in the veld, she sees their arrival as a sign:

> This was not the old house, the Stilwell house where life was various. This place was completely inhabited, for the present, by *her being*; couldn't they sense it?—she thought: it must fill the place, like a smell. If they came to her here, it must be through some special and deeply personal connection with that being. (pp. 212–13)

This connection is revealed to be the bond of a more intimate, if transient community, prefigured by the family of porpoises, than she had known before: "The presence of a man rounded out the group into a family; other evenings she had not expected to join in the little girls' games: they had almost forgotten about her, sitting in the dark near them" (p. 209). Withdrawal has been Jessie's characteristic posture throughout the novel; she had feared having the life "sucked out of her" and evaded the intimacy on which a family depends. Through this occasion at the beach, Jessie experiences a kind of family life for the first time, for there had been a Stilwell house but no Stilwell family. This term is applied to the Stilwells for the first time when Jessie returns to Johannesburg, where "they were a family in spite of failures and evasions" (p. 280).

Jessie's readiness for mature family life is seen most clearly in her acceptance of Morgan, the child she has evaded and often failed. During their talk of the affair's aftermath—a grown-up's discussion—she tells him, "You've got nice hands. I wonder where you got them from?"

(p. 285). She gives Morgan not just her love and her acceptance of his manhood but, in the question, the freedom to explore his past and seek his own future. She gives him the freedom to leave his mother's house.

This acceptance of Morgan's maturity ends the tyranny of Jessie's own childhood. The cries of children are heard for the last time at a party near the novel's close:

> The far-off wail of a baby—a child of the house—seemed to be heard, like a noise in the head, between the music, the talk and the movement, but was always lost before it attracted attention; it was inconceivable, it had no more relevance, in the clamour of politics, liquor and sex, than the call of a bird in a thunderous machine-shop. (p. 287)

This passage summarizes Jessie's development in the novel much as the balcony scene in Durban does Helen Shaw's. Both scenes are correlatives for emotional states: Helen's begins with "the ringing of my ears" which becomes the black children's song, and Jessie's "noise in the head" is the child's cry. But Jessie's noise, unlike Helen's, reflects her liberation from the world of children. Throughout the novel the unwelcome sounds of "a child of the house" had assailed Jessie, but finally the call of the child—another's, her children's, her own "noise in the head"—fails to attract attention. Unlike Helen, Jessie does not end listening to sad children's voices; her claim to an adult's life is secure.

But if Jessie's personal past has "no more relevance," the "politics, liquor, and sex" do. The novel closes at this party with Gideon drunk and in despair after Ann has left the country with Boaz. Jessie feels "a deep, uncomplicated affection for this man," but he does not recognize her (p. 287). She ends mourning the loss of this man, who had seemed at the beach to be a member of her family. Her affection for Gideon, which "flowed in peace," comes from his role in her most private life. Gideon had allowed her to broaden her sense of family beyond what, she realized when reading Thomas Mann at the beach, was "the 'safety' of middle-class trappings" (p. 198). Jessie no longer has the "safe" middle-class home; she has welcomed into her house Gideon and even Jason, the beach-house servant, who "took her hand awkwardly" in parting. But her occasion for loving at the beach does not "flow" to the future. Her house has been unable to hold Gideon and, by extension, Jason and her other black countrymen.

The novel therefore has two endings, the establishing of continuity and community in Jessie's personal life, the failure to do so in her public life. Since the two lives have been intertwined—at the mine dance, in the transient contact of hands, in the failed affair—Jessie is still not at ease. While she achieves the freedom in her private life that Helen failed to, Jessie ends feeling not just regret but rage. White privilege, which she sees as "a silver spoon clamped between your jaws," leaves her gagged and impotent, locked in "silence and motionlessness" as she had been for private reasons at the novel's outset (p. 279). Early in the novel she had seen "her life as a bird let into a series of cages, each one, because of its comparative freedom, seeming, for a while, to be without limit, without bars" (p. 22). By the close, she has left her mother's house and liberated Morgan from the bars of his childhood, but she still finds herself in a new cage. In the metaphor used at the final party, she is "a bird in a thunderous machine-shop." The personal life—the primary subject of *The Lying Days* and *Occasion for Loving*—has been dealt with, but Jessie is silenced and powerless in what Lewis Nkosi called that "public area where the noise is."

Jessie fails because, as Helen had with Mary Seswayo, she has attempted to integrate her private and public lives by bringing Africans into the white house. Until the law is changed, Africans simply cannot be brought in. Gideon tells Jessie as much one morning at the beach when she talks of the need to keep on proving one's humanity. He responds, "You might have to prove it in jail one day. You know? Your house won't be big enough any more" (p. 244). Jessie has learned that her house isn't big enough, but she is not ready for jail. She might, Gordimer writes, blow up a power station "perhaps, in time" (p. 279). Only with Rosa Burger fifteen years later would these qualifications about public action disappear.

IV

Gordimer has said that *Burger's Daughter* was inspired by the children of South African Communists, whose parents were recurrently on trial or in prison. She was struck by these "children or teen-agers, left with the responsibility of the whole household and younger children. It must have affected their lives tremendously; it must have been a great intrusion on the kind of secret treaties that you have when you're an adolescent."[10] At the outset of *Burger's Daughter*, one of those waiting outside a prison with the fourteen-year-old Rosa Burger to deliver goods to the detainees says that "the child was dry-eyed and composed, in fact she was an example to us all of the way a detainee's family ought to behave. Already she had taken on her mother's role in the household" (p. 12). The novel is about the discovery of "secret treaties" by this child whose parents have taught her so well how she "ought to behave."

The household the child takes over is better described as a political institution than a family. Lionel Burger was born in 1905, the year of the revolt against the czars; he married Cathy Burger during the 1946 African mineworkers strike; and their daughter Rosa was born in May 1948, the very month the Nationalist party assumed power. Rosa is in-deed apartheid's child; the stages in her life are marked not by gradua-tions or proms but the 1956 treason trial and the 1960 Sharpeville mas-sacre. Even her fondest childhood memory, taking refuge in her father's hairy chest as she swims in the family pool with Baasie, the child of an African nationalist reared by the Burgers, is put in a political context: "In 1956 when the Soviet tanks came into Budapest I was his little girl, dog-paddling to him with my black brother Baasie, the two of us reach-ing for him as a place where no fear, hurt or pain existed" (p. 115). Rosa will need to assess the Burger Communist vision, called into question by the Russian tanks, but she will have much more difficulty ceasing to be Burger's "little girl." Like Helen and Jessie before her, Rosa will remain bound to her parents' house, as her continuing perception of her father as a haven from the world's pain indicates. Rosa will find it especially difficult to confront, much less express, her own feelings, for she has been disciplined to remain "dry-eyed" in the face of such painful experiences as two called up by the pool scene. The black brother had been cast out of the Burger house at the age of eight, shortly after this remembered scene, when no schools could be found

10 Gardner, "'A Story for This Place and Time,'" 100.

for him nearby, and her brother Tony had drowned in the pool some years later. The confrontation of such private issues awaits Rosa, the exemplary radical child.

Unlike the earlier novels, *Burger's Daughter* is given shape by the presence of a strong man. Lionel Burger is a public man who is the peer of Nelson Mandela and Bram Fischer, a private man who could expand the boundaries of his house to truly take in an African child.[11] It is the unrelenting attention to Rosa as this martyred man's daughter that most stifles her attempts to become Rosa Burger. She must assist her father's biographer; a Swede enters a love affair with her in order to further work on a Lionel Burger documentary; "it is understood" among her friends that she will dedicate her life to the struggle as Lionel Burger did his. But like Helen Shaw and Jessie Stilwell, Rosa attributes her loss of freedom as a child and young woman largely to her mother. The novel's opening scene reveals Rosa's desire to express her personal self to her mother even as she fulfills the political responsibilities given her. As she waits outside the prison, she holds a hot-water bottle with a concealed message indicating that her father has not yet been detained. But Rosa seeks to convey a private message as well; experiencing menstrual cramps for the first time, she has chosen the womblike hot-water bottle to carry the message. Standing "in that public place on that public occasion," Rosa makes a small gesture to express her private self (p. 16).

Rosa's mother does not apprehend such gestures, large or small. Her preoccupation with the Communist struggle leaves her oblivious to her daughter's private needs. She requires Rosa, in the most bitter incident of her young life, to pose as the fiancée of a detained comrade, Noel de Witt, so that Rosa will be allowed visitor's privileges and can once again carry messages in her parents' cause. Rosa will later reflect bitterly, "Those were my love letters. Those visits were my great wild times" (p. 69). She comes to see herself not as her mother's daughter

11 Fischer's life served as a model for Lionel Burger's, from his family background and trial to his death in prison, and the original for the woman who turned state's evidence against Burger is the woman who did so against Fischer. See Nadine Gordimer, "The Fischer Case," *London Magazine*, V (March, 1966), 21–30 and "Why Did Bram Fischer Choose Jail?" *New York Times Magazine*, August 14, 1966, pp. 30ff.

but simply one of those who can be used in the Burger cause, "one of my mother's collection of the dispossessed, like Baasie or the old man who lived with us" (p. 84). Rosa is particularly struck by her mother's use of another member of this collection—an old-maid schoolteacher, who is detained and, lacking the Burgers' strength of purpose, turns state's evidence against Lionel Burger. Rosa accedes to her mother's demands as thoroughly as this woman and finds them as difficult to fulfill. Where this woman turns state's evidence, Rosa will pathetically fall in love with Noel de Witt and attempt to join him abroad to develop a private life. Rosa will later actually defect from the Burger cause, for a time, to southern France. Like this woman who couldn't meet her father's face in court, Rosa will not be able to address him— the novel is constructed around her addressing others in the attempt to define herself—until her return to South Africa at the novel's close.

Initially, Rosa simply seeks escape in a private world by living with Conrad, a wanderer with no political interests, indeed no strong commitments of any kind. His garden cottage, soon to be destroyed to make way for a freeway, appeals to her because it is "nowhere," a private place for a private occasion. Through Conrad, Rosa is able to distance herself from her parents' house and begin to feel some of the anger which, as "an example to us all," she has repressed. This process is at its most intense in her recollection of "the engagement" to Noel de Witt:

> Mine is the face and body when Noel de Witt sees a woman once a month. If anybody in our house—that house, as you made it appear to me—understood this, nobody took it into account. My mother was alive then. If she saw, realized—and at least she might have considered the possibility—she didn't choose to see. Alone in the tin cottage with you, when I had nothing more to tell you, when I had shut up, when I didn't interrupt you, when you couldn't get anything out of me, when I wasn't listening, I accused her. I slashed branches in the suburban garden turned rubbish dump where I was marooned with you. (p. 66)

Conrad has helped Rosa to distance herself from her home, making it "that house," and to rail at her mother. But Rosa's persistent use of negatives—she knows what wasn't done for her, and she defines her behavior to Conrad by what she doesn't do—reveals her lack of alternatives to "that house." Indeed, Rosa projects its atmosphere onto the world of the tin cottage; Conrad becomes someone, like her mother, who is interested in getting things "out of her." She will finally conceive her relationship with Conrad in terms of her upbringing. Because of their closeness she views them as siblings, "treating each other's dirt, as little Baasie and I had long ago," and she stops making love to Conrad, "aware that it had become incest" (p. 70). Even before she leaves him, she begins again to refer to "that house—our house," reversing the formulation she used when expressing anger toward her mother. Clearly, she still carries "our house" with her.

Rosa's behavior is not simply a compulsion, like Helen's, to relive an unhealthy past; for the world of her parents, unlike the Shaws or Fuechts, has much to offer. Rosa recurrently thinks of the sense of community in "our house," most often of the close and broad circle of friends who gathered there on Sundays. Even more, she misses the sense of what she calls "being connected," in contrast to being "marooned" at Conrad's, that her parents' struggle provided. This "connection," what Helen and Jessie termed "continuity," derived from the Burgers' sense of a life's purpose, the Communist vision of a just society growing from the past and extending to the future. But Rosa's selfhood has been so thoroughly denied in the service of this vision that she cannot claim it until she has developed a sense of personal worth. She needs, in short, first to become Rosa Burger before she can again be the Burgers' daughter.

Rosa finds establishing a life of her own particularly difficult because, having been used so much in the service of her parents' cause, she has no friends of her own. After her parents' deaths when Rosa is in her teens, her only associates, excepting Conrad, are their long-time comrades who have the same expectations of her as her parents. Of Ivy Terblanche, the most important of them, Rosa tells Conrad, "In the enveloping acceptance of Ivy's motherly arms—she feels as if I were her own child—there is expectance, even authority. To her warm breast one can come home again and do as you said I would, go to prison" (p. 114). Behind the unwillingness to be enveloped by a surrogate mother lies Rosa's awareness that commitment to her parents' cause means prison, where her father died an early death and she had already wasted the sweet times of her youth.

The first book of the novel shows Rosa looking for "connection," the sense of a future growing from her past. The only other past Rosa has been exposed to is the Afrikaner past of the Nels, her father's relatives, whom she had visited at the age of eight when her parents were imprisoned during the 1956 treason trial. Not only her father's but her aunt's tradition is reflected in Rosa's name. She assumes she has been named after Rosa Luxemburg, "But my double name contained also the claim of MARIE BURGER and her descendants to that order of life, secure in the sanctions of family, church, law" (p. 72). At the Nels, Rosa feels the seduction of a life governed by an order so clearly lacking in her private life:

> All this ordered life surrounded, coated, swaddled Rosa; the order of Saturday, the order of family hierarchy, the order of black people out in the street and white people in the shade of the hotel stoep. Its flow contained her, drumming her bare heels on Daniel's box, its voices over her head protected her. (p. 61)

She fleetingly enjoys this new feeling of being protected and "swaddled"; like Jessie, she desires the "flow" of a peaceful life. Yet she is not free to explore this claim, for choosing the Nel order would be a betrayal—a word often summoned up in the novel—of everything the Burgers have fought for. But betrayal, public and private, is at issue in a society so polarized by two orders, the Nels' and the Burgers', each demanding unquestioned adherence. The picture of young Rosa surrounded by this order is followed by reference to it as "the heritage of his people that Lionel Burger betrayed" (p. 61). Rosa will, in turn, temporarily betray his heritage by seeking a private life in France which offers a serene order such as this. Indeed, the schoolteacher, with whom Rosa identifies, cannot "look at him whom she had betrayed" in court (p. 87). And the Burgers have betrayed Baasie, as he will remind Rosa later, by casting him out just before her visit to the Nels. Rosa's exploration of her place is hindered by the severity with which any deviation from the group will be judged; her world seems to offer only choices for betrayal.

Rosa is forced to confront betrayal only later, for at first her two heritages offer no images of herself worth claiming. Their restrictiveness is revealed through the use of the rose, the flower associated with her name. She recalls sitting across from de Witt in prison, "a flower standing for what lies in her lap. We didn't despise prostitutes in that house— our house—we saw them as victims of necessity while certain social orders lasted" (p. 69). Set against this prostitution masquerading as engagement is an image of even greater inauthenticity at the Nel farm, where the grave of Rosa's grandmother is decorated with a glass dome "under which plastic roses had faded" (p. 77). Rosa feels her identify to be, like the roses, artificial and faded, removed from the world under glass. Neither the Burger nor the Nel past offers a sense of what she desires to be, a beautiful girl whose symbol is a living rose.

An incident during a party in the Orlando location links Rosa's search for meaning in her name in her future as well as her past. As so often, Rosa is treated as Burger's daughter and has to "describe again, as Lionel told a political anecdote, a family chronicle, what was really his love affair with my mother" (p. 168). During her recounting, an African grandmother gives a baby a cap with a rosette on it to present to Rosa. The hat—a sign of acceptance and, in the grandmother and baby, of the continuity of past and future—pleases Rosa. But it is given to the daughter of the Burger love affair, not to a woman valued for herself, as Rosa realizes; she puts it away in a drawer on returning home.

The possible futures, much discussed in the novel, seem to exclude her as well. The most important is, once again, her parents': the future, often italicized or capitalized, of Communist victory. "*That house*," Rosa thinks, "made provision for no less than the Future. My father left that house with the name-plate of his honourable profession polished on the gate, and went to spend the rest of his life in prison, secure in that future" (p. 111). Aunt Nel offers "the future—it's the same as now. It will be occupied by her children, that's all" (p. 131). For Africans, "through blackness is revealed the way to the future. The descendants of Chaka, Dingane, Hintsa, Sandile, Moshesh, Cetawayo, Msilekazi and Sekukuni are the only ones who can get us there" (p. 135). The first future, with its prospect of prison, Rosa fears; the second she denies; and the third, as the disdain with which all whites are held by the young Africans at the Orlando party indicates, seems to be denied her.

Her attempts to find a private life in the present are unsuccessful as well. "Now you are free," she thinks again and again after her parents' deaths, but she is disconnected, as the setting of her new job indicates: "Up on the twenty-sixth floor the smoked glass windows made the climate of each day the same cool mean, neither summer nor winter, and the time something neither night nor day" (p. 77). In this world divorced from environment and time she remains a rose behind glass. When she descends for lunch in a park one day, she experiences the first of the two events, both marked by disconnection and stasis, which are to precipitate her "betrayal" of the Burger cause. In the park Rosa and the other lunchers find one among them suddenly and inexplicably dead. The entire scene is marked by immobility and frustrated action: the dead man sits "solid as the statue of the landrost"; a pantechnicon is unable to turn at the traffic light; an errant child is caught by its mother; two young lovers display a "fondling half-mating." Rosa can find no context for this event, a death without ostensible cause or meaning. Rosa, formed entirely by her parents' code of opposition to institutional injustice, is arrested by this action in the present, this simple death. The second event, the beating of a donkey, has no spatial context; it occurs as Rosa drives through the fringes of an African location, a place "not on any plan of the city environs" (p. 207). Again, the incident is marked by arrested motion. She sees a donkey, cart, and driver "convulsed, yet the cart was not coming any nearer" (pp. 207–208). As she becomes aware of the senseless beating of the exhausted beast, which she calls a "mad frieze," she too becomes immobilized: "the car simply fell away from the pressure of my foot and carried me no farther" (p. 209).

Rosa senses that her life in "our house" is the cause of her paralysis in the face of death and pain. Shortly after leaving the dead man in the park, she recalls "the paralysis that blotted out my mother limb by limb," and she makes a more specific connection, that her mother despised "those whites who cared more for animals than people," to explain her failure to stop the man from beating the donkey. Rosa has sought in part one of the novel to break free from her parents by searching for a past from which her future can grow. Failing to find this connection, she remains the little girl, Burger's daughter, who sought her father in the pool as "a place where no fear, hurt or pain existed."

Rosa's condition at the time of the donkey beating recalls Helen Shaw's at the close of *The Lying Days*. Both women are disconnected and, consequently, paralyzed; both remain in their parents' thrall; both run. But where Helen failed to acknowledge her parents' influence and simply sought to "go away," Rosa realizes, "I don't know how to live in Lionel's country" (p. 210). Rosa's formulation, implying that it is his country, not her own, which she seeks to inhabit, shows her incipient awareness of her problem's cause. And where Helen made cheery claims about accepting disillusion as a beginning rather than an end and exited claiming she would return, Rosa leaves disillusioned, knowing that her running will be seen as betrayal.

Rosa's vehicle for escape from Lionel's country is Brandt Vermeulen, a cosmopolitan Afrikaner with influential government connections. Like the Burgers and Nels, he offers Rosa another version of a continuous history, "dialogue, beginning with Plato, the dialogue with self, culminating in 'the Vorster initiative,' the dialogue of peoples and nations" (p. 194). A more intellectual version of her employer on the twenty-sixth floor, Vermeulen has shut himself off from the South African environment by accepting the ingenious notions of the verlighte. Afrikaners. Where the Burgers have fought for "Peace, Land, Bread," Vermeulen uses what Rosa calls "the long words"—separate freedoms, multilateral development and the like—in a vain attempt to reconcile the viewpoints of the Burgers and Nels.

Set against Vermeulen's constructs is the real South African environment, which Rosa observes on her first trip to his house. She perceives in the landscape the history which had informed her parents' lives and which, in the end, will inform hers—the history of a land in which the only legitimate home is prison. Her drive takes her toward Pretoria, where she sees "Ndebele houses like a mud fort" and "the monumental shrine of the volk," signs of the African battle against domination and the molding of the victorious Afrikaner nation, and then

> in past the official's house in the fine old garden, the trunk of the huge palm-tree holding up its nave of shade, the warders' houses in sunny domestic order, the ox-blood brick prison with the blind façade on the street—the narrow apertures darkened with bars and heavy diamond-mesh wire, impossible to decide, ever, which corresponded with which category of room for which purpose, and along which corridor in there, to left or right, there was waiting a particular setting of table and two chairs; the police car and

van parked outside, a warder come off duty flirting with a girl with yolk-colored hair and a fox terrier in her arms; the door; the huge worn door with its missing studs and grooves exactly placed for ever. (p. 178)

The historical allusions continue in this depiction of the prison, "the ox-blood brick" recalling the Afrikaner teams trekking north from the Cape and "the diamond mesh" recalling the discovery which led the whites to settle the veld. The huge door is what confronts those, like Rosa, waiting to deliver parcels to the detained at the novel's outset, those waiting to deliver them to Rosa at the close. That door is there "for ever" for Lionel Burger after his life sentence. That it will be for Rosa as well is further indicated by the "narrow apertures," which provide a small patch of light for those inside, a detail with which the novel closes. The description of the prison is bracketed by allusions to gardens, the private life Rosa has sought in order to escape it. The "sunny domestic order," a contrast with the darkness behind the apertures, recalls the order of the Nels' life which had entranced Rosa, and the flirtation of the man and girl, the pleasures of a young woman she was denied and still craves. The landscape thus calls up at once the harsh realities of South Africa history, the private life Rosa has been denied in the past, and the future in prison she is trying to escape.

For Rosa to seek a passport through one such as Vermeulen is betrayal of the Burger cause with a vengeance. By putting her defection in such stark terms, Gordimer makes her strongest statement of the need, whatever the consequences, of a child to claim a life of her own. Rosa seeks that life with Madame Bagnelli (nicknamed Katya), the first wife of Lionel Burger, who had bridled under the discipline of the Communist party and betrayed its cause by establishing a personal life in southern France. For most of the novel's second part, Katya is the vehicle for Rosa's search for a private life; Rosa now addresses her, as she had Conrad in part one. The initial appeal of Katya's world is the liberty it allows Rosa to experience the childhood she was denied in a house dominated by stories of the Sharpeville massacre and prison visits. As Rosa thinks, "I giggle with *their Katya* like the adolescent girls at school, who were in that phase while Sipho Mokema was showing Tony and me the bullet hole in his trouser-leg and I was running back and forth to visit prison, the first prison, where my mother was" (p. 326).

Katya also offers Rosa a world, unlike South Africa's, in which an historical continuity can be assumed. "If you live in Europe . . . things change," Katya says, "but continuity never seems to break. You don't have to throw the past away. If I'd stayed . . . at home, how will they fit in, white people?" (p. 249). The breaks in her speech—a parenthetical glance, the ellipses—are an early sign of the problems with continuity in Katya's life that Rosa will see later. But at the outset of her visit, Katya presents, and Rosa eagerly accepts, a society in which continuity never "seems" to break. This sense of continuity has allowed Katya to live for the present, and as the room she has prepared for Rosa indicates, Katya knows the need of present, sensuous experience for a young girl.

> It was a room made ready for someone imagined. A girl, a creature whose sense of existence would be in her nose buried in flowers, peach juice running down her chin, face tended at mirrors, mind dreamily diverted, body seeking pleasure. Rosa Burger entered, going forward into possession by that image. Madame Bagnelli, smiling, coaxing, saw that her guest was a little drunk, like herself. (pp. 229–30)

Rosa doesn't need much coaxing; she has wanted to take possession of a room catering to her senses, a room in which her face, not Lionel Burger's, is attended to.

Already on her first day in France, Rosa, the model of restraint, is intoxicated. The development of the latent desire for pleasure in the sensual world of the present comes through a love affair with a married French professor, Bernard Chabalier. The sense of Rosa's luxuriating in the present is evident as she observes the furnishings of the bar which is their *rendez-vous*: "All these were strongly the objects of Rosa's present. She inhabited it completely as everything in place around her, there and then. In the bar where she had sat seeing others living in the mirror, there was no threshold between her reflection and herself" (p. 272). "Everything in place around her," Rosa is beginning to see herself as the focal point of her world; and for the first time in her life she finds no disparity—no threshold—between what she is and what her appearance shows her to be, as she so painfully had when posing as de Witt's fiancée.

Chabalier offers Rosa love simply for herself unalloyed with feelings about her august father, but when he proposes a life together for them, it is simply a continuation of the present they share. The prospect of Rosa's living in Paris as his mistress—what more private life could there be, she thinks—is introduced as they view two Bonnard canvases, one from 1894, the other from 1945. The women in them, Chabalier holds, were the same to Bonnard, as if fascism, two wars, the Occupation had never occurred, because they have no "existence any more than the leaves have, outside this lovely forest where they are. No past, no future" (p. 287). Rosa's response, "If I did come to Paris," shows her assumption that it holds a life with "no past, no future." She tries out the idea soon after, watching people from a hill "as if completing a figure that was leading to a tapestry on a museum wall" (p. 288). But the prospect of this life doesn't hold her. As she and Chabalier lie together, she gives a glance down "in a private motivation of inner vision as alert and dissimulating as the gaze her mother had been equally unaware of" (p. 290). This is the look Rosa noticed when her mother suddenly realized she would make use of someone, like the pathetic schoolteacher, in her cause. Instead of being used as she had been throughout her early life, Rosa acts as her mother had; she uses Chabalier in her cause, the affirmation of her desirability as a woman. She will not join him in Paris.

Katya has given Rosa a sense of herself as well—as Rosa, so proper and withdrawn when Burger's daughter, thinks, "I've never talked with anyone as I do with you, incontinently, femininely" (p. 262). Rosa has realized that "something is owed us. Young women, girls still"; what she felt owed—what she has now claimed—is the right to be girlish, incontinent if she pleases (p. 300). But the dangers of being only this are conveyed to her in a chance meeting in the street with an old woman, who "didn't know, couldn't remember what was wrong" (p. 300). Her problem is the same, if more extreme, as Mrs. Fuecht's, whose life changed "suddenly" for no apparent reason. Both of them have lived without looking for a pattern in their lives; having no sense—no remembrance—of the past, they live a series of isolated presents. After calming the woman in her room, Rosa takes her leave:

> I wanted to go and she wanted to keep me with her in case the woman I had met in the street took possession of her again. I came flying up the hill to look for you singing while you upholster an

old chair or paint a brave coat of red on your toenails. I wanted to ask who she was and tell you what happened. But when I saw you, Katya, I said nothing. It might happen to you. When I am gone. Someday. When I am in Paris, or in Cameroun picking up things that take my fancy, the mementoes I shall acquire. (p. 301)

Unstated is Rosa's realization that the life of the present in Paris means it might happen to her. In short, there is a fine line between entering into possession of rooms made for the moment's pleasure as Rosa did on arrival and being taken possession of by a discontinuous series of them. At best, what might appear as taking possession can, without a purpose to one's life, become merely "taking a fancy." Rosa has needed the life of the present that Katya has given her, but she sees that its prospect may be worse than the prison she has fled. She doesn't tell Katya about this incident; indeed, Rosa will address her no longer in her thoughts.

Before returning to South Africa, Rosa encounters Baasie at a gathering in London. He phones her later that night, drunk and denouncing the past they had shared. The confrontation is, in short, the same as Gideon and Jessie's at the close of *Occasion for Loving*. But the effect is not elegiac as it had been for Jessie, who waits, helpless, for Gideon to remember their time together, when he certainly will not. For Rosa, by contrast, the confrontation is cathartic. She cries for only the second time in her life—the first was on leaving Chabalier—over the loss of her black brother Baasie and of her drowned brother Tony, whose death her vomiting sausage and "gasping between spasms" recalls. She realizes that in the house pool where she and her brothers swam, Lionel Burger had only seemed to provide "a place where no fear, hurt or pain existed." By accepting that her father did not have the power to nullify the pain of Tony's death and Baasie's rejection, Rosa ceases to see him as the "place" defining her life. In the words of the novel's epigraph, she now feels that "I am a place in which something has occurred."

Only through her private time in France, Gordimer stresses at the close of part two, could Rosa sever the hold of her father and feel herself as the place at the center of her world: "Love doesn't cast out fear but makes it possible to weep, howl, at least. Because Rosa Burger had once cried for joy she came out of the bathroom and stalked about the flat . . . sobbing and clenching her jaw, ugly, soiled, stuffing her fist in her mouth" (p. 324). Her private occasion of loving and being loved as

Rosa Burger allows her to mourn the end of the Burger house, to leave behind the composed, dry-eyed, girl—Burger's daughter—who waited, motionless and silent, before the prison door.

Having become Rosa Burger, she is free to return to South Africa to fashion her own life. Rosa cannot say why she returned, but she is clearly changed by her confrontation of her past through Baasie's phone call, the experiencing of a private life of the present she can claim as her own, and the understanding that without a sense of continuity one may become the woman she met in the street. Rosa's own sense of this continuity is shown in the peace she finds at the Nels' farm after her return: "I went to bed in the rondavel and slept the way I had when I was a child, thick pink Waverly blankets kicked away, lumpy pillow punched under my neck. Anyone may have come in the door and looked down on me; I wouldn't have stirred" (p. 352). Her blankets kicked away, she is no longer "swaddled" as she had been by the Nels' order of Afrikaner life. This change derives, in part, from the deflation of her aunt's vision of the future. She had been certain it was to be the present, only "occupied by her children," but her daughter Marie has been implicated in terrorist activities. For Rosa Marie Burger, the two heritages in her name have become one, both heralding the same future. Certain of her heritage and future, it no longer matters to the girl who was so concerned with what people saw in her—the girl whose first words in the novel are *"When they saw me outside the prison, what did they see!"*—should they happen to look at her sleeping (p. 13). She knows; she sleeps secure in an African hut, in place.

Having found in France a life of her own, Rosa is now undaunted by those who controlled her past. She can finally address her father as an equal, telling him that his vision of the way to "the future" was wrong. Rosa sees the future in the revolt of the Soweto children in 1976. The spontaneity of their action, unguided by the discipline urged by the older opposition leaders, carries a condemnation of not only her parents' political methods but the discipline imposed on the young Burger daughter. Rosa says to her father: "The sins of the fathers; at last the children avenge on the fathers the sins of the fathers. Their children and children's children; that was the Future, father, in hands not foreseen" (p. 348). This is at once a statement about historical change and an assertion by Rosa Burger, his child, that the future lies in her hands.

Her sense of self secure, Rosa can now carry on, in her own way, the struggle to which Lionel Burger dedicated his life. She chooses his profession, working with crippled children: "I am teaching them to walk again, at Baragwanath Hospital. They put one foot before the other" (p. 332). In this calling she has found a means of alleviating the paralysis she had felt as a child under parents' demands. She can act when faced with the inexplicable suffering of crippled and wounded children. One can be sure she would not run from a dead man in a park or a tormented donkey.

During the October 1977 school boycott, Rosa is one of the many detained. In a women's prison at the novel's close, she has assumed the position of her mother at the outset. Having learned how to act on her own volition, Rosa has claimed her maturity. Other women are no longer the massively powerful figures that they had been for Helen Shaw. Rosa is their equal; as she says, "My sense of sorority was clear." Rosa gets permission to draw pictures, which visitors recognized as the women inside "and understood that these women were in touch with each other, if cut off from the outside world" (p. 356). Rosa is once again "connected," but she is not carrying messages from and about others—her father's not yet being detained, her parents' news to de Witt. She now sends her own.

The importance of her private time with Katya remains clear as well. Rosa draws, again and again, childlike sketches of a hill by a sea filled with bright, tiny boats, renditions of Katya's village. The most striking aspect of the drawings is the light "which appeared to come from everywhere; all objects were sunny" (p. 355). In her dark cell, Rosa is sustained by the bright private time she had spent in southern France. But she does not mourn its loss, realizing that it belongs to a world with different codes, different possibilities than the one into which she was born and has now claimed as her own. In a letter to Katya which closes the novel, the prison censor deletes Rosa's reference to the "watermark of light" which is reflected into her cell every evening. Katya is simply perplexed by his deletion, where Lionel Burger had taken delight in trying to decipher the censored material. He, and now Rosa after him, have accepted and managed to find small pleasures in their chosen world; he had described the watermark as "delicate pearly light" (p. 64). Rosa had realized while at Katya's that "there is a certain range of possibilities that can occur within the orbit of a particular order of life" (p. 238). Rosa ends accepting the possibilities allowed by her order: the few sensual pleasures like that watermark of light, her sorority, and a belief in her future. The view may not be as good as from the hill in southern France—or even the twenty-sixth floor of the office building—but Rosa's company is better and her sense of place, and time, secure.

V

July's People brings to its logical conclusion the theme of leaving the mother's house developed in Gordimer's extended *Bildungsroman*. The novel begins with Maureen and Bam Smales and their three children exiled in July's village some sixty kilometers outside Johannesburg, an embattled city which has suddenly become "back there," as it is repeatedly called in the novel. In the opening days of their stay, Maureen and Bam remain confident in the power their parental roles have always conferred. When the oldest child, Victor, wants to show his racing car set to the village children, Maureen responds,

> —To whom?—
> The black children who watched the hut from afar and scuttled, as if her glance were a stone thrown among them, re-formed a little way off.
> —But tell them they mustn't touch it. I don't want my things messed up and broken. You must tell them.—
> She laughed as adults did, in the power they refuse to use. —I tell them? They don't understand our language.—
> The boy said nothing but kicked steadily at the dented, rusted bath used for their ablutions.
> —Don't. D'you hear me? That's July's.—[12]

The family unit is very much as it was in Johannesburg. Maureen is secure in the adult power she really doesn't refuse to use; she protects the possessions of other adults, like July's tub here. Victor and the

---

12 Nadine Gordimer, *July's People* (New York, 1981), 14. Subsequent references in the text are to this edition.

black children contest this power only by sulking. The racial boundaries from "back there" remain intact as well. Those black children flee as much from the white as the adult presence, and while Victor has the impulse to mix with them, he still wants the prerogatives, enforced by his mother, that he has been used to in dealings with them. Indeed, Victor's concern with the racing car set is the best sign of his identification with the old white order, for Maureen and Bam fix on their vehicle as the symbol of their power which had gone unquestioned "back there."

But this old order is quickly undermined along both generational and racial lines. In their new surroundings, the children soon begin to equate their parents' treatment of them and the Africans. During an early quarrel between the parents and their sister Gina, the boys observe "their parents closing in on one of their own kind." This is an echo of the language used to designate Africans, specifically of the novel's opening in which July "began the day for them as his kind has always done for their kind" (pp. 42, 1). We also look from the children's point of view when Bam patronizes the man whose orange sack the children had made use of by patting him on the back; then Victor is aware that "his father laid the same calming hand on him" (p. 86). A counter process is already under way, for in his homeland July naturally becomes the provider; he has begun to patronize Bam, for example, in his comments to the children about Bam's small contribution to village life of a tank to catch rain water: "You lucky, you know your father he's very, very clever man. Is coming plenty rain, now everybody can be happy with that tank, is nice easy, isn't it: You see, your father he make everyone-everyone to be pleased" (p. 63). But it is really July who is the clever man here, for he finds food from the neighboring town and instructs the children in the ways of the village.

The merging of the children into the life of the village is not due so much to these perceptions of their parents' attitude toward them or of the changed power structure. The children change quite simply because they are young enough not to have been completely formed by the world of "back there" as their parents have. Gina, the youngest, adapts almost immediately; the Smales can't have been in the village more than a few days—time isn't clearly marked in the novel—when she enters the hut carrying an African baby on her back "with the old woman's sciatic gait of black children who carry brothers and sisters almost as big as they are" (p. 41). For the two boys, about six and nine, the transformation is slower. But by the time Bam's gun disappears near the novel's close, the children observe his distress as the African children would. Bam seems to sense their greater allegiance to the village world when he accuses the boys of having divulged the gun's hiding place; for their part, "neither would dare risk telling their father everybody knew it was there, every chicken that scratched, every child whose eyes went round the interior of the hut, *mhani* Tsatswani's hut, where the white people stayed" (p. 144). The boys clearly see their hut with the eyes of the other African children, and Victor, the older, at once surreptitiously pinches his brother's leg to keep him from implicating their sister and mocks his father by advising, "You c'n tell the police, dad" (p. 145). Victor, of course, has learned that the police are useless here and that his parents are powerless as well—as the contrast to the scene with the racing car indicates. Indeed, his ability to put that racing car aside, where his parents remain preoccupied with their vehicle, is the best indication of his greater acceptance of village life.

The Smales may continue to speak "in the sub-language of hints and private significance foreign to children," but it is clearly not that "sub-language" which figures most in the children's lives by the novel's close (p. 67). The language of the community, by contrast with their parents', seems less and less "foreign" to them; when the *gumba-gumba*, a musical amplifier from the city, arrives, it is "something for which Victor, Gina, and Royce knew the name in the village people's language but not in their own" (p. 40). The children are becoming bilingual; they don't try—in one of the most loaded words in the novel—to translate from one culture to another as their parents do. They are not preoccupied with new contexts, with comparisons with "back there," with the different life they might have lived had they run from South Africa in time. The last image we have of them is of the oldest unselfconsciously receiving a gift from July with the traditional African gesture: "Victor is seen to clap his hands, sticky with mealie-*pap*, softly, gravely together and bob obeisance, receiving the gift with cupped palms" (p. 157). Throughout the novel, for something to "be seen" is for it to be experienced, taken into oneself—the landscape around the village is "not seen" by Maureen as the city is "never seen" by Martha,

July's wife. The authenticity of Victor's response is emphasized by its juxtaposition with a picturesque view characteristic of European photographs, a panorama of the African village "held in the pantheistic hand" (p. 156). Victor, unlike such photographers, does not view his village from afar; his hands are smeared with mealie-*pap*. He and the other Smales children have acquired new "ways of seeing" during their youth which, as Gordimer said, will stay with them always. These children will, in time, be dreaming dreams in the language and the gestures of the village as the truly bilingual, those who have immersed themselves in another world, are said to do.

3

Landscapes as Outward Signs in the Early Novels

I

From the outset of her career through the 1960s, Gordimer was "chosen" by two aspects of her situation. The most influential in the fifties was what Guy Butler described as a "dismal dependent colonialism," which led to "a lack of curiosity about one's past and one's surroundings."[1] As Gordimer has noted, she initially found it hard to be curious because her own reading had been about "the life and the physical background of England and America and France and Germany and Russia," which caused her to feel that "what I was writing couldn't have been of interest to anybody, because it was so *ordinary*."[2] Gordimer made it her interest: her own world's "physical background" was a major concern in *The Lying Days* and the very subject of *A World of Strangers*. In these novels she did for Johannesburg what Defoe had done for London, Balzac for Paris, Dreiser for Chicago and New York. A second aspect of her situation, the increasingly brutal implementation of apartheid, claimed her attention in the sixties. The pattern of the novels of the fifties was repeated: *Occasion for Loving*, which grows from an exploration of private life, was followed by *The Late Bourgeois World*, which, as the title implies, takes its impetus from her situation, the South African "world." Indeed, from the mid-sixties on, Gordimer's fiction was to reflect the political developments of the South African situation in an unusually specific way. *The Late Bour-*

1 Quoted in Sands, "The South African Novel," 93.
2 Gray, "Writing in South Africa: Nadine Gordimer Interviewed," 2.

geois World treats the frustrated impulse of the 1963/64 radical white sabotage movement; *A Guest of Honour* records the difficulties posed to the many African states which gained independence in the sixties; *Burger's Daughter* develops from the life of the barrister Abram Fischer, an Afrikaner who renounced his heritage to become a radical opponent of apartheid during the early sixties. *July's People* shows Gordimer reacting to a subject of particular contemporary concern; the novel is one of a number, including J. M. Coetzee's *Waiting for the Barbarians* (1981) and Karl Schoeman's *Promised Land* (1976), set during the interregnum following white rule in South Africa. But Gordimer's situation "chose" her in an even more pronounced way than it did such contemporaries. Hers has been a realist's art set in the present, where her most accomplished contemporaries, like Coetzee and Sheila Fugard, have treated the tensions of South African society metaphorically, often through events set in the historical past.[3]

Gordimer has provided a record of her society's background in a remarkably consistent way throughout her career: through describing the surface features of the South African landscape. She has spoken of her attempt to capture the "surface shimmer" of her world in her fiction in the fifties. She did so admirably. Even in the most negative appraisal of her early fiction, Anthony Woodward allowed that her work provides "a genuinely vivid impression of the living texture of South African landscape and society: its dry heat, its dorps, its suburban homes, its noisy towns, its multi-racial tensions. An authentic feeling of *place* is built up in all her fiction; . . . to register the surface-texture of life with her degree of vitality is a genuinely impressive accomplishment."[4] So pronounced is Gordimer's skill in creating a sense of place

---

3 The style of such writers as Coetzee and Fugard is accurately discussed under the heading "Fabulation" in Sarah Christie, Geoffrey Hutchings, and Don Maclennan, *Perspectives on South African Fiction* (Johannesburg, 1980), 159–83. They discuss Gordimer under "Realism," a placement supported by her claiming the tradition Lukács has termed "critical realism." Faithful rendition of her situation was so important an aspect of her novels that Gordimer undertook extensive research of the African trade union movement for *A Guest of Honour* and of the South African Communist party for *Burger's Daughter*. Indeed, she replied to a reviewer to justify her sources for *Burger's Daughter* in *African Communist*, LXXX (1980), 109.

4 Woodward, "Nadine Gordimer," 2. Gordimer's reference to the "surface shimmer" is in Ravenscroft, "A Writer in South Africa: Nadine Gordimer," 28. The documentation continues through the seventies. See Frank Tuohy, "Breaths of Change," *TLS*, April 25, 1980, p. 462.

through the accumulation of surface details that her early fiction recalls no novelist so much as Balzac. Rarely since him has a writer been so relentless in documenting a world.

Since Bernard Sachs's late fifties essay "Nadine Gordimer: Writer with the Eye of a Camera," reviewers have noted that Gordimer used her verbal photography most often—and most effectively—to describe her situation. As the South African critic Colin Gardner generalized, she is "good at depicting societies, not so good at creating people—an expert at backgrounds, but rather less happy in her foregrounds. Or to put it another way, she seems often to prefer surfaces (which she registers with a coolly loving care) to inwardness."[5] Gardner is right both ways: in her fiction through *The Late Bourgeois World* Gordimer was concerned with "registering" surfaces, and she devoted most of her attention to creating "backgrounds," the situations in which her characters moved. Indeed, in 1961 she justified both tendencies when she contrasted the role of the South African writer with that of the European, who is "too stuffed with facts about himself":

> In South Africa, in Africa generally, the reader knows perilously little about himself or his feelings. We have a great deal to learn about ourselves, and the novelist, along with the poet, playwright, composer and painter, must teach us. We look to them to give us the background of self-knowledge that we may be able to take for granted. Consequently, the novel-in-depth—what one might call the "pure" novel of the imagination—cannot be expected to flourish in Africa yet. We are still at the stage of trying to read ourselves by outward signs.[6]

This statement stands as a manifesto for Gordimer's novels through the mid-sixties. Particularly in her two novels focusing on "worlds," but to a surprising degree in *The Lying Days* and *Occasion for Loving*, she would be concerned with providing this "background of self-

5 Bernard Sachs, *South African Personalities and Places* (Johannesburg, 1959), 83–89; Colin Gardner, "Nadine's World of Strangers," *Reality: A Journal of Liberal and Radical Opinion*, VIII (January, 1977), 15. References to Gordimer's verbal photography are numerous. See Abrahams, "Nadine Gordimer: The Transparent Ego," 87–88; Girling, "Provincial and Continental: Writers in South Africa," 113; Haugh, *Nadine Gordimer*, 30–31. Readers of Gordimer's fiction will find it appropriate that her son Hugo is a filmmaker and that she devoted a year to advising on the production of the seven films collected in *The Gordimer Series*.

6 Nadine Gordimer, "The Novel and the Nation in South Africa," 523.

knowledge" through photographing the "outward signs" of South African society.

To define this as the South African novelist's task was one thing, to find a pattern that defined her culture in these signs another. Gordimer was "still at the stage of trying to read" these signs in 1961, well after she had completed her first two novels. *The Lying Days* reflects a relatively salutary view of this undertaking—that a pattern is there but not yet readable—yet it fails to appear in *A World of Strangers* even though the novel is carefully structured to afford a clear reading of the "outward signs." The problem, of course, was that as the Forsterian "only connect" proved less and less applicable in the South African situation, Gordimer was left without a sense of pattern in her world. None emerges in the novels of the sixties either, but the seeds of a new cultural view are apparent in the changing background of the novels. While Johannesburg remains the primary setting, Gordimer's characters increasingly seek a cultural pattern in the veld, an African land informed by an African culture.

The novels of the sixties also show Gordimer feeling toward the resolution of a related problem, described well by a complaint of a character in *A World of Strangers* that "there are too many landscape painters here. They don't know how to deal with man so they leave him out."[7] Gordimer found it difficult to "deal with man" without a sense of a world with which characters could engage. Her discovery of that world in the veld is accompanied by a modification of her photographic perspective which was predicated on observers registering a world discrete from themselves. By the late sixties she had developed what can be called a painterly attitude, which would allow her characters to enter the worlds they confront.

The first two decades of Gordimer's career show not just an uncommon curiosity about her world but a singular tenacity in searching for its distinctive form. The four novels through *The Late Bourgeois World* serve as a kind of public apprenticeship, in which she explores her culture's "outward signs," discovers a new landscape offering a culture with which her characters can engage, and fashions a new perspective

---

7 *A World of Strangers* (1958; rpr. London, 1976), 81. Subsequent references in the text are to the 1976 edition.

which would allow them to do so. This apprenticeship lays the ground-work for *A Guest of Honour,* the first of Gordimer's "pure novels of the imagination."

II

As Helen Shaw stands outside the concessions in the first chapter of *The Lying Days,* she realizes that there were no images of her world in the literature about "the English children for whom the books were written":

> I had never read a book in which I myself was recognizable; in which there was a "girl" like Anna who did the housework and the cooking and called the mother and father Missus and Baas; in which the children ate and lived closely with their parents and played in the lounge and went to the bioscope. (p. 20)

Young Helen senses that, lacking images of her world—what Gordimer later called a "background of self-knowledge"—she knows perilously little about herself and her environment. *The Lying Days* is a record of her search for that knowledge. While she fails to find a native culture to replace the European world that is reflected not only in her books but in the mining society in which she was raised, Helen is as curious about her surroundings as even Professor Butler could wish his countrymen to be. Helen provides a wide-ranging record of the "outward signs" of her society. But she does even more. As the numerous self-conscious references near the novel's close point up, the writing of the novel is itself a sign of the colonial's self-conscious attempt to forge a native view of her world. *The Lying Days* is the creation of what Helen lacks outside the concessions—"a book in which I myself was recognizable."

The most obvious constraint on Helen's creation of her book is that all her models are European. She reads Lawrence, Eliot, Auden, Smollett, and Donne, but she is exposed to no South African or other colonial literature. Young Helen, in fact, defines her world by its failure to conform to the literature she has read; at the novel's outset she stands before the concessions "knowing and flatly accepting it as the real world because it was ugly and did not exist in books" (p. 21). Her first, predictable reaction is to escape from this ugly world through European literature. On her train trips from Atherton to Johannesburg when she first attends the university, Helen sits each day across from a man identified only by the English novels he reads, and after they finally converse one day, "He returned to Trollope, I to George Eliot," until "the sooty, antiseptic scent of the city came in at the window" (p. 107). Neither passenger has observed the dirty yet sterile South African world outside.

Helen returns repeatedly to those European books:

> But in nothing that I read could I find anything that approximated to my own life; to our life on a gold mine in South Africa. Our life was not regulated by the seasons and the elements of weather and emotion, like the life of peasants; nor was it expressed through movements in art, through music heard, through the exchange of ideas, like the life of Europeans shaped by great and ancient cities, so that they were Parisians or Londoners as identifiably as they were Pierre or James. (p. 96)

When Helen looks at the sixty miles between Johannesburg and the open veld along the railway, she finds an anti-pastoral, "the hills made of sand from the Mine dumps, the chemical-tinted water bringing a false promise of river-greenness, cool, peace of dripping fronds and birds" (p. 97). The landscape, far from bringing a pastoral merging of rural and city life, reveals neither the "regulated" life of the peasants nor the "shaped" life of the great cities. Helen sees

> The wreckage of old motorcar parts, rusting tin and burst shoes that littered the bald veld in between. The advertisement hoardings and the growing real-estate schemes, dusty, treeless, putting out barbed-wire fences on which the little brown mossies swung and pieces of torn cloth clung, like some forlorn file that recorded the passing of life in a crude fashion. The patches of towns, with their flat streets, tin-roofed houses, main street and red-faced town hall, "Palace" or "Tivoli" showing year-old films from America. We had no lions and we had no art galleries, we heard no Bach and the oracle voice of the ancient Africa did not come to us, was drowned, perhaps, by the records singing of Tennessee in the

Greek cafés and the thump of the Mine stamp batteries which sounded in our ears as unnoticed as our blood. (p. 97)

The world Helen perceives is most notable for its disconnectedness, "the patches of towns," "pieces of torn cloth," and the barriers of the fences reflected in the fragmentary sentences. The passage itself records "the passing of life in a crude fashion" as well in the choppy series of negations, a distinct contrast with the sophisticated negations in the passage on European life. What begins as litter on the veld becomes a cultural dumping ground of Tivoli, American films and Greek cafés. But for all its ugliness, this native landscape is alive: the real-estate dealers "put out" fences and the mossies "record." And if "the oracle voice of the ancient Africa" does not come, it is still presumed to exist.

The whites in Helen's mining community cling to what she terms their "eternal colonialism" to ensure that the African oracle voice goes unnoticed. Their response to a mild protest by the African mine workers early in the novel is characteristic: the whites concern themselves with the absence of the proper paraphernalia for the tea served by the mine manager's wife, "an exiled Mrs. Dalloway." Those mine workers are pathetically docile here, but they pose a real threat; indeed, they will go on strike by the novel's close. This attempt of the whites in the mine to hide from the world without is described especially well in Gordimer's 1968 essay "The Witwatersrand: A Time of Tailings":

> One could go from christening to old age pension within the shelter of the company plantation of blue gums that surrounded the property. One need never be aware of the threatening space of the veld without. Inside the magic circle of blue gums everything was decided for one, from annual leave to social status. (p. 25)

Here, as so often in her fiction, Gordimer uses the landscape to capture the insular quality of that "magic circle" meant to block awareness of the threatening veld outside. Indeed, she uses the same "outward signs" to emphasize the boldness of Helen's initial venture outside to the concessions:

> The Mine houses had their fences and hedges around them, their spoor of last summer's creepers drawn up about their walls. I

went down the dust road through the trees and out onto the main road that shook everything off from it, that stood up alone and straight in the open sun and the veld.

It was different, being down on the road instead of up in the bus or the car, seeing it underneath. (p. 17)

The barriers of trees and fences, the houses drawing the creepers around them, capture the isolation of the mine world from the veld, which is almost always viewed from the safety of bus or car.

Helen comes to perceive the insularity of this colonial outpost through her sporadic forays outside its bounds. Her awareness is developed through a series of contrasts between the narcissistic impulses fostered by her mine society, revealed in her preoccupation with mirrors, and the ability to view it with detachment, seen in the pictures of the mine she provides after each movement outside its "magic circle." The opening scene of the novel introduces these contrasting impulses; the self-engrossment of Mrs. Shaw and Helen looking in mirrors is set against Helen's perceiving her parents' tennis group "suddenly as a picture" as she returns through the mine barriers of "the pines and the clipped hedge" (p. 24). This pattern is repeated when Helen rejects her parents' invitation to a barbecue, as she had the tennis gathering, for a date with Joel Aaron, whose Jewishness places him outside the mine society. As Helen's mother looks in the mirror, insisting that Helen give more attention to "her own kind of people," she conjures up another colonial scene, a garden party with the participants standing within a circle of trees:

> They would be standing under the trees, the corseted women, the thin, gracious women who always dressed as if for a garden party, the satellite young daughters in pastel frocks. . . . I had been there many times. I knew what it was like; a small child in white party shoes that made my feet big and noisy, tearing in and out among the grown-ups, wild with the excitement of the fire and the smoky dark; and then grown-up myself, standing first on one foot, then the other, drawing patterns with my toe on the ground, feebly part of the feebleness of it all, the mawkish attempts of the boys to entertain, the inane response of the girls: the roasting of meat to be torn apart by hands and teeth made as feeble as a garden party. That was what these people did to everything in life; enfeebled it.

Weddings were the appearance of dear little girls dressed up to strew rose petals, rather than matings; death was the speculation about who would step up to the dead man's position; dignity was the chain of baubles the mayor wore round his neck. (p. 136)

One can see Helen's imagination taking hold, the picture forming, in the phrasing "I had been there many times. I knew what it was like." She depicts an enervated society, even the bacchanalian tearing of meat by hands and teeth "made feeble as a garden party." Helen feels toward a sense of what this life has held and will hold for her by recalling her roles as a child and adolescent, then projecting her future by imagining marriage and finally death. Her feeling of entrapment in this world is captured not just by circular images—the surrounding trees, the "satellite young daughters," the absurd chain around the mayor's neck—but by the circular temporal pattern of the passage: the wedding represented by the little girls strewing roses near the close recalls the small child with which the progression through life began. Helen presents at once a portrait of the mine's rigid, insular social structure and her own frustrated position in it.

Helen provides numerous other portraits of the mine society functions—the sundowner gathering, the women's afternoon tea parties, and the displaying of goods collected on the ritual trip to England. A final portrait, during her return home for the last time, begins as she tries on jewelry before the mirror, realizing that she has merely assumed a role dictated by conventions of a new era. She sees "the outfit, the face, that any one of the women I knew at Isa's or the Marcuses' might be wearing at this moment" (p. 307). The realization that she has merely assumed a place within another "magic circle" causes her to accept her place in the evening party at the mine manager's, where she is once again enveloped by "the warm buzz of talk that had surrounded my childhood" (p. 308). Helen has presented the "outward signs" of this mine society, but she still remains within its circle.

At the other extreme from the world of the "magic circle" is the most foreign and threatening world of all, the African location. Both depictions of it in the novel take a markedly different form than the novel's other settings. The carefully ordered pictures of the location derive partly, no doubt, from Gordimer's awareness that it was not well known to her readers. But the orderliness of Helen's depictions has a more fundamental cause: her need to keep this feared world at bay. Thus, the very means she uses to comprehend her world, providing still-lifes of it, is called into question. Her pictures of the location, in fact, are shown to be simply a more sophisticated means of distancing herself from the African world than the colonial tea ritual used by the mine community during the initial protest. These location descriptions are the first indication in Gordimer's fiction of the limitations of "picturing."

During both of Helen's location visits, the neat models she constructs to control a world she fears prove insufficient to contain her threatening subject. The first, occasioned by Helen's providing a ride home for Mary Seswayo, reveals not only Helen's motivation for the pictures she provides but their inefficacy in depicting this foreign ground. As they enter, Helen is momentarily reassured by her isolation from the location as the car "seemed to descend into noise that sealed us up inside it" (p. 173). Her picture of the location, the most structured of any setting in the novel, reveals her underlying fear:

> First we passed the administrative offices. . . . Then the usual small street of shops, homemade and pushed tightly one against the other so that you felt that if the first were taken away, the whole lot would slowly keel over and collapse. . . . After the shops there was an empty space covered with ashes, mealie cobs, dogs and children, and at the far end, a tiny church. (pp. 173–74)

This orderly description, with its careful use of place markers, reflects Helen's concern that if one of those shops were removed, if the location ceased to be "pushed tightly" into shape, the whole structure might collapse. And when she loses her way when leaving the location, it does:

> The closeness of the place, the breath-to-breath, wall-to-wall crowding, had become so strained that it had overflowed and all bounds had disappeared. The walls of the houses pressed on the pavement, the pavement trampled into the street, there were no fences and few windows. (p. 176)

When her construct becomes too strained, the whole rickety structure falls toward Helen in the street. Without those fences that had protected the mine properties, no longer feeling sealed away from this world, Helen flees, realizing that "the awfulness of their life filled me with fear" (p. 177).

Helen had tried to use the same mirror/picture construct she had employed within the magic circle to capture Mary Seswayo's personal surroundings. When she first meets Mary, before the mirrors in the university lavatory, Helen feels that "what I saw on her face now was what was on my own" (p. 105). Her presumed identification with Mary actually reflects the narcissism of the colonial. Mary is simply another mirror for Helen, who will continue to see Mary's experience as a reflection of her own. Both of them, Helen thinks, are estranged from the European literature they read, both are rebelling against the values of their parents. But Helen is too presumptuous, as her inability to construct a picture of Mary's world reveals. After dropping her off in the location, Helen "had suddenly a great regret and curiosity for the room of Mary Seswayo that I had not seen; I wanted to make it up for myself out of the raw material which I saw in flashes in the other houses all about me" (p. 175). Helen feels that the task will be easy; she will simply act "like an archaeologist restoring the arms, trinkets and drinking vessels to the excavated city." But like the location streets, Mary's room is not amenable to the model Helen wants to impose. When she tries to create a picture of it, "the thousand differences in the way she is compelled to dress, wash, eat—they piled up between us and I could scarcely see her, over the top" (p. 175). As in Helen's attempt to picture the location outside, the environment asserts itself. Indeed, numerous experiences such as these, in which the South African environment proves intractable to the colonial's perspective, precipitate Helen's decision to flee the country.

While Helen makes a concerted effort to make up an image of South Africa from "the raw material" around her, she is frustrated again and again by her colonial perspective. Another of Helen's depictions of the railway near Atherton begins with a colonial perspective which is fractured, as in the location, by the force of the native environment:

> The quiet, steeped autumn days passed, as if the sun turned the earth lovingly as a glass of fine wine, bringing out the depth of glow, the fine gleam; the banks of wild cosmos opened like a wake, with the cream and pink of an early Florentine painting, on

> either side of the railway cutting from Atherton to Johannesburg
> and spattered, intoxicating bees with plenty in the bareness of flat
> veld and mine dumps, out of ditches and rubbish heaps; the last
> rains brought the scent of rot like a confession from leaves that
> had fallen and lain lightly as feathers; the cold wind of the high-
> veld, edged with the cut of snow it had passed on the Drakens-
> berg, blew round the house, blowing bare round the bare Mine,
> blowing the yellow cyanide sand into curling miasmas and mis-
> trals over the road; the Mine boys walked with only their eyes
> showing over blankets. (p. 95)

The passage shows Helen's attempt to make the transition from a European to a South African perspective. She begins by trying to recast
the Witwatersrand in the image of England's green and pleasant land.
Framed by the Florentine painting is a truly pastoral scene: an autumn
of gentle, natural intoxication, bees, and a land of plenty. With the allusion to the leaves of the epigraph, there is a "withering into the truth"
as the native climate, the cold wind from the Drakensberg, blows
death to the pastoral idyll. We are left at the "wake" of the orderly European "cosmos" in the South African climate. The pleasant, intoxicated aura yields to images of encompassing death and alienation as
the cold wind blows round the house and the shrouded mine boys try
to escape its "curling miasma." Helen observes the dissipation of the
colonial's European world, but the native environment offers no alternative, simply another world of circular isolation in place of the "magic
circle" she has tried to escape.

When leaving Atherton for the last time, Helen searches for a sense
of the town's pattern of growth, as she had her own in the still-life
of the garden party. As there, she suddenly perceives an image of development:

> But this evening I had the shock of discovering that in my mind
> the idea of Atherton carried with it a complete picture of the town
> the way it must have been when I was nine or ten years old: it rose
> up in connotation like a perfectly constructed model, accurate in
> every detail. And I saw that now it really was nothing more than a
> model, because that town had gone. The vacant lots blocked in
> concrete, the old one-storey shops demolished; with them the
> town had gone. A department store was all glass and striped awn-

ings where two tattered flags, a pale Union Jack and a pale Union flag, had waved above the old police barracks. A new bank with grey Ionic columns and a bright steel grille stood on the corner where my mother's grocer had been; the grocer was now a limited company with a five-storey building. . . . In the shadow of two buildings a tiny wood-and-iron cottage lived on, a faint clue. Here at least, the one Atherton fitted over the other, and in relation to this little house I could fade away the tall irregular buildings, and place the vanished landmarks where I had looked or lingered. (p. 310)

This is Helen's most self-conscious attempt to find a pattern in her world. She fashions "a complete picture," a "perfectly constructed model" of her childhood landscape. With the Union Jack now removed, Helen's task is to find a native model which provides a sense of continuity between past and present Atherton. But she focuses merely on the loss of the past town, which "had gone," and tries to "fade away" the new buildings. The new Atherton offers no meaning; it is "blocked in concrete," and she implies that there are no new landmarks—the bank is hidden by columns and grille—only those which had "vanished."

The scene in which Helen decides to leave South Africa is foreshadowed by both the railway and Atherton pictures. Helen sits on the balcony of her Johannesburg flat, to find, as by the railway, that "the autumn was suddenly gone" (pp. 332–33). The chill of winter winds she feels is due as well to the completion of a new building five stories high (like the one in Atherton), "which blocked out much of the sky" (p. 333). As in Atherton, Helen is left lamenting the loss of the past view, for before the building was constructed, "you could see right over the hill, you could see the Magaliesburg" (p. 333). Each scene reveals Helen's search for a native culture in the South African landscape. Each shows her frustration: at the Atherton railway the cold South African wind creates another encircling, divisive world; the new Atherton has no connection with the past; on the balcony the landscape is blocked by the new buildings. With the passing of autumn, Helen is left in the cold to wither into the truth.

Helen's regret over the blocking out of the Magaliesburg reveals her intuition that meaning might lie there. Indeed, she had come closest to fashioning a model of a South African formed along other than colonial lines during an afternoon trip with Joel Aaron to such a setting. They had driven into the veld to McDonald's Kloof, where "it was as if the earth, ugly, drab, concealing great riches for sixty miles, suddenly regained innocence where it no longer had anything to conceal, and flowered to the surface" (p. 141). No longer blocked away, the land "gave us pleasure by reminding, in its own poor way, how beautiful the country could be" (p. 141). On the Kloof, Joel traces an imaginary map of the world on a rock; its final detail is "a huge, rich country, an Africa and America rolled into one, with a bit of Italy thrown in for charm" (p. 145). This is the picture Helen has sought in her world: an Africa which, like America, has found a native identity, with the influence of Europe diminished, a bit of charm. Fashioned from the rugged veld, this is a different cosmos from the Florentine pastoral Helen conjured up at the railway. But the ending is the same as there, in the new Atherton, and on the balcony where the cold wind blew and the five-storey buildings left Helen in shadow: "Quite suddenly, but with authority, the Kloof's own shadow fell upon us. Enough, it decreed. It had closed like an eyelid over the sun. The rock faded; we felt our elbows and hipbones sore" (p. 145). The feeling toward a native cosmos is blocked once again, but the setting in which it is closest to being apprehended, the African veld, points to it as the landscape where the ancient oracle voice will emerge in Gordimer's later novels. But at the outset of Gordimer's career, the landscape of veld as well as city says, as it did to Aziz and Fielding at the close of *A Passage to India*, "No, not yet."

Still, the novel ends with some promise. If Helen has not found "a background of self-knowledge," she has provided a native South African's view of what her country is, and could be. The novel opened with young Helen's lament that her world had not been portrayed in books. But while she refers almost obsessively to European writers at the novel's outset, they disappear entirely in the novel's later sections. By the close, the only novelist remaining in *The Lying Days* is Helen herself. In the final scene in Durban she refers again and again to her writing of the novel. She talks to Joel "as I have talked to this pen and paper"; she writes of envying Joel, who is about to embark for Israel, his "purpose and the hope of realizing a concrete expression of his creative urge, in doing his work in a society which in itself was in the live process of emergence, instead of decay. All this came to me in shock and turbulence, not the way I have written it here" (pp. 357, 366). The juxtaposition of the comments shows the linkage in Helen's mind of the creative urges to build a society and to portray it in literature. While Helen discovers no basis for the creation of a native culture and seeks refuge in England, she leaves behind not just a record of her country's outward signs, but a concrete expression of her own creative urge: a book in which she herself is recognizable.

III

Whereas Gordimer incorporated a record of South African society into Helen's narrative in *The Lying Days*, "the background of self-knowledge" becomes the foreground in *A World of Strangers*. As Robert Green recently concluded, the strength of the novel is "documentary, its creation of the *external* world." But that documentation also reveals the novel's weakness: despite Gordimer's relentless recording, the details coalesce into no coherent vision of a developing society. The novel's world is accurately described by Dan Jacobson's remark that "a colonial culture is one which has no memory"; in it "blankness rules; blankness perpetuates itself." In *A World of Strangers* there is no "memory," not even the hope that the ancient oracle voice of Africa may be heard or a map of a new South African world sought in its landscape. Presenting as it does a dead colonial world but no alternative to it, *A World of Strangers* offers particularly clear testimony to the frustrations posed to Gordimer by her situation in the late fifties.[8]

The novel is best seen as Gordimer's attempt to explore Johannesburg once again, but from a better vantage point than Helen's afforded. The narrator is Toby Hood, a twenty-six-year-old Englishman, who is temporarily assuming control of the South African office of his family's publishing house. He arrives with letters of introduction to a broad segment of white society and, only vaguely aware of South African codes, quickly develops friendships across the color bar. Having done so, his lack of roots in the country minimizes the pressure against

8 Robert Green, "Nadine Gordimer's *A World of Strangers*: Strains in South African Liberalism," *English Studies in Africa*, XXII (1979), 45; Dan Jacobson, Introduction to Olive Schreiner's *The Story of an African Farm* (London, 1971), 7–8.

continuing those contacts. Moreover, as a foreigner he can view South Africa with a detachment Helen never gained. As the South African journalist Nat Nakasa noted, he is the perfect vehicle "to illuminate all aspects of our life from a central point in the social structure."[9]

By contrast with Helen, Toby's personal background affects him little during the course of the novel. His grandfathers were servants of the Empire; his parents had reacted, predictably, by espousing anti-colonial causes, taking in "an overwhelming supply of victims and their champions from Africa" (p. 30). As Toby's sneering tone suggests, he has reacted, in turn, against their values. He recalls proudly proclaiming to his mother and a visiting victim that he wants to display the sword his grandfather used in the Anglo-Boer War in homage for his having killed "a hell of a lot of Boers." The lightness with which he recounts this episode indicates that Toby's period of personal rebellion is past. His view of the world is not colored, as Helen's was, by animus toward his parents. Even when his experiences in South Africa lead him to affirm his parents' liberal views, he does so casually, concluding "I supposed my mother's and father's definitions were my own" (p. 231).

The novel takes its impetus, however, from his grandfathers' colonial definitions. Toby's fellow passengers on the boat to South Africa are all colonial types: a consul from the Belgian Congo, who is first observed prodding bundles of elephant tusks; a lady who "had been something called 'household advisor' to some Indian prince"; and the wife of a Rhodesian farmer, whose first impression of Mombasa is "exactly like something out of Somerset Maugham!" (p. 7). Toby initially finds these companions congenial, precisely the sort whose friendship his grandfathers would have cultivated, and he views himself, in good colonial style, as a young man "going out to live in Africa." Throughout the novel this colonial viewpoint serves as the norm against which his behavior is measured. Letters from England refer to "the life out there," and even late in the novel, indeed its entire fourth part, he participates in a colonial hunting expedition, complete with "savage" Nyasa attendants.

Toby attempts to apprehend Africa through its "outward signs," but

9 Nat Nakasa, "Writing in South Africa," *The Classic*, I (1963), 59. Others who called for such a perspective are Plomer, Krige, Paton (*Proceedings of a Conference*, 70–71, 82, 156), and Ezekiel Mphahlele (*The African Image*, New York, 1974, p. 75).

his lack of familiarity with the continent makes his readings of them much simpler, if more objective, than Helen's. The first picture Toby provides is the Africa of popular myth. After a trip into Mombasa, he returns to the ship for a nap induced by too much pink gin. As he begins to doze, he revels in new sensations:

> I saw for a moment in my porthole the round, brilliant picture of the shore, a picture like those made up under glass on the tops of silver dressing-table utensils, out of butterfly wings. Glittering blue sky, glittering green palms, glittering blue water. . . . Suddenly I felt the warm turquoise water swinging below me as I kept myself afloat. Sand like the dust of crystals was pouring through my fingers, hairy coconuts, like some giant's sex, swung far above my head, under the beautiful scimitar fronds of a soaring palm, Sinbad, Sinbad, Sinbad the Sailor. (pp. 18–19)

Toby clearly begins with a cliché-ridden view of Africa, which he associates with decorative exotica, National Geographic scenery, hypersexuality, and fairy tales. Absurdly stereotyped as this view is, he will find it confirmed after his arrival in a tourist pamphlet in his hotel and, much more extensively, in the views of the circle of upper-class whites he enters.

Gordimer presents a picture of Toby feeling his way toward a more accurate view of the landscape's "background of natural features" as he takes a train through the East Rand shortly after his arrival in South Africa:

> I was struck at once by the queerness of the landscape: man-made to a startling degree—as if the people had been presented with an upland plateau and left to finish it, to create a background of natural features instead of to fit in with one—and at the same time curiously empty, as if truly abandoned to man. Between the factories that thinned out from the perimeter of one town, almost meeting the last industrial outpost of the next, there was a horizon of strange hills. Some of them were made of soft white sand, like the sand of the desert or the sea, piled in colossal castles. Others looked like volcanoes on whose sides the rolling yellow lava had petrified; fissures stained rust-colored, and eroded formations like the giant roots of trees, marked their bases. There were others, cream, white, buff-coloured and yellow, and worn into rip-

pling corrugations by the wind, built up in horizontal ridges, like the tombs of ancient kings. Where coal mines had been, black mountains of coal dust glittered dully.

There were no valleys between these hills, for they were simply set down on the flat veld. Patches of tough green grass and short waving grasses showed, but mostly the growth was weird, wet and thin; a few cows would stand in the reeds of an indefinite swampy patch where the ooze shone mother-of-pearl, like oil; a rectangular lake out of which pipes humped had sheets of violet and pink, like a crude water-colour. In some places there was no earth but a bare, grey scum that had dried and cracked open. And there was black earth, round a disused coal mine, where someone had once thrown away a peach pit, and it had grown into a tree, making out of the coal dirt some hard, hairy green peaches. (pp. 109–10)

At the outset South Africa remains the land of the tourist brochure. Toby initially notes only the queerness of the landscape; he focuses on the "soft white sand," such as he had seen through his porthole, and he imposes similar comparisons, the sand formations reminding him of "colossal castles" and "the tombs of ancient kings." But the landscape soon proves unable to sustain such an exalted view. The "glittering" sky, palms and blue water of Mombasa become coal dust which "glittered dully"; "warm turquoise water" becomes a pipe-filled rectangular lake with oily "sheets of violet and pink"; the "hairy coconuts" under the beautiful soaring palms become "hard, hairy green peaches" in a tree rising from coal dust. In short, that porthole view, a delicate picture under glass, becomes "a crude water-colour." As in Helen's view of the same setting, Toby begins with inappropriate models—the stereotyped view of Africa and, in the "upland plateau," the English country-side—and moves toward an anti-pastoral of cows in a manufactured and polluted landscape.

Throughout the novel Toby provides such pictures of the surface of the South African world. But unlike Helen, he never attempts to engage with it. Even late in the novel he holds the Transvaal veld at bay by imposing a formal European pattern on it:

Walking through this landscape, so thinly green, so hostile with thorn that the living growth seemed a thing of steel rather than sap, I thought of old religious pictures, with their wildernesses and their bleeding, attenuated saints. This was a Gothic landscape, where the formalized pattern of interwoven thorns that often borders such pictures was real. (pp. 211–12)

Toby's detached view, evident in the framing of the landscape here, is reflected more pervasively in his frequent adoption of an omniscient vantage point. In the midst of a party, for instance, "the garden and the people sprang up with a strong variety and brightness, a deep texture of colour and shadow through which I seemed to look down" (p. 86). Here and throughout the novel, he remains a recording spectator masquerading as a participant in the action.

Despite his excellent perspective for providing a picture of his world, Toby does little more than show that South Africa is not the Africa of popular myth. Even though over three-fourths of the novel is set in Johannesburg, one could go much further toward constructing a map of the city's physical features from *The Lying Days*. This is partly so because Gordimer takes pains in *A World of Strangers* to show that the city is structured to hide the racial repression on which it is based. In Toby's phrase, the city is "muffled in a conspiracy of stuffs to keep the atmosphere anonymous" (p. 42). But while he will notice such details as an all-black bus queue hidden down below a railway cutting, Johannesburg remains essentially like the European cities Toby has known. Walking about, he is engulfed by "the sounds generic to a city," and at a concert he hears "the same talk, with different place-names, that you hear at any concert in London" (p. 42). Johannesburg is described as new by contrast with London, and unlike most other cities, it closes down early in the evening; but for all of Toby's one-year stay, no sense of its shape emerges. The point, indeed, is that the city has no perceptible form; as one of its inhabitants says, "Johannesburg seems to have no *genre* of its own" (p. 75). The absence of a *genre* in the central setting of a novel based on the evocation of the external world prohibits the kind of search for a native tradition undertaken by Helen.

To be sure, Gordimer does describe a broad range of social groups within Johannesburg—from the wealthy High House world of the Hamish Alexanders, to multiracial gatherings of artists or of liberals euphoric over the prospect of entertaining Africans "as equals," to gatherings in shebeens, the houses in which Africans congregate to partake of illicit liquor. But these groups offer no prospect of being melded into a coherent society. Lionel Abrahams has aptly described the novel as "a satirical travelogue of Johannesburg."[10] As his designation "travelogue" implies, the novel seems to be composed by a sojourner gathering brief, isolated impressions of a world he passes through. The satiric impulse is frustrated because he develops no sense of how a better society can be formed, or even sought.

After Toby has been in South Africa about three weeks, the novel begins its major theme, the contrast between the standards of High House and African township life. The world of the upper-class whites who congregate at the High House is presented in much greater detail, probably because it is a milieu which falls more within Gordimer's experience than the township. Toby's first verbal photograph of the High House interior introduces the dominant traits of this world:

> The entrance hall led away down a few broad, shallow steps to the left; I got the impression of a long, mushroom-coloured room there, with gleams of copper and gilt, flowers and glass. In the hall there was a marquetry table under a huge mirror with a mother-of-pearl inlaid frame. Further back, the first steps of a white staircase spread in a dais; carpet seemed to grow up the stairs, padding the rim of each step like pink moss. An African appeared soundlessly; I followed him soundlessly (I found later that the entire ground floor of the house was covered with that carpeting the colour of a mushroom's gills) past the mirror that reflected three new golf balls and a very old golf glove, sweated and dried to the shape of the wearer's hand, on the table below it, and through a large living-room full of chairs covered in women's dress colours, that led to a veranda. If you could call it that; a superior sort of veranda. The entire wall of the room was open to it, and it was got up like something out of a film, with a barbeque fireplace, *chaises longues*, glass and wrought-iron tables, mauve Venetian glass lanterns and queer trailing plants. (p. 46)

This interior evokes the same sense of queerness and emptiness as the man-made landscape on the East Rand, as it well might since both are the creation of the High House magnates. The similarity is given support in the picturing of the room as a landscape, the carpet growing like moss and its mushroom colors noted twice. Like the East Rand,

10 Abrahams, "Nadine Gordimer: The Transparent Ego," 149.

this house lacks a pattern, the formal hall leading to the "women's dress colours" of the living room furniture and it, in turn, to the *chaises longues* and barbecue fireplace. The allusions to the natural world are undercut by the artificiality of this film-inspired mélange. One can be sure that this film was European since the High House set will be seen as formed, as were the Shaws, by its attempt to ape a European culture it doesn't fully comprehend. This group might be able to assimilate the *chaise longue* and Venetian glass, but Toby later describes a "masterpiece" Mrs. Alexander had located in Johannesburg as "a small and dingy Courbet, deeply set in a frame the colour and texture of mud" (p. 58). Clearly, the native landscape asserts itself in less prepossessing ways than the delicate moss and mushroom colors of the High House interior. The soundlessness emphasized during Toby's entrance reveals another trait of which its inhabitants are unaware—their repulsion, for all their hearty athleticism (reflected by the golf glove and balls), from sensual experience. Toby will soon find them alluding squeamishly to the hideousness of crocodile and fish odors.

The African location is a contrast in every respect. When Toby first visits one with Steven Sitole, who comes to epitomize its world, he finds a world of noise, odors, disorder, and unselfconscious sensuality. The first shebeen Toby enters is, by contrast with the High House, "the barest room I had ever been in in my life; it depended entirely on humans" (p. 94). In numerous subsequent visits to this world, Toby focuses on the abandon and naturalness of urban African life. By contrast with the jazz-crazy youths at home in England, writhing "like chopped-off bits of some obscene animal," the jazz in the locations "was not a frenzy. It was a fulfillment, a passion of jazz. Here they danced for joy. They danced out of wholeness, as children roll screaming down a grass bank" (p. 121). Throughout the novel Toby records the joy in this world with all the fervor of Jack Kerouac on a lilac evening in Denver.

Toby provides numerous descriptions of parts of this high-spirited, under-furnished world. Only once does he give an extended description of the location as a whole as he looks over it from the front yard of his friend Sam Mofokenzazi:

> I would walk with Sam in the early evening out on to the waste ground near his house. It was a promotory of ashes and clinker, picked bald, by urchins and the old, even of the rubbish that was

dumped there, and it looked back over most of the township. At that time, the day seems to relent, even the dreariest things take on disguising qualities in the soft light. The ashheap took on the dignity of loneliness; we might have been standing on the crater of a burnt-out volcano, the substance beneath our feet gave no life to anything, animal or vegetable, it was a ghost of the fecund earth. Behind, and down below, everything teemed, rotted and flourished. There were no street-lights, and in the night that seemed to well up like dark water round the low, close confusion of shacks and houses—while, higher up, where we were, the day lingered in pink mist—cooking fires showed like the flame of a match cupped in the hand. (p. 152)

Like the description of the interior of the High House, this impressionist landscape reveals an attitude. While the location isn't quite viewed through rose-colored glasses, it is seen through a pink mist. The passage begins on waste ground, but even its negative qualities are subsequently transformed in the "soft light." The land beneath their feet gives "no life to anything," yet the earth is "fecund"; it teems and flourishes. The "dignity of loneliness" is affirmative in itself, but even the loneliness is mitigated by the "close confusion" of shacks and the warmth and communion promised by the cooking fires.

Given these two worlds, Toby easily chooses Steven's and Sam's. "The life of the township," he says, "did for me what Italy and Greece had done for other Englishmen, in other times," exposed him to an abundance of vitality and emotion. He easily rejects the artificial and unexamined colonial world of the High House. During the hunting trip in the Transvaal veld, Toby thinks "of the Alexanders' world, the curiously dated world of the rich, with its Edwardian-sounding pleasures. They thought of courage in terms of gallantry, spirit in terms of gameness; in the long run, I supposed my mother's and my father's definitions were my own, I could really only think of these things in terms of political imprisonment and the revolt of the intellect" (p. 231).

Gordimer attempts to make Toby's final commitment to the world of the location plausible by setting the unattractive High House as its alternative. But Toby's commitment lacks credibility not just because of his excessive detachment from the society he observes but because Gordimer has attempted to impose a value system which will not

hold. As the references to Englishmen in Italy and the Edwardian period imply, *A World of Strangers* is Gordimer's attempt to transpose
Forsterian values onto a South African world. The contrast between
the search for connection in Gordimer's and Forster's worlds is instruc-
tive. Even in *Howards End*, in which connection finally proves impossible, the prospect of connecting is a real one: between what Margaret
Schlegel calls "the prose and the passion," between the Schlegel German and British heritages, between Schlegels and Wilcoxes, even between Schlegels and Basts. Such possibilities for connection do not exist in *A World of Strangers*. This is partly because the two worlds of
the High House and the location are so radically disjunct. Moreover,
even Toby cannot connect with either of them; he scorns the super-
ficiality of the High House, and it becomes increasingly difficult to align
himself with Africans, as the breakup of a multiracial party in his
house near the close indicates. But the problem is even more fundamental: no group in the novel offers a sense of place. The High House
is based on a clearly futile attempt to perpetuate an Edwardian world,
and for all the vibrancy and feeling Toby perceives in the townships,
they offer a world of parties and joy, but no community. The reason the
world Gordimer portrays in this novel offers no place is best indicated
by Toby's description of his street, "one of those newly old streets that
I saw all over Johannesburg—a place without a memory" (p. 61). Toby's
coming to an awareness during a hunting trip in the veld that his values were those of his parents is but a faint hint of where a society with
a memory, a society with which one can connect, may be found. But
only with *Occasion for Loving* will the urban society be clearly rejected and the veld sought as the landscape where a society may be
formed.

IV

In 1954 Gordimer wrote of Johannesburg and the surrounding
mining towns of the Witwatersrand, the dominant setting in her novels
of the fifties, that "any feature of the landscape that strikes the eye always does so because it is a reminder of something else; considered on
its own merits, the landscape is utterly without interest—flat, dry and

barren." While her own attention to this landscape in *The Lying Days* and *A World of Strangers* belies the claim that it is without interest, her comment does point up the problem her protagonists faced in discerning a native history in it: the "something else" was too often the Europe that had formed Gordimer's colonial world. Neither Helen Shaw nor Toby Hood can gather from the "outward signs" of their world a sense of a developing culture which Dan Jacobson has described well. "The 'human reality' of a civilization," he wrote in the late fifties, "is a reality only if there is some continuity to it, only if it is present in the consciousness of the people as a force controlling, guiding, and inspiring them, in a way that they themselves are aware of."[11]

In the fifties not only Gordimer but most of her contemporaries sought this continuity in Johannesburg. Sarah Gertrude Millin had asserted in 1940 that "most of the things that happen in South Africa have their origins in Johannesburg," and the refrain "All roads lead to Johannesburg" punctuates *Cry, the Beloved Country*. Paton's novel was simply the best known of the many works based on the massive migration of Africans to the city. What became known as the "Jim Goes to Joburg" theme provided the impetus for numerous other works, most notably Peter Abrahams' *Mine Boy* (1946) and, in autobiographical form, Es'kia Mphahlele's *Down Second Avenue* (1962). The pervasive chronicling of this movement to the city of gold is, indeed, the best example of how thoroughly the writers of the "first birth" were "chosen" by the themes of their society.

Gordimer echoed the view of Millin and Paton in 1953 when she asserted that "the *real* South Africa is to be found in Johannesburg and in the brash, thriving mining towns of the Witwatersrand. Everything that is happening on the whole emergent continent can be found in microcosm here." Describing the city proved difficult because it offered no sense of continuity, of a developing history. As Gordimer noted, nobody knows after whom the city is named, and even in the late sixties Lionel Abrahams could find no organizing principle to it:

11 Gordimer, "A South African Childhood," 121; Dan Jacobson, *Time of Arrival and Other Essays* (London, 1962), 172.

She has been so recently imposed on the empty veld that we think of her—more emphatically than other cities—as a product of human determination, yet her defining attributes all elude design, her features are improvised by cold contingency; she has no plan, no enduring form, no works of permanent nobility or interest, to express man's freedom of choice. Change according to commercial need is her only constant; demolition her only tradition.[12]

Gordimer's novels of the fifties depict a search for meaning in this world without form or plan, nobility or interest. The primacy of Johannesburg in her search was reflected in the place designations which provide headings for the three parts of *The Lying Days*; after two brief sections, "The Mine" and "The Sea," fully two-thirds of the novel takes place in "The City." Even more emphatically, after a brief prologue *A World of Strangers* is a concerted but futile search for "the Johannesburg *genre*." These novels fail to depict an enduring design in the city not simply because of the formlessness Abrahams noted but for a more central reason: Gordimer was to find in the mid-sixties that the city was not the microcosm of her society she had believed it to be. Johannesburg, she would realize, was a European city, a colonial creation "imposed on the empty veld." On that veld, long the province of the Africans, the features of a native tradition were to be found.

It is tempting to view Gordimer's shift to the veld as the primary setting for her novels (beginning with *A Guest of Honour*) as yet another example of her reaction to her situation, for two developments in the sixties could have suggested this focus. One was the implementation of the Bantustan policy, based on the rescission of the right to freehold land tenure by urban Africans and their removal, often on a massive scale, to what the Nationalist government designated as their "tribal homelands" in the veld. Senseless and unworkable as this policy was, it still mandated at least a short-term reversal of the migratory pattern and the end of such African urban cultural communities as Sophiatown. The other development pointed to the past: the discovery of ancient African kraals on the Witwatersrand which proved con-

12 Lionel Abrahams, "The Idea of Johannesburg," *Purple Renoster*, VIII (Winter, 1968), 2. Gordimer's reference to the "*real* South Africa" is in "A South African Childhood," p. 143.

clusively that, contrary to government assertions, the Johannesburg area had originally been settled by Africans. Indeed, both developments are reflected in *Occasion for Loving*. Gideon Shibalo's perception during a visit to a location that it will shortly be bulldozed out of existence might well serve as an emblem of the death of Johannesburg as the center of Gordimer's world. And Jessie Stilwell's identification with the African mine dancers, whom she sees trampling the past under their feet, recalls those ancient kraals, a rural African society which would inform Gordimer's future works.

But these developments only intensified a basic impulse which had been present though submerged in Gordimer's depiction of her world. There are important signs that Gordimer sensed that the veld could be a source of cultural meaning from the start of her career. *The Lying Days* opens with Helen Shaw's venture outside the colonial compound to the veld, an area with which she cannot negotiate but which is everywhere alive. And it is in the veld that Helen and Joel Aaron come closest to creating a map of a native world. The long hunting trip in Part IV of *A World of Strangers* requires a strange deflection of the narrative to allow Toby's central moments of perception to occur in the veld: his acceptance of his parents' liberal standards as his own and his premonition of his friend Steven Sitole's death through the death of a hunting dog at the section's close.

Only with *Occasion for Loving* does the veld emerge as the landscape which can provide a sense of a continuous native history. This change in emphasis is most evident in the pattern of the narrative. Whereas the novels of the fifties chronicle movements into the city where social meaning is sought, in *Occasion for Loving* the characters begin in the city and feel toward a sense of their society during attempts to escape its bounds. The Ann Boaz–Gideon Shibalo affair is developed through outings to the veld, which is also the scene of their three-week wandering when they fail in their attempt to escape the country; Jessie Stilwell perceives a native history in it on her return from the Fuechts' South Coast cottage. While neither Jessie nor the other characters are able to connect with this native history, the veld is clearly the setting in which it must be sought.

The first indication in *Occasion for Loving* that a native history may be read in the veld landscape comes during Gideon and Ann's travels in the Northern Transvaal:

> Ann and Gideon could not have been further from the world of ordinary appearances, earth covered with tar, space enclosed in concrete, sky framed in steel, that had made the mould of their association. They walked over the veld and already it seemed that this was as it had always been, before anyone came, before the little Bushmen fled this way up to Rhodesia and the black man spread over the country behind them, before the white man rediscovered the copper that the black man had mined and abandoned—not only as it had been, but as it would be when they were all gone again, yellow, black and white. They did not speak, as if they were walking over their own graveyard. (p. 230)

The veld offers Gideon and Ann a sense not only of the past but the future, its openness presenting possibilities, especially by contrast with the enclosed city which had "made the mould" of their relationship, as it had the lives of Helen Shaw and Toby Hood. Ann and Gideon are awed by the sense of history in the veld but, molded by city life, they can picture this scene only as a graveyard, of the past generations and their own to come.

The clearest expression of the veld's significance as a historical repository comes as Jessie observes it on her drive back to the city from the Fuechts' cottage near the novel's close:

> Little groups of huts were made out of mud and the refuse of the towns—rusty corrugated iron, old tins beaten flat, once even the head of an iron bedstead put to use as a gate. The women slapped at washing and men squatted talking and gesticulating in an endless unimaginable conversation that, as she passed, even at intervals of several miles, from one kraal to another, linked up in her mind as one. In this continuity she had no part, in this hold that lay so lightly, not with the weight of cement and tarmac and steel, but sinew of the earth's sinew, authority of a legendary past, she had no share. (p. 269)

Jessie first sees the veld as composed of "the refuse of the towns," a view similar to Helen's of the fragmented colonial dumping ground in *The Lying Days*. But where Helen found only the cast-off culture of

Europe, Jessie sees signs of a native history. The passage turns on the African word *kraal*; after perceiving the African basis of the landscape, Jessie finds the settlements "linked up," part of a "continuity," and bound together by "sinew." The lightness of this linkage holds the prospect of liberation from the "weight of cement and tarmac," the mold of city life. The passage recalls the African mine workers dancing on the tarmac, having lost their kingdom like a "crazed Lear of old Africa." That tarmac is gone here, and Jessie can hear "the oracle voice of the ancient Africa" Helen sought. Instead of "the dignity of loneliness" Toby found on Sam's ash heap, Jessie finds a communal dignity, "the dignity of the poor about to inherit their earth" (p. 269).

Finding herself in a township a few days later, Jessie feels that "the continuity of the little communities of mud and tin on the road was picked up again" (p. 270). But as she looks more closely, this urban scene becomes a place

> where people were born and lived and died before they could come to life. They drudged and drank and murdered and stole in squalor, and never walked free in the pleasant places. When they were children they were cold and hungry, and when they were old they were cold and hungry again; and in between was a brief, violent clutch at things out of reach, or the sad brute's life of obliviousness to them. (p. 270)

Jessie's anger at the waste of this world is intensified by its failure to reveal the continuity she had found in the veld and sought again here. The only continuity in urban life is a succession of "ands," beginning and ending with cold and hunger. Unlike Ann and Gideon on the veld, these people "never walked free in the pleasant places."

The veld is the only pleasant place in the otherwise somber landscape of *The Late Bourgeois World*. Liz Van Den Sandt drives through the veld to the school of her son Bobo with the unpleasant task of informing him that Max Van Den Sandt, her former husand and his father, has committed suicide, probably because of the guilt he felt at turning state's evidence when the sabotage activities of his radical cadre were uncovered. But the high veld plain momentarily lifts her spirits. Its open space, the morning's "calm, steady sunlight" and "fresh smell" offer a relief from her urban world—the cramped quarters of her flat, the "supersunset" which she and her friend Graham will attribute to nuclear test fallout, and her job as a technician examining feces. As she drives, Liz thinks of her husband's death and the failure of the past generation's suburban code—the "kindness to dogs and neighbors, handouts to grateful servants" which has brought her only bewilderment while failing to provide for the many it excluded (p. 12). But on this morning she also thinks of new beginnings. She hopes that the code of Bobo's generation will be an improvement over her own or at least that he will seek security "elsewhere than in the white suburbs." Her reason for having some hope for him is revealed when she continues, "He wasn't made there, thank God. It was in a car—which is where the white suburbs keep their sex. But at least it was out in the veld" (p. 12). What she terms her "unreasonable confidence in Bobo" derives, in short, from his conception in the veld (p. 22).

The veld also serves as a link between father and son, for the first sign of Max's disaffection from his Afrikaner background was when as "a child he would come back from solitary games in the veld and at a certain point suddenly hear the distant quacking of the ducks like a conversation he couldn't understand" (p. 9). This solitary child first heard different voices than those within his home on the veld, and this experience is implicitly the beginning of his rebellion, for "he experienced the isolation of his childhood become the isolation of his colour" (p. 60). Max's attempts to overcome his isolation may have been pathetic, but he could at least heed other voices than those of the smug and repressive society of his bourgeois world. Like Helen at the outset of her novel, Max hears them outside the "charmed circle" in the veld. Liz connects this impulse from the past with the hope that Bobo, conceived on the veld, will find a better world in the future. Max's frustrated impulse and her "unreasonable confidence" in Bobo make for a tenuous continuity indeed. But it is the only one she perceives in the novel's dying world.

The perception of continuity in the veld in Gordimer's novels of the sixties is clearly not strong enough to stand as an affirmation of a native order in her society. But in these novels the veld does at least hold the promise of an alternative to the colonial world. This tentative but still credible affirmation is an improvement over those advanced in Gordimer's first two novels. The declarations of commitment to South

Africa at the close of *The Lying Days* and *A World of Strangers*—
Helen's promise to return from exile and Toby's decision to remain in
the country—had struck her critics, quite correctly, as unconvincing.
Many of them found that she recorded well but to no discernible end.
The *Commonweal* reviewer of the 1952 short story collection *The
Soft Voice of the Serpent* lauded her "intensely perceptive observation"
but concluded that she fails to "convey" much. In 1961, Anthony
Woodward made the same point in a decidedly less restrained manner
when he concluded, "She is a marvellous, vivacious observer with
nothing very subtle or important to say, and with an ever-growing fa-
cility for saying it."[13] Certainly these appraisals would require modification by the late sixties. If Gordimer had failed to "convey" much,
she had, to paraphrase Jacobson, tried with uncommon tenacity to become aware of a force controlling, guiding, and inspiring her people.
Gordimer's first four novels stand as a concerted search for something
she could not quite articulate: the presence of a native cultural continuity in her world. The suggestion in these novels that she would convey it on the veld finds clear confirmation in her later novels.

V

Where Jessie Stilwell and, less consciously, Liz Van Den Sandt
perceived a historical continuity in the veld, neither could claim it as
her own. They, like the earlier protagonists, provide pictures of their
worlds but rarely engage with them. Gordimer's fiction through *The
Late Bourgeois World* reveals not just the search for a landscape in
which a continuity could be found but for the kind of perspective
needed to allow engagement with it. This search took the form of a
contrast between what I have termed photographic and painterly approaches to the world. While "the writer with the eye of the camera"
continued to present pictures of her world, her early fiction reveals
both a developing criticism of a photographic perspective and the exploration of a painterly approach, which would allow for a radically different relationship of protagonist and landscape in the later novels.

Photographic and painterly perspectives represent fundamentally

13 Richard Hayes, Review of Nadine Gordimer's *The Soft Voice of the Serpent*,
Commonweal, LVI (May, 1952), 204; Woodward, "Nadine Gordimer," 12.

different ways of viewing the world. A narrator who functions as a camera's eye is essentially a scribe, an acute but noninterfering observer. He records a discrete world "out there" with which he need not engage; indeed, this perspective, as in Helen's visit to the location in *The Lying Days,* may reveal the desire to keep from doing so. In extreme cases, the photographer, as Susan Sontag has reminded us, manifests "a chronic voyeuristic relationship to the world."[14] This tendency is quite clear in such narrators as Toby Hood, who acknowledges as much when he fears adopting the role of "a *voyeur* of the world's ills and social perversions" (p. 33). By contrast, a painterly attitude requires a more pronounced interplay between the perceiver and his world. In Gordimer's fiction this interplay develops not so much from the narrator's imposition of an attitude on the landscape—the formation of "psychologized landscapes"—as from qualities inherent in the landscape itself. That is, the impetus for engagement arises from a landscape which has more depth and fluidity—is more alive—than a photograph allows.

"Photographic" and "painterly" refer to attitudes. Scenes described as paintings but conceived as artifacts disjunct from the viewer reveal a photographic attitude. The most prevalent examples of this kind in Gordimer's fiction are pictures which are framed and therefore perceived as something "out there." The frame of the Florentine pastoral in Helen's description of the Atherton railway, the frame of the porthole as Toby views Mombasa, and the border of thorns typical of gothic landscapes he provides during the hunting trip to the veld all serve this function. This kind of viewing is given the most conscious expression in the scene which summarizes the attitude of the inhabitants of the late bourgeois world. Liz and her friend Graham sit looking at the sunset, "a romanticized picture," through the frame of her apartment window. She replies to his query about how it looks to her,

> "Like the background to a huge Victorian landscape. Something with a quotation underneath with lots of references to the Soul

---

14 Susan Sontag, *On Photography* (New York, 1977), 19–21. Gordimer's concern with the voyeuristic tendencies of her society has become increasingly pronounced since the great increase in the use of paid political informers in South Africa since the mid-sixties. Indeed, *Something Out There* takes voyeurism as a major unifying theme; see especially "Crimes of Conscience," "Rags and Bones," and "A Correspondence Course."

and God's Glory and the Infinite. Something that ought to have a scrolled gilt frame weighing twenty pounds. It's what my grandmother would have been taught was beautiful, as a child. You know, that style. What's it got to do with us. And with bombs."

"It's a bit picture-postcard, but still."

"All the dawns and sunsets in all the albums rolled into one. The apotheosis of picture-postcard. Just imagine a colour photograph of that, exhibited in a hundred-years' time. Things are not like that with us at all." (p. 83)

The attitudes of Liz, who first uses a painting analogy to describe the sunset, and Graham, who introduces the photographic comparison, are essentially the same. Both approach the sunset as something to be viewed, an artifact, as Liz says, which might be "exhibited" a hundred years hence. Indeed, that she sees it as lifeless is reinforced by her thinking just before this interchange that, unlike a Chagall landscape, there aren't "any floating lovers or fiddles or cows" in it. It is, in short, uninhabited by life.

Gordimer's later fiction would reveal an emphatic rejection of such camera-eye views. It is of no small import in *Burger's Daughter* that Orde Greer, an ineffectual revolutionary similar to Max Van Den Sandt, is a photographer and Rosa Burger an artist. And one can find few comparable depictions in fiction of the callousness of the detached photographer as Gordimer provides in the late seventies story "A Hunting Accident." The story's climax is a photographer's reaction to a dying hartebeest as his female companion looks on:

He went straight up to the beast and, down on one knee, began to photograph it again and again, close-up, gazing through the camera, with the camera, into the last moments of life passing in its open eyes. His face was absolutely intent on the techniques he was employing; there was a deep line she had never seen before, drawn down either side of his mouth from the sucked-in nostrils. He placed filters over his lens, removed them. He took his time. The beast tried to open its mouth once more but there was no sound, only a bubble of blood. Its eye (now the head had lolled completely into profile, he could see only one) settled on him almost restfully, the faculty of vision bringing him into focus, then fading, as he himself looked steadily into it with his camera.[15]

15 Nadine Gordimer, *A Soldier's Embrace* (Harmondsworth, 1982), 64–65.

The emphasis on technique, the clinical view of death, and the pathos of the beast's view at the close combine to make this event seem an act of violence, even torture.

The 1984 novella "Something Out There" is a more concerted examination of the kind of knowledge yielded by pictures like this photographer's. The novella develops into a criticism of picture taking as a process of unsuccessful reification—an attempt to convert the essence of a subject into a thing, a snapshot. The novella opens: "Stanley Dobrow, using the Cannonball Sureshot, one of three cameras he was given for his barmitzvah, photographed it" (p. 118). Stanley and his countrymen are armed to the eyebrows, but neither he nor many others—golfing doctors, illicit lovers, housewives—are successful in capturing "it." The attempts like his to reduce "it" to a verifiable image are so prevalent in the novella that the society comes to resemble, in one image used, "a camera gone berserk, lens opening and closing" (p. 139). At first thought to be a marauding gorilla, orangutan, or monster, "it" gradually comes to represent the unarticulated white fears of black rebellion. "It," finally photographed after death, is merely a baboon, a common "native species," as the narrator calls it. The picture yields no useful knowledge for at least two reasons. One is that the reified image does not accurately reflect the white fears, which are so massive that only King Kong, as "it" was sometimes called, would be an appropriate manifestation of them. Another is that pictures are not absolute truths, as the society wants to believe. Pictures require interpretation, and this society's pictures deny the truth of its situation, for the whites need to see the baboon as an intruding beast from abroad rather than a "native species." In other words, the people deny that the white fears the baboon represents are caused by internal forces.

These white fears quickly become an irrelevant issue, for on the very night that the futile scramble to picture this racial bogey man ends, a power station is blown up by saboteurs. This event sets off a new round of photographing in a vain attempt to reify the new "something out there." The reification is unsuccessful once again. The photographs of the saboteurs' arms cache which appear in the papers are misleading government-prepared displays. Moreover, the pictures don't finally help to answer any questions about the development they purport to represent. Despite the photographs, "no one knows," in a phrase Gordimer employs repeatedly at the novella's close, who let the baboon loose, who blew up the power station, how the saboteurs operated, let alone the underlying questions of what forces molded the saboteurs or what their actions say about the past and future of this society. In fact, the photographs keep the white population from acknowledging that the threat is not really "something out there"—a beast lurking outside Johannesburg houses or communist-inspired terrorists from across the border. The threat has its roots within, in the subconscious need of whites to see the native black population as prowling subhuman invaders, in the native history which has produced the native saboteurs. The "out there" that cameras capture is not where the problems or the solution lie; indeed, the images the photographers bring back allow this society to avoid facing its home-grown problems.

"A Hunting Accident" and "Something Out There" are but two examples of how completely Gordimer rejects picturing in her later fiction. Her severe criticism is in part a reaction to her own photographic perspective in her early works. "The writer with the eye of the camera," it is true, was providing a function quite different from the photographers in these later works, namely describing a society previously unapprehended in literature. But even in the fifties Gordimer was uncomfortable with the kind of knowledge provided by picturing. Her discomfort is most obviously indicated by the kinds of characters associated with photography. Toby's choice of Steven and Sam's world at the close of *A World of Strangers*, for instance, is objectified by two newspaper clippings—a list of those who had been arrested on a treason charge set against a picture from the social page of a vapid High House woman Toby had dated. Ann's affair with Gideon Shibalo introduces the most common criticism in Gordimer's early fiction of a photographic perspective: its association with failures to connect. At the boxing matches which afford their first intimate contact, "the looks, the casual remark of faces in the crowd, set them together; it was a picture imposed from the outside, like a game that partners off strangers" (p. 100). The picture suggests the barriers to their relationship. Ann will view it only as an interesting diversion, "a game." And this picture implies that their union will be transient, for the racial attitudes of those who "set them together" here will soon serve to set the pair apart from the rest of the South African world.

The use of photographs to objectify a failure to connect finds a more central place in Gordimer's stories from the late fifties. In "The Bridegroom," for instance, a young Afrikaner in an isolated work camp is offered two worlds: the one he has known with his Tswana workers, exemplified by the music he shares with them at night; the other that of the girl he is soon to marry, represented by the photograph of her which he observes on his desk at the outset of the story.[16] The young man clearly loves the company of the Africans, most notably his personal servant who is portrayed as a wife of sorts, but he realizes that the presence of his new bride will make continued intimacy with them impossible. After telling them that he will return from the wedding with a radio they will all enjoy together, he flushes with emotion, but "he shut down his mind on a picture of them, hanging round the caravan to listen, and his coming out to tell them—" (p. 162). What he will tell them, of course, is that they cannot continue to fraternize in the old way due to the presence of his wife. The story ends with his packing the photograph of "the coy, smiling face of the seventeen-year-old girl" (p. 163). The addition of "coy" to the description indicates his subliminal awareness that his new position will be less fulfilling than the old.

The implication that a world viewed photographically doesn't foster connection is given more complex treatment in "Little Willie." The story begins with a ruse perpetrated by an uncle. He tells his niece that Little Willie, a scruffy white boy from the wrong side of the tracks, has fallen wildly in love with her after her photograph has fallen into his hands. For young Denise, this admiration raises the prospect of her relationship to Willie's outcast community. When the uncle contrives the delivery of a magnificent box of chocolates with a card, reputedly from Little Willie, Denise reacts by conjuring up a picture of his society: "She thought of a group of ragged children; of a bony-headed boy, looking on at her pleasures and triumphs. A dirty boy without shoes. She was ashamed of him. She would never speak to him or look at him; and he knew this" (p. 66). Denise uses a photographic perspective in

16 "The Bridegroom" is reprinted in *Selected Stories*. The references to "Little Willie" below are from *Friday's Footprints* (New York, 1960). Stories in the sixties which treat the limitations of a photographic perspective include "One Whole Year and Even More" and "Vital Statistics" (both in *Not for Publication*) and "A Meeting in Space" (in *Livingston's Companions*).

much the same way as Helen did in the location. Each sees photographs as instruments of power which provide control of her world.
Denise attributes a voyeuristic power to Little Willie, whom she imagines "looking on at her pleasures and triumphs." And the picture of his
world she creates in her mind's eye is an antidote of sorts; the objec-
tification of it in a picture allows her to reject it, never "to look at" it
again.

Helen's location visit and "Little Willie" suggest Gordimer's awareness that the photographic capturing of "outward signs" may often be
used to reject, not develop, "a background of self-knowledge." By *The
Late Bourgeois World*, photographs are clearly used not to foster such
knowledge but rather to maintain a comforting view of a world in
which the white inhabitants feel insecure. When Liz tells Bobo of his
father's suicide, the boy, who had seen him only infrequently since his
parents' divorce, replies that he can't remember what his father looked
like. Liz responds,

> "You've got a photograph, though," There on his locker, the up-
> right leather folder with mother on one side, father on the other,
> just as all the other boys have.
> "Oh yes."
> There didn't seem to be anything else to say; at least, not all at
> once, and not in that room. (p. 18)

Clearly, Bobo is not convinced; indeed, the photographs of parents
which all the boys have are apt icons of Liz's late bourgeois world. The
association of photographs with a dying order is made once again as Liz
briefly attempts that evening to take solace in the idea of putting together an album: "Sticking Bobo's pictures into an album and recording the dates on and places where they were taken suddenly seemed
enthusiastically possible, just as if the kind of life in which one does
this sort of thing would fly into place around us with the act" (p. 93).
Not just her phrasing but the sudden knock of Luke Fokase, who offers
the prospect of a life dramatically opposed to one based on "this sort of
thing," is a commentary on the futility of using photographs to maintain possession of space in contemporary South Africa.

Gordimer's fiction through *The Late Bourgeois World* is not simply
a rejection of a photographic approach to the world; it also reveals her

exploration of the painterly perspective she would employ in her later novels. This exploration begins with her attempt to liberate the photograph, a discrete moment, from its spatial and temporal limitations. In a snapshot of Ludi, the man who first awakened Helen's sexuality, and some of his friends in *The Lying Days*, for instance, the photograph strains to become a more fluid representation:

> Ludi, who, like most short-sighted people, did not photograph well, stood scowling at the sun in the artificial camaraderie of a garden snapshot. Two little boys grinned cross-legged in the foreground, a dog was straining out of the arm of a young woman with a charming, quizzical smile that suggested that she was laughing at herself. A badly cut dress showed the outline of her knees and thighs, and with the arm that was not struggling with the dog, she had just made some checked gesture, probably to push back the strand of curly hair standing out at her temple, which the photograph recorded with a blur in place of her hand. (p. 84)

The attempt to free the photograph from the restraints of its form is evident in the movement from the artificiality, characteristic of a snapshot, at the outset—the uncomfortable, scowling Ludi and the boys posed cross-legged—to the natural, even disheveled young woman. But the picture shows a more emphatic fracturing of the discrete photograph. Instead of capturing a single moment frozen in time, the photograph pushes into the past in the gesture the young woman just checked before the camera clicked, into the future with the dog straining out of the picture. The picture, like that dog, strains for a life not restricted to the photographic impression.

The fracturing of a picture actually occurs in the early fifties story "The Smell of Death and Flowers."[17] It originates in a *tableau vivant*. Young Joyce McCoy is introduced as "a girl who had been sitting silent, pink and cold as a porcelain figurine, on the window sill" behind her brother's back. That the window serves as a framing device for this art object—a usage Gordimer might well have observed in Katherine Mansfield—is made clear by the description of Joyce which follows. She has the short nose of "a Marie Laurenican painting" and "an essen-

17 References to "The Smell of Death and Flowers" and "Is There Nowhere Else Where We Can Meet?" below are from *Selected Stories*.

tially two-dimensional prettiness: flat, dazzlingly pastel-coloured, as if the mask of make-up on the unlined skin *were* the face; if one had turned her around, one would scarcely have been surprised to discover canvas. All her life she had suffered from this impression she made of not being quite real" (p. 106). The story details her stepping out of this precious, pastel-colored existence—out of the painting in which she is restricted—to join a group of Europeans protesting the color bar in an African location. As her group is being arrested, three Africans look at her, causing her to feel "suddenly, not *nothing*, but what they were feeling at the sight of her, a white girl" being so treated (pp. 123–24). We might only infer that she strikes them as "real," but we know she has come alive through identifying with their world.

These two examples show the impulse in Gordimer's early fiction toward bringing worlds which are frozen, photographically conceived, to life. A third depicts this process much more emphatically. Like "The Smell of Death and Flowers," the 1949 story "Is There Nowhere Else Where We Can Meet?" begins with a picture. The effect is the same but the movement is reversed; the story depicts not a liberation from the constraints of a pictured world, but a two-stage process—the picturing of a world followed by a painterly engagement with it. The setting is the veld, the meeting of the title presented as a young woman's entry into a landscape which begins as something she conceives of as a picture "out there." The story opens on a morning in which all is muted, indistinct; the sky is "grey, soft, muffled." The young woman walks across a field:

> Away ahead, over the scribble of twigs, the sloping lines of black and platinum grass—all merging, tones but no colour, like an etching—was the horizon, the shore at which cloud lapped.
>
> Damp burnt grass puffed black, faint dust from beneath her feet. She could hear herself swallow.
>
> A long way off she saw a figure with something red on its head, and she drew from it the sense of balance she had felt at the particular placing of the dot of a figure in a picture. She was here; someone was over there. (p. 15)

Here the young woman remains detached from a landscape "over there." Not just the references to an etching and a picture, but the use of terms which are appropriate to drawing—"scribble," "sloping lines"—insist upon this means of viewing the scene. The calmness of the young woman is linked to her control over her pictured world: the red patch gives her the same sense of balance which she achieves through placing a dot in a picture. This sense of control is quickly undercut as the man with the red hat accosts her as they pass:

> There was a chest heaving through the tear in front of her; a face panting; beneath the red hairy woollen cap the yellowish-red eyes holding her in distrust. One foot, cracked from exposure until it looked like broken wood, moved, only to restore balance in the dizziness that follows running, but any move seemed towards her and she tried to scream and the awfulness of dreams came true and nothing would come out. (p. 16)

The attack is presented as the young woman's entering the picture, the surface of which "tears" before her. She finds a world of powerful feeling, suggested by the primary colors which replace the greyness and the probable allusion to Edvard Munch's *The Scream*. Even during this brief tussle, she becomes, like the man with the foot of weathered wood, enmeshed in the landscape:

> She ran and ran, stumbling wildly off through the stalks of dead grass, turning over her heels against hard winter tussocks, blundering through trees and bushes. The young mimosas closed in, lowering a thicket of twigs right to the ground, but she tore herself through, feeling the dust in her eyes and the scaly twigs hooking at her hair. (p. 17)

She tears herself out of this picture, this landscape with which she has merged. She runs from a world of which she has become part, a world in which others cannot be kept "over there."

Such fleeting engagements of character and landscape recur, if in less overt form, in Gordimer's early fiction. Joel Aaron and Helen Shaw had come closest to creating a picture of a distinctively South African world in the veld at McDonald's Kloof, but fled when the Kloof spoke to them. Even Toby Hood had conceived of the kind of meeting required to overcome the divisions of South Africa as a union of character and landscape. One evening after discussing her political activities with Anna Louw, a renegade Afrikaner working as a legal aid advocate for Africans, he provides a picture of her:

> Her face, chin lifted to pull at a cigarette, or bent, with the shadows streaking down it, over the glass cupped in her hands, was the face of burned boats, blown bridges; one of those faces you suddenly see, by a trick of the light, in the rock formation of the side of a mountain. I felt suddenly afraid of her, I put out my hand and touched, with the touch of fear, the thing I fled from. (p. 174)

The union of character and landscape—the face embedded in the mountain—is a concrete representation of the situation not being held at bay as it had been in Toby's photographic images of the landscape. He might well feel afraid of her, for this kind of meeting proves dangerous; Ann Louw will be imprisoned by the novel's close. It is just such a union of character and landscape, developed in the later novels, which often leads to psychic collapse or death. But for those who engage with their worlds rather than fleeing as quickly as Toby, such meetings will lead to a sense of place achieved by none of Gordimer's earlier protagonists.

4

Landscapes Inhabited in Imagination: *A Guest of Honour*, *The Conservationist*, and *July's People*

I

In Gordimer's later novels the landscape ceases to serve as a background in which the characters attempt to read "outward signs." It becomes a living force—the moving force—in her fictional world. Indeed, there had been indications from her earliest years that Gordimer had seen the landscape of her world as inhabited by life. In "A South African Childhood: Allusions in a Landscape," she recalls being aware as a child of the vast system of mine tunnels beneath the ground, which would periodically send tremors throughout the Witwatersrand. In 1968 she would draw on these mines again in "The Witwatersrand: A Time of Tailings" as a metaphor for the suppressed imperatives of her society. "The social pattern," she wrote, "was, literally and figuratively, on the surface; the human imperative, like the economic one, came from what went on below ground. Perhaps it always remained 'below ground'; in men's minds too. It belongs to the subconscious from where what matters most in human affairs often never comes up to light." In her later novels "what matters most"—the human imperatives buried in the landscape—does come up to light. Gordimer would begin the 1981 essay "Apprentices of Freedom" by asserting that essential questions burst "with the tenacity of a mole from below the surface of cultural assumptions in a country like South Africa." In *A Guest of Honour*, *The Conservationist*, and *July's People*, Gordimer no longer attempts to capture the "surface shimmer" of her world's landscape; she uses it to embody a living, tenacious force—the human imperatives of her world.[1]

This metaphor of suppressed forces emerging from below ground finds most explicit expression in *The Conservationist*, in which the pig-iron magnate Mehring discovers shortly after buying a farm that an African buried in its third pasture is already "something inhabited in imagination." The narrative centers on his growing identification with this African until, after a flood near the novel's close, the African is washed up, causing what goes on "below ground" in Mehring's mind to surface. But the force of the landscape is emphasized from the outset of the other later novels as well. The protagonists of *A Guest of Honour* and *July's People* awake at the start of the novels to confront landscapes which are radically disjunct from those they had previously known. James Bray awakes to the heat of an African afternoon from which he recalls the placid English countryside "lying, now, deep in snow of a hard winter"; the Smales awake not to the "governors' residence, commercial hotel rooms, shift bosses' company bungalos, master bedrooms *en suite*" to which their kind had been accustomed but to thick mud walls and a thatched roof. They, like Mehring, are forced to confront new, living landscapes which deflect their lives into radically new paths.

While Gordimer had sensed the power of her landscape throughout her life, it finds expression in these later novels largely because of her claiming of an African history, which, as her use of the dead African indicates, she embodied in the landscape. But the increased role of place in her later novels was likely prompted as well by her increased interest in the literary-cultural views of Georg Lukács and Antonio Gramsci, who emphasize the role of broad cultural trends in shaping identity.[2] *Occasion for Loving* had revealed the need for cultural, as op-

1 Gordimer, "A South African Childhood," 121; Gordimer, "The Witwatersrand: A Time of Tailings," *Optima*, XVIII (January, 1968), 22; Gordimer, "Apprentices of Freedom," 12.

2 For the influence of Lukács, see Gordimer, *The Black Interpreters*, 32; Gordimer, "98 Kinds of Censorship in South Africa," *Hekima*, I (December, 1980), 115–16, and Gordimer, "The Idea of Gardening," 6. Gordimer took the epigraph for *July's People* from Gramsci's *Prison Notebooks*. Her later work illustrates well his theory on "hegemony," that the rule of one group over another depends not so much on economic or political power but on persuading the ruled to accept the cultural beliefs of the ruling class. Like both Lukács and Gramsci, Gordimer sees the under-

posed to personal, definition of self through Jessie Stilwell's failure to find a sense of place after resolving her familial problems. By the later novels, the family, which was the formative influence for Jessie and Helen Shaw, is of negligible significance.[3] We learn nothing of Bray's or Mehring's parents, and little of the Smales'. For Bray and Mehring, spouses and children are of little importance; both men are separated from their wives, and only Mehring tries, briefly, to establish contact with his son. Even though the Smales family lives together, by the novel's close husband and wife come together at a public event "as divorced people might meet on their regular day to keep up a semblance of family life" (p. 140).

Instead of these dead bourgeois structures, the later protagonists are defined by the way they relate to their physical world, a repository of cultural history. Bray puts this focus in the simplest way when he states that in Africa "you realize how hard it is to grasp change except in concrete terms."[4] It is characteristic of these later novels that Maureen Smales pictures her dislocation in very "concrete terms," as the destruction of "the background" of her world:

> She was not in possession of any part of her life. One or another could only be turned up, by hazard. The background had fallen away; since that first morning she had become conscious in the hut, she had regained no established point of a continuing present from which to recognize her own sequence. The suburb did not come before or after the mine. 20, Married Quarters, Western Areas, and the architect-designed master bedroom were in the same rubble. (p. 139)

Maureen sees hers as a shattered physical world, from which she can "turn up" only random parts of the "rubble" it has become.

Like the other later protagonists, Maureen is judged by her ability to identify with the landscape, which holds the imperatives of her world.

---

standing of one's historical situation as a precondition for action and accepts this understanding as the reality (none of the three would put the term in quotes) from which self-definition derives.

3 This generalization applies to *Burger's Daughter* as well, since the family there, as I discuss in Chapter Two, section four, is defined as a political institution.

4 *A Guest of Honour* (New York, 1970), 223. Subsequent references in the text are to this edition.

She fails to find what she calls "a continuing present"—what other Gordimer protagonists called "continuity" or "connection"—because she sees the landscape as "a background" discrete from herself. She persists in seeing herself as the center of her world; she needs to be "in possession of *her* life," which reveals "*her* own sequence." Similarly, Mehring attempts to possess his farm from the novel's outset, when he is concerned with the pilfering of eggs by African children. Both Maureen and Mehring attempt, at best, to record the salient features of their landscapes in order to maintain a controlling personal vision of them. Only Bray renounces his role as an observing "guest of honour" and accepts the imperatives in the landscape. He alone flourishes.

II

Gordimer described the setting of *A Guest of Honour* in 1970 as "a nonexistent, composite central African country. Imagine a place somewhere between Kenya, Tanzania, Zambia, Rhodesia, and Angola—you know, just make a hole in the middle of Africa and push it in—that's where it takes place."[5] It's a large hole, particularly by contrast with the limited urban settings of earlier novels. And the filling is different. For the first time in Gordimer's novels, the central figures are political men and the major events public spectacles, from the independence celebrations which open the novel to the party congress near the close. As in many of the states Gordimer mentions, these spectacles are the battleground for factions advocating different shapes for this new African state. The faction in power, led by Adamson Mweta, accepts, if reluctantly, a continued reliance on colonial economic and social structures; the opposition, led by Mweta's former mentor Edward Shinza, urges an African socialist path. Gordimer proves surprisingly deft in introducing not only the large cast of characters on both sides

5 E. G. Burrows, "An Interview with Nadine Gordimer," *Michigan Quarterly Review*, IX (Fall, 1970), 233–34. Gordimer traveled extensively in Southern Africa in the decade prior to the novel's publication. See "Report and Comment: Tanzania," *Atlantic*, CCXXXI (May, 1973), 8–18; "Zambia," *Holiday*, XXXIX (June, 1966), 38–47.

but of the many disoriented by the rapid transition to self-rule, like the servant that James Bray greets on his return as a guest of honor for the independence celebrations:

> Bray greeted the servant in Gala with the respectful form of address for elders and the man dumped the impersonality of a servant as if it had been the tray in his hands and grinned warmly, showing some pigmentation abnormality in a pink lip spotted like a Dalmatian. The ex-Governor looked on, smiling. The servant bowed confusedly at him, walking backwards, in the tribal way before rank, and then recovering himself and leaving the room with an anonymous lope. (p. 28)

Gordimer includes scores of characters like this servant in a vast canvas covering Mweta's capital, Shinza's rural Bashi Flats, and the old colonial outpost of Gala to which Bray returns.

Bray, who had been a district commissioner in Gala but removed ten years previously for supporting African demands for self-rule, is himself transformed during the course of the novel by learning how to participate in Shinza's attempts to transform the new country. He begins by assuming that his role in the new state will be simple: with the colonial era ended, he will facilitate the foundation of a new African society by serving as Mweta's educational advisor. His response during the celebrations to the servant in the traditional African way and his perception of the ex-governor as a smiling on-looker are but two small indications of his certainty that one era has passed, another begun. Bray eventually learns, however, what is most succinctly put in a passage from Frantz Fanon that he reads midway through the novel: "Everything seemed so simple before: the bad people were on one side, and the good on the other. The clear, the unreal, the idyllic light of the beginning is followed by a semi-darkness that bewilders the senses" (p. 292). Bray, a friend of both Mweta and Shinza, must learn to first accept this semi-darkness, then act within it, as he finally does by trying to assist Shinza. Indeed, the novel opens with him in the semi-darkness between waking and sleeping: "A bird cried on the roof, and he woke up. It was the middle of the afternoon, in the heat, in Africa; he knew where he was" (p. 3). This claim is unconvincing, for Bray immediately drifts into an extended recollection of the English country

estate he has just left. It will take most of the novel for him to renounce the moderate, liberal values that are appropriate in that setting
but finally, he learns, inappropriate in the new African country.

For most of the novel, Bray persists in a mediatory posture between
two sets of contradictory allegiances: on the one hand, Mweta and his
wife Olivia, whom he finally realizes were "linked at some level of his
mind"; on the other, Shinza and Rebecca Edwards, a woman through
whom the fifty-year-old Bray finds a revivified sensuality (p. 377). The
depth of conflict he feels is indicated by Mweta's given name, Adamson. Which son of Adam is he, Bray tries to see, a betrayed Abel to
Shinza's Cain or vice versa? From these two pairs grow other larger oppositions: between Mweta's city and Shinza's country worlds, neo-
colonialism and socialism, rationalism and intuition, a life of the present and a life governed by a sense of history. Bray must learn to operate
in the world of semi-darkness these oppositions create. He finally does
so when he comes to understand shortly before his death "that one
could never hope to be free of doubt, of contradictions within, that this
was the state in which one lived" (p. 465).

Bray learns how to act in the face of these contradictions through a
process which is the reverse of Gordimer's early protagonists. He begins by attempting to read the "outward signs" in the landscape, but he
gradually finds that only by allowing the landscape to inhabit him can
he sense a role for himself. He comes to trust less in his vision of the
landscape, more in envisioning within its presence. He articulates this
change near the novel's close when he realizes that his future with
Rebecca had been presaged by his first view of the lake near Gala:

> If he had been able to see it, the girl was there ahead in that pres-
> ence. He had the feeling that the area of uncertainty that sur-
> rounded him visually when he took off his glasses was the real
> circumstance in which he had lived his life; and his glasses were
> more than a means of correcting a physical shortcoming, they
> were his chosen way of rearranging the unknowable into a few
> outlines he had gone by. (p. 431)

The external world, the lake here, holds signs, but they must be sensed
as a "presence," not through acuity of sight which gives the false promise of a pattern which can be read in a discrete landscape. Bray finally

learns to accept that his world is an "area of uncertainty" which can be negotiated only by means of what he terms "a kind of second intelligence." He finds that a developing history can be sensed in such presences as the lake; the continuity Jessie Stilwell found in the African kraals cannot be seen or described, only felt.

From the novel's outset, environment plays a much more significant role than in the earlier works. It is not simply something that can be observed; rather, it enforces a kind of life. The environment has the same insidious power that the personal bonds to mothers had for Helen Shaw and Jessie Stilwell. Its power is first revealed through the effect of Olivia Bray's furnishings of the Wiltshire house that she and Bray were to inhabit during their retirement. She had taken out her family's furniture and possessions "and, putting them in place, inevitably had accepted the life the arrangement of such objects provided for":

> In the room they had decided on for his study, the desk from her great-grandfather that had naturally become his—a quiet field of black-red morocco scratched with almost erased gold—was a place to write the properly documented history of the territory (Mweta's country) that had never been done before. (p. 7).

This description gives the sense that not just the furniture but the inhabitants are "put in place." Not simply a kind of life, but the very way one looks at the world seems determined by this external order. Bray is "naturally" put in the role of the detached observer when put at "a place to write the properly documented history." Even when Bray imagines the house, after months away from it in Gala, its power of place reasserts itself:

> The house in Wiltshire with all its comfortable beauty and order, its incenses of fresh flowers and good cooking, its libations of carefully discussed and chosen wine came to Bray in all the calm detail of an interesting death cult; to wake up there again would be to find oneself acquiescently buried alive. At the same time, he felt a stony sense of betrayal. Olivia moved about there, peppermints and cigarettes on the night-table, her long, smooth-stockinged legs under skirts that always drooped slightly at the back. A detail taken from a painting, isolated and brought up close to the eye. (p. 130)

Bray's very thoughts of the house's order cause it to come to him in "calm detail" and finally to resolve itself into the detail from a painting. The sense of the environment's dominance is created by presenting the atmosphere of the house, then describing Olivia's place in it, ending with her legs as a detail taken from the larger whole of Bray's "painting."

By the time of this recollection, Bray has obviously begun to reject, because it is unchanging, this world which can be pictured, in which Olivia's skirts "always" drooped. This house is not somewhere Bray can "wake up"; in this passage "wake," bracketed by "death cult" and "buried alive," clearly suggests a funeral. His movement away from this visioning of life is made possible by Gala's environment in which he becomes, less and less, a detached observer. His movement toward merging with what he observes is revealed in thoughts of Rebecca occasioned by his use of the phrase "for a lifetime" in a letter to Mweta:

> For a lifetime—lying suddenly in his mind, the word associated with advertisements for expensive Swiss watches: lifetime. The habits of a lifetime. He felt himself outside that secure concept built up coating by coating, he was exposed nakedly as a man who has been shut away too long from the sun. The girl presented herself face-to-face, fact-to-fact with him, a poster-apocalypse filling the sky of his mind. Thought could crawl all over and about her, over the steadfast smile and the open yellow eyes and in and out the ears and nostrils. (p. 269)

Bray's engagement in this scene is revealed most obviously by the two references to its being in his mind, the trite phrase "lying" there, Rebecca more actively "filling" it. The choppy phrasing and the abrupt transitions reinforce the sense of internal images, feeling rather than intellect, in operation. The pictorial comparison remains, but the picture is without form and certainly not seen from the detached perspective of the Wiltshire house; rather, Rebecca is taken into Bray, face-to-face. This world of engagement has its dangers too. In fact, this vision foreshadows Bray's own apocalypse, his being murdered while attempting to leave the country to raise funds for Shinza. Rebecca's "yellow eyes" suggest Balzac's *La Fille au Yeux d'Or* that Bray will use as the password for securing funds in Switzerland. As in his thoughts about the lake above, this scene—"if he had been able to see it"—portends not only his private engagement with Rebecca but engagement in a Sartrian sense as well, for the trip to Switzerland is in aid of Shinza's political cause. The scene thus reveals a future intuitively apprehended, a claiming of a life-in-death with Rebecca and Shinza, a rejection of a death-in-life with Olivia and Mweta.

Reaching this point requires a radical change in Bray. At the novel's outset he attempts to comprehend the current condition of the African state, from which he has been absent ten years, through picturing it in much the same way as Toby Hood had Johannesburg in *A World of Strangers*. During the independence celebrations Bray provides descriptions of the town's buildings, such as the Great Lakes Hotel and the Silver Rhino bar, which, as their names imply, embody the colonial era which Bray assumes will soon cease to exist. On his first visit to Mweta's new house, Bray finds yet another colonial remnant:

> It was neo-classical, with a long double row of white pillars holding up a portico before a great block of local terracotta brick and mica-tinselled stone, row upon row of identical windows like a barracks. The new coat-of-arms was in place on the façade. The other side, looking down upon the park as if Capability Brown had been expected but somehow failed to provide the appropriate sweep of landscaped lawn, artificial lake, pavilion, and deer, was not so bad. The park itself, simply the leafier trees of the bush thinned out over seven or eight acres of rough grass, was—as he remembered it—full of hoopoes and chameleons who had been there to begin with, anyway. (p. 56)

Bray is unsettled by Mweta's having occupied the governor's mansion, especially perhaps because of the uncanny resemblance of this mansion to the house Bray himself has left behind. The Wiltshire house also has an imposing façade and an extended grassy look-out down through a long valley behind it. Bray takes solace in the African aspect of the park, which seems to be merely thinned-out bush. Yet, while he refuses to acknowledge them, the details reveal the beginning of Fanon's semi-darkness. The mansion and grounds have more of an English than an African aspect. Not just the neo-classical portico but even the so-called local aspects have a European flavor: the local brick is terracotta; the hoopoes and chameleons are European as well as African animals. Bray thinks that this house can be easily ignored. At the end of a walk in the park with Mweta, Bray concludes, "It was so easy, very tempting—he looked at the empty house looming up in their way— one could walk round the past they had inhabited, as one does round a monument" (p. 69). As in so many of the novel's descriptions, this house carries signs of a future as yet unapprehended by Bray and indications that the past cannot be walked around. The house, as the depiction of the windows indicates, will become a barracks during an insurrection near the novel's close. And the house is one means by which Mweta will show his desire to continue the colonial regime he inherited; he will later reject the non-English aspects of the park by closing a window looking on to it and commenting, "We're not in the bush in Gala anymore" (p. 162). Mweta does seem to expect that an architect like Capability Brown, so named for his finding "capability" in the most unprepossessing sites, might yet transform the African bush into an English country garden.

As Bray leaves the capital for Gala, where he has agreed to serve as Mweta's educational consultant, the landscape he observes also reveals his desire to see the colonial era as coming to a neat close. The pattern he perceives in the landscape is the same pictured by Helen Shaw and Toby Hood—the city, then the encircling gold mines, and finally the mine properties:

> Then there were the landscaped approaches to the mine proper-
> ties themselves, all flowery traffic roundabouts, sign-boards, and
> beds of cannas and roses, and then the stretches of neat colour-
> washed rectangles of housing for the African miners, a geometric
> pattern scribbled over by the mop-heads of paw-paw trees, smok-
> ing chimneys, washing lines, creepers and maize patches, and bro-
> ken up by the noise and movement of people. In twenty minutes it
> was all gone; he passed the Bush Hill Arms, its Tudor façade
> pocked with wasp nests and a "For Sale" notice up (someone else
> "getting out"), and then there was nothing at all—everything; the
> one smooth road, the trees, the bamboo, and the sudden open
> country of the *dambos* where long grasses hid water, and he saw
> at last, again, the single long-tailed shrike that one always seemed
> to see in such places, hovering with its ink-black tail-plume like
> the brushstroke of a Chinese ideograph. (p. 76)

Bray is quick to notice that the Bush Hill Arms (like his own and Mweta's residences) has an English façade, which marks it as a superficial remnant of empire left by another colonial "getting out." This end of the colonial era is signaled to him as well by the intrusion of the African landscape and people into the neat "geometric pattern" of housing created by the mine owners, which is "scribbled over" by indigenous trees and "broken up" by the Africans' noise and movement. Bray's need to see the country's history in such neat terms is also revealed as he moves out into the veld. Its formlessness causes him to distance himself by resolving it into a composition, the bird giving it the form of a Chinese ideograph. He still feels the need to control "the sudden open country" by keeping it at a distance, a picture to be viewed. It will require time for him to come up close to this world as he does, for instance, when that phrase "for a lifetime" lay "suddenly in his mind," leading to his vision of merging with Rebecca. Here he reacts as Helen Shaw did to the sudden stretch of open veld outside the mines; his conceiving it as a composition is the counterpart of her retreat to the order of the clearly focused picture of the colonials playing tennis.

On entering the town of Gala, Bray finds a history in the landscape which shows even more emphatically his belief that the colonial era need no longer be reckoned with. He thinks of the outpost Tippo Tib established nearby as part of his slave network, then of the British colonial settlement:

> Walls had fallen down in the village but trees remained; too big to be hacked out of the way of the slave-caravan trail; too strong to be destroyed by fire when British troops were in the process of subduing the population; revered by several generations of colonial ladies, who succeeded in having a local by-law promulgated to forbid anyone chopping them down. Their huge grey outcrops of root provided stands for bicycles and booths for traders and craftsmen; the shoemaker worked there, and the bicycle and sewing-machine repairer. (p. 90)

This landscape shows not just that the colonial era has passed but that it never really took effect. The slave caravans, British troops, and colonial ladies made no lasting impact on the native environment, for those trees remained. The two references to bicycles also show Bray's attempt to deny the continuing colonial presence, for his allegiance to Mweta, long after his maintenance of colonial policies should be clear to Bray, is due to his image of Mweta as "the boy on the bicycle" journeying from village to village in the campaign for self-rule. Bray has indeed walked around that governor's mansion to avoid seeing that the boy on the bicycle has become part of the colonial system he previously fought. Bray, in short, persists in viewing the colonial era as past. As he thinks shortly afterwards, his own role before independence had been dictated by "a particular historical situation, a situation that no longer existed. Not objectively, and not for him; he had been away and come back clear of it" (p. 92). This easy and tempting view is clearly bound up with his lack of involvement with the society to which he returns. So long as he persists in separating what is "objectively" out there from himself, he will remain "clear of" the troubling semidarkness around him.

Soon after Bray's arrival, Gordimer introduces the beginnings of the engaged perspective which will lead to his choice of Rebecca and Shinza. This new perspective, prompted by Bray's first thoughts of the lake, serves as a comment on the simple historical view he has maintained thus far:

> As he went in and out of the Fisheagle Inn he was sometimes arrested, from the veranda, by the sight of the lake. The sign of the lake: a blinding strip of shimmer, far away beyond the trees, or on less clear days, a different quality in the haze. For a moment his mind emptied; the restless glitter of the lake, the line of a glance below a lowered lid—for it was not really the lake at all that one saw, but a trick of the distance, the lake's own bright glare cast up upon the heated atmosphere, just as the vast opening out of pacing water to the horizon, once you got to its bush-hairy shores, was not really the open lake itself at all, but (as the map showed) only the southernmost tip of the great waters that spread up the continent for six hundred miles and through four or five countries. It was then, just for a moment, that this symbol of infinity of distance, carrying the infinity of time with which it was one, released his mind from the time of day and he was at once himself ten years ago and himself now, one and the same. It was a pause not taken account of. (p. 93)

Instead of two separate roles in two different historical situations, Bray is at once himself then and now. He is led to this feeling of a continuing history, "an infinity of time," through experiencing the lake, "an infinity of distance," which casts its glare around him in the atmosphere. This change derives from the disillusion of his observer role; he is captured ("arrested") by the lake, which is not kept "out there," as the two references to his mind indicate, but experienced within. This vision, moreover, prefigures the form of his future awareness. The "blinding" lake foreshadows that his awareness will come not through observing but when, his glasses removed, he will merge with the landscape he inhabits. The passage, more specifically, points to the consequences of this more involved perspective, for the reference to "the line of a glance below a lowered eyelid" is echoed by his appearance after his murder (p. 474). The passage thus reveals Bray experiencing his past, present, and future as one through a new participatory mode of perception. That this mode requires development is indicated by the momentary intrusion of an objective construct in the reference to the map. Bray's development will come as such pauses, unlike here, are "taken account of" without such distancing.

A more conscious acknowledgment of this change in perspective comes to Bray as he arrives in Shinza's Bashi Flats after a long trip:

> On the morning of the sixth day the Volkswagen was poled across the river and the silent motion, after the perpetual rattling of the car, was a kind of presage: Shinza was on the other side. In the light, sandy-floored forest he came upon movement that he thought, at a distance, was buck feeding; it was women gathering sour wild fruit, and they turned to laugh and chatter as he passed.
>
> The trees ended; the scrub ended; the little car was launched upon a sudden opening-out of flowing grass and glint of water that pushed back the horizon. He had always felt here, that suddenly he saw as a bird did, always rising, always lifting wider the ring of the eyes' horizon. He took off his glasses for a moment and the shimmering and wavering range rushed away from him, even farther. (p. 115)

The passage incorporates many of the same elements as the moment of arrest at the Fisheagle Inn, from the "glint" and "shimmering" qualities to the premonitions of death in the removal of his glasses and the Charon-like poling across the river. The passage points up the consequences of two modes of perception he might choose to employ. His attempt to observe this scene fails—he mistakes the women for bucks—whereas the movement culminating in the removal of his glasses provides a broadened viewpoint within himself. Two contrasts with his earlier observations reinforce this sense of change: instead of using a bird to create a portrait as he had on leaving the city, he identifies with it, and the "sudden opening" of the landscape here provokes him to "suddenly" see. In short, this landscape is not viewed; it evokes a sympathetic response in him.

The consequence of this moment's being "taken account of" is immediately apparent in his perception of a different history in the landscape than he had on first entering Gala:

> Feeling his way through the past, he drove, without much hesitance at turnings, to Shinza's village. A new generation of naked children moved in troops about the houses, which were a mixture of the traditional materials of mud and grass, and the bricks and corrugated iron of European settlement. Some of the children were playing with an ancient Victorian mangle; Belgian missionaries from the Congo and German missionaries from Tanganyika had waded through the grass all through the last decade of the nineteenth century, dumping old Europe among the long-horned cattle. (p. 116)

In equating wading "through the grass" with "through the last decade of the nineteenth century," Bray conjoins landscape and history much more concretely than in his view from the Fisheagle Inn. This landscape, unlike those Bray had previously perceived, shows a continuing colonial presence, with Europe and Africa mixed in the houses, the "Victorian mangle" with the cattle. And, unlike the first view of Gala, in which the trees overshadowed European attempts at intrusion, Bray does not present a simple argument about the country's history. He is "feeling his way through the past" without the false security of a single bicycle in sight.

Bray's development is occurring through a series of contrasts between his initial tendency to observe his world and his taking into account "sudden" moments in which he internalizes the landscape.

Gradually the tendency to observe dissipates and the power and concreteness of the envisioned scenes increase, carrying with them more explicit presentiments of his future. Looking at Gala from his desk outside his bungalow one day, he begins once again by establishing a detached perspective; he sees "foreshortened" figures in the village below, and he finds "himself held in a kind of aural tension—something cocked within him, as in an animal in the dream that is grazing" (p. 201). Bray uses Henri Rousseau's "The Sleeping Gypsy" to give his feeling shape, but the picture is internalized, a correlative for his condition. And instead of distancing him from the scene, the picture leads him into a dream vision:

> Nothing happened in the open in this small, remote, peaceful crossroad. All change was a cry drowned by the sea of trees. A high-pitched note, almost out of range. (In a noon pause, one morning, he experienced in fantasy this same quiet of sun and heavy trees existing while things went wrong—he saw a car burning, bleeding bodies far down under the shifting shade-pattern of the trees. It lasted a vivid moment; his skin contracted—it seemed prompted physically, like the experience of *déjà vu*. . . . (pp. 201–202)

As at the novel's outset, Bray is awakened by a bird's cry, which leads here to a vivid presentiment of the scene of his death, where his body will lie bleeding near a burning car. Again, the landscape evokes a corresponding state in Bray. Its timelessness—it is morning at noon—induces him to experience in the present his future death which has the feeling of *déjà vu*. He not only perceives but experiences the continuity Gordimer's earlier characters sought.

This scene reflects as well Bray's growing acknowledgment that the process of change as he had first conceived it is too simple, for nothing happens "in the open" at this crossroad. Bray reveals a more conscious sense of a complex historical pattern when he states shortly afterward that "a profound cycle of change was set up here three or four hundred years ago with the first of us foreign invaders. We're inclined to think it comes full stop, full circle, with Independence . . . but that's not so . . . it's still in process—that's all" (p. 210). With this statement, Bray renounces his easy certainties about historical stages. Moreover, the statement shows Bray's inklings that his own personal history, which he had foreseen when "things went wrong" in his vision above, is connected with a history "in process" since he is responding here to a query of Rebecca's about his use of the phrase "when things go wrong."

Bray can never articulate what this "cycle of change" is, but he does know that it involves change, not Mweta's attempts to frustrate it by shoring up colonial structures. His coming break with Mweta, which does not find expression until the party congress near the novel's close, is indicated in another scene in which observing yields to an inner landscape. Bray and Rebecca stand "looking out across the neat *boma* garden . . . down the slope to the town half-hidden by the cumulus evergreen," where the activities of the town are "all in the frame of vision":

> The usual bicycles and pedestrians moved in the road, bicycles bumping down over the bit where the five hundred yards of tar that had been laid in front of the *boma* ended and there was a rutted descent to the dirt. He had the feeling—parenthetic, precise—that they were both suddenly thinking of the lake at the same time. The lake with its upcurved horizon down which black pirogues slid towards you. The lake still as a heat-pale sky. (p. 295)

Here the neat, observed view, with its allusions to "the boy on the bicycle," is replaced by the lake, which begins to inhabit Bray's imagination as the pirogues slide toward him.

While Bray supports Shinza at the party congress and agrees to aid him by going to Europe, the attraction of Mweta does not fade until literally minutes before Bray's death. Appropriately, his final dispatching of Mweta comes as he thinks of the obliteration of Mweta's colonial residence from his consciousness. He envisions himself "actually walking up the steps to the red brick façade," but supposes that this image will fade "into an empty wall" (p. 466). Only with Mweta's habitation removed from his own inner landscape can Bray tell Rebecca that he will do whatever he can for Shinza.

Bray can act for Shinza because he has accepted the uncertainties of the world with which he has engaged. Shortly before his death, Bray thinks, "There was no finality, while one lived, and when one died it would always be, in a sense, an interruption"; and his final thought while being bludgeoned to death is "I've been interrupted, then—" (pp. 465, 469). This acceptance is credible because Bray's development has occurred through many sudden interruptions of what had been his accepted way of viewing life: his being "arrested" by the lake, the "sudden opening out" when removing his glasses at Shinza's, the "vivid moment" when he envisioned his death, the "parenthetic" appearance of the pirogues. These moments have given him a sense of a continuous personal existence and of his life's accord with a cycle of history, which allows him to act in the semi-darkness he inhabits. As Gordimer said of his death, "He's killed by mistake, it's gratuitous, fortuitous, it doesn't make sense to the world. But it would have made sense to him, because he'd made his moral choice there, he'd accepted the risks it carried. He'd accepted the fact that what he had to offer the country was no longer sufficient, and ineffectual. He had taken the risk, moral and physical, of *action*."[6]

A Guest of Honour could well end with Bray's life being interrupted, but Gordimer chooses to emphasize the worth of his moral choice through a long coda to the novel. She begins by giving him an honorable mourning ceremony by the local Africans. She underscores the consequences of failure to develop a sense of felt history and act in accord with it through two of Bray's friends: one chooses a private retreat and ends doddering about Bray's garden in Gala; the other remains in the thrall of Mweta and increasing amounts of alcohol. But Gordimer affirms Bray's choice best in a portrait of the man he might have become had he continued simply to observe, not act in, his world. While waiting in Mozambique for a plane to Europe, Rebecca sees a man sitting at a nearby table. He had "a very dark Mediterranean face, all the beautiful planes deeply scored in now, as if age were redrawing it in a sharper, darker pencil. Brilliantly black eyes were deep-set in a contemplative, amused crinkle that suggested disappointed scholarship— a scientist, someone who saw life as a pattern of gyrations in a drop under a microscope" (p. 489). The man is clearly what Bray was likely to become had he remained in Wiltshire with Olivia: a contemplative scholar writing his "carefully documented history," observing the patterns of life, and hardening into a picture, a product of the kind of perception he has had of the world. For the child with him, the man has drawn "a picture of great happiness, past happiness, choppy waves frill-

6 Gray, "Landmark in Fiction," 81.

ing along, a gay ship with flags and triumphant smoke, birds sprinkled about the air like kisses on a letter" (p. 489). Rebecca's sense that the child is "all he has left" is confirmed by this picture, a happy child's picture. Its "past happiness" and the man's focus on the child reveals a life drawn back into the past without the sense of a future. The picture shows, in short, the contemplative death-in-life which Bray, writing at the desk of Olivia's grandfather, forsook for a life of action, his own.

The very fact that Bray's death is so consistently misunderstood serves only to highlight, as Gordimer stated, that *his* choice was what mattered. *Time* labels him Mweta's "trusted White Man Friday"; an acquaintance calls him one of "those nice white liberals getting mixed up in things they don't understand" (pp. 488, 502). Bray, accepting the uncertainties of the semi-darkness in which he lived, had anticipated such responses when he observed of his choice of Shinza, "It was either a tragic mistake or his salvation. . . . I'll never know, although other people will tell me for the rest of my life" (p. 465). Indeed, when Bray thought that the party congress "would be swept up in the historian's half-sentence some day," he foresaw the kind of attention he is given by a British writer who gives him fleeting attention as one of those who renounced "empirical liberalism" and was prepared to accept "apocalyptic solutions, wade through blood if need be, to bring real change" (pp. 359, 503). This historian's half-sentence is half-right. Bray renounces liberalism and accepts the apocalypse. But he has learned to proffer no solutions, and the blood is his own.

III

The landscape of *The Conservationist* is much like that of the Central African state of *A Guest of Honour* before its independence. A large European city, the center of power, is set in the veld; roads radiate out from it past mines and African locations to the farms beyond. At the novel's outset, the Europeans control the city; they control the locations and farms. Most importantly they control the roads, for the most observable symbol of their power is the vehicles they use to move from city to veld and to set themselves apart from the Africans on the farms. In the novel's opening scene, as a farmer surveys his recently acquired land from his Mercedes, "the emblem on the car's bonnet, it-self made in the shape of a prismatic flash, scores his vision with a vertical-horizontal sword dazzle" (p. 8). The emblem confers more than just a sword's might; its "prismatic flash" correctly implies his Zeus-like power in this world. He will later appear as an Old Testament god within the whirlwind of dust the Mercedes creates on a dirt road.

During the novel the Europeans are weakened by the arrogance growing from their power, as the farmer is blinded by the Mercedes emblem. They begin to lose control of the roads. A tropical storm washes out large sections of them; neighboring Africans do not heed the signs forbidding their use of the farm's roads, and the African farm laborers begin to use the farm vehicles at will. In the first of the climactic scenes of the novel, the farmer's Mercedes rolls to a halt when hailed by a young woman who entices the farmer into a tryst at one of the abandoned mine dumps between the city and the farm. There, off those well-traveled roads, he will succumb to a paranoid delusion: He imagines the girl to be "Coloured" and their liaison a sign of depravity disclosed for all to see. The second climax, with which the novel closes, shows the farm tractor rolling slowly on, carrying an African to burial, "to take possession of this earth."

Through the decay of the tenuous European superstructure and the transfer of power on the farm, *The Conservationist* depicts the re-claiming of the veld by the Africans who first settled it. Even though this transformation is given more metaphorical treatment than the major theme of any of Gordimer's other novels, it still carries quite specific allusions to the South African situation. The flood which ushers in a new order is caused by a tropical storm which originated in the Mozambique channel, near the Portuguese territory which was soon to claim independence. The novel closes with the statement that the dead African had "come back" to his people, a clear echo of the African National Congress slogan "Come Back, Africa." A broader historical context is provided as well. In the opening scene, for instance, the major figures are designated "the farmer" and "the herdsman," recalling the usurpation of land by the white farmers, the Boers, from the cattle-raising Africans. When the herdsman greets the farmer with the news that a dead African has been found on his property, his hand "with an imperious forefinger shaking it, stabs the air, through chest-level of the farmer's body," a gesture which evokes the thrust of a Zulu assegai. The transformation of power is, however, developed mainly through the demise of the arrogant farm owner Mehring, "an archetypal white South African," as A. E. Voss has called him. Mehring's representative status is indicated, for example, in the form his seizure takes at the mine dumps, where he imagines himself to be apprehended for breaking the society's central taboo of interracial sex, and in Gordimer's equation of his fears of death with the mining system on which the whites have built their power. Indeed, the mine dumps scene has the feel of a psychodrama: the Afrikaner whom Mehring perceives waiting to expose him is seen as a "thickheaded ox, guardian of the purity of the white race," playing the super-ego to the "Coloured" girl's lascivious id. But Mehring's character has wider associations. Indeed, he is not a native—he was born in South West Africa (now Namibia). He is depicted as a latter-day colonialist, the narrative an account of his brief colonizing of the farm. He is an international businessman, often abroad in Japan and Europe; he attempts to preserve the farm for future generations by planting European trees. And Mehring conceives his position not in South African but broadly historical terms, as evidenced when he thinks early in the novel, "How long can we go on getting away scot free: When the aristocrats were caught up in the Terror, did they recognize: it's come to us" (p. 42). Even after a brief period on the farm, Mehring senses that he is, in Paul Theroux's words, "a doomed man, the last alien."[7]

By the novel's close he accepts that the Africans on the farm "have been there all the time and they will continue to be there" (p. 246). Mehring acknowledges here a condition which Christopher Hope has expressed well: "He is *the* white man . . . among people who cannot be said to be hostile but who are increasingly indifferent to his survival." If Mehring realizes, like those in the Terror, that "it's come to us," the end is, as Hope implies, not going to come as a mass uprising. Indeed, the farm workers, led by Jacobus—the "herdsman" of the opening

7 A. E. Voss, "The Conservationist," *Reality*, VII (May, 1975), 16; Paul Theroux, "The Conservationist," *New York Times Book Review*, April 13, 1975, p. 4. Christopher Hope's comment below is from "Out of the Picture: The Novels of Nadine Gordimer," *London Magazine*, XV (April/May, 1975), 54.

chapter—realize that Mehring is superfluous. They get what they need from him, while simply waiting for him to take himself out of the picture. Jacobus, the farm's foreman, provides for its extended family and presides over its rituals—a dance, the ritual slaughter of a calf, a Christmas celebration, and finally the burial of the dead African at the close. The descriptions of these activities serve partly to point up the lack of basis to Mehring's life; the Christmas parties in his community are drunken, throw-people-in-the-pool affairs, and its only funeral, a suicide's, is ignored. The largely separate treatment in the narrative of these two separate worlds creates a strong impression of the decline of the urban white, the vitality of the rural African cultures.

But if Mehring is a doomed alien, his tale is of interest largely because he overcomes some of the limitations of "his kind." This is no mean fact in a world where characters do not change, indeed rarely have the impulse to. The novel depicts a world, as Gordimer notes in reference to the Indian store near the farm, where "contexts were . . . unvaryingly established, grooved by time and sameness" (p. 114). To be sure, Mehring takes refuge in the grooves his society mandates. After a visit to the Boer farm nearby and a talk with Jacobus, for example, he thinks with relief that "the well-regulated demands and responses between the Boers and himself, the usual sort of exchange between his black man and himself have re-engraved the fine criss-cross of grooves on which his mind habitually runs" (p. 54). But he does have the impulse, even if he fails to acknowledge it, to escape his "well-regulated" life. The very root of his German name suggests as much: he wants "more," not just more possessions but more experience and more of a community than his segregated society has afforded him. The most obvious sign of this impulse is his having taken a mistress with liberal/radical views; their past conversations—she has left the country on an exit permit—come to dominate his thoughts. But Mehring also wants to appreciate the beauty of the farm, he wants a more intimate bond with Jacobus, and he wants relations with black women. At a very basic if unacknowledged level, Mehring has the same vitality and urge for a broader experience as Saul Bellow's Henderson the Rain King. Like him, he says "I want. I want."

But strong as this impulse is, Mehring spends much of his time avoiding the identification he inwardly desires with the farm and the workers. What Gordimer's earlier, liberal protagonists sought, he resists. This is partly because the fifty-year-old Mehring is too thoroughly a city man to adapt to the rhythms of farm life. Gordimer emphasizes early on how radically dissociated he is from the farm life he confronts by introducing him as "the farmer," then undercutting such pretentions by opening the second section, "Mehring was no farmer." At the novel's outset he is so much a creature of commercial city life that its jargon informs even his idle thoughts. As he takes a shower at the farm, for instance, he automatically thinks that the fixture "may be secured in a bracket on the wall or held in the hand," the very language used to advertise it (p. 44). Moreover, his life, as this thought implies, has been informed by a purely functional ethic, most significantly his society's rigid code of black-white interaction. It is characteristic that when Jacobus requests a new worker for the farm, "the response falls into the place that has been made ready for it, just as, at the telephone exchange that connects two voices, certain metal levers have had to drop into slots in order to establish communication" (p. 84). This is the kind of "engagement" with the African world Mehring has been accustomed to, the interfacing of separate parts in a purely mechanical way. The disjunction between the world he comes from and the new world he encounters in the novel is markedly greater than that faced by any of Gordimer's earlier protagonists.

So unaccustomed is Mehring to engaging with Africans in an African landscape that his growing identification with this new world takes a particularly radical form. It is best described as a tension between his urge to possess the farm and the farm's power to possess him. Mehring resists the farm's power, but it increasingly gains control over his subconscious as he cuts loose from the well-traveled roads. Indeed, the novel's opening scene shows him observing an incident which calls into question his assumed possession of the farm that he conceived as an enterprise "in which reasonable productivity prevailed" (p. 20). The novel opens,

> Pale freckled eggs.
> Swaying over the ruts to the gate of the third pasture, Sunday morning, the owner of the farm suddenly sees: a clutch of pale freckled eggs set out before a half-circle of children. Some are squatting; the one directly behind the eggs is cross-legged, like a

vendor in a market. There is pride of ownership in that grin lifted shyly to the farmer's gaze. The eggs are arranged like marbles . . . . The bare soles, the backsides of the children have flattened a nest in the long dead grass for both eggs and children. (p. 8)

Like the woman Mehring sees soon thereafter who "stands quite still, one of those figures with the sun in its eyes caught in a photograph," this view has the clarity of a picture seen by one safely distanced in his car (p. 9). To Mehring, the children's appropriation of the eggs is a trifling instance of the transgression of his power, which he will simply tell Jacobus to stop. But to give this command, he uncharacteristically leaves his car and the safety of the road's familiar pattern for the fields. There he finds Jacobus waiting with his own message, that an unknown African has been found dead in the third pasture. Mehring wants to leave this problem "to the proper channels that exist to deal with such matters," but he is already becoming involved: the dead body "is a sight that has no claim on him. But the dead man is on his property" (p. 12). The dead man, like the children, has made a claim by fashioning "a nest" in the farm's grass. The dead man has claimed Mehring as well. It is largely through the power exercised by the body beneath the land's surface that Mehring will come to realize that "there are kinds of companionship unsought. With nature" (p. 190).

The buried man quickly comes to claim what lies beneath the surface of Mehring's mind. Lying one afternoon in the third pasture, Mehring begins to be aware of "something already inhabited in imagination":

> I have my bit of veld and my cows . . . Perhaps he has dozed; he suddenly—out of blackness, blankness—is aware of breathing intimately into the earth. Wisps and shreds of grass or leaf stir there. It is the air from his nostrils that moves them. To his half-open eye the hairs that border it and the filaments of dead grass are one.
> There is sand on his lip.
> For a moment he does not know where he is—or rather who he is; but this situation in which he finds himself, staring into the eye of the earth with earth at his mouth, is strongly familiar to him. (p. 37)

Mehring has merged with the land, his hair blending with the "dead grass" and "earth at his mouth." He does not yet associate this experience explicitly with the dead African, which is, Mehring finally comes to think, "who he is." His linked fears of blackness and death erupt completely into consciousness only when the African is washed up following the apocalyptic flood near the novel's close. This occurrence is already foreshadowed during Mehring's experience on this afternoon: "The sense of familiarity, of some kind of unwelcome knowledge or knowing, is slow to ebb. As it does, it leaves space in his mind; or uncovers, like the retreat of a high tide, carrying away silt" (p. 37). It is this space which Mehring will take solace in re-engraving with the criss-cross of grooves through his talks with the Boers and Jacobus. But he is soon to find that all roads lead not to Johannesburg, as they had in Gordimer's early novels, but to the third pasture where this African lies buried.

The narrative, then, takes its impetus from the farm's landscape, more specifically from the claim to the farm made by this dead African beneath its surface. Mehring resists this claim vigorously. His attempts to counteract the farm's power sometimes take the form of picturing it as the earlier protagonists and, at the outset of his narrative, Bray had. But the farm is, as even Mehring's insipid Johannesburg friends realize, "a landscape without any picture-postcard features (photographs generally were unsuccessful in conveying it)" (p. 22). It is, by implication, a landscape from which one cannot remain detached. Nevertheless, Mehring has an active, resourceful mind, which he has long put in the service of distancing himself from his surroundings. His encounters with the farm become a kind of sparring in which he uses a wider variety of methods than the earlier protagonists to keep the landscape "out there." The following passage early in the novel is characteristic of the ebb and flow of Mehring's attempts at detachment and the landscape's exercising of its own power, in other words, the tension between possessing and being possessed:

> Even the most random-seeming creatures are shown by studies to have a topography of activity from which they never really depart, although they may appear to casual observation to weave and backtrack aimlessly, almost crazily, free. From the flat to the car to the office, from tables to beds, from airports to hotels, from city to country, the track like the etching something (worms? ants?) has left on this tree-trunk amounts to a closed system. No farther. Wherever he sets out for or from, or however without di-

rection he sets out to roam, on his farm, it's always here that he ends up. Down over the third pasture at the reeds. (p. 69)

The attitude of clinical observation so evident at the opening finds concrete expression in a pictorial image, "the etching" on the tree trunk. Instead of distancing Mehring from his world, however, this picture connects it with his own situation, prompting his desire to go "no farther." Yet he still ends in that third pasture. The novel will show him being led away from "a topography of activity"—the city and the well-grooved tracks of South African life—governed by restrictions on activity and perception. Again and again Mehring's road—his "closed system"—is associated with barriers, from the city where the Zulu garage attendant draws open "the loop of chain that bars unauthorized entry" to the Indian store near the farm, where the guard dogs refuse to leave after the restraining gates are opened, "as if, for them, the pattern of closed gates was still barred across their eyes" (p. 119).

Under the influence of the farm's topography, the gates across Mehring's own eyes begin to open, but only slowly and against his will. The farm's growing power is evident during his walk one morning when he uncharacteristically disrupts his pattern and delays going to the city:

> Look at the willows. The height of the grass. Look at the reeds. Everything bends, blends, folds. Everything is continually swaying, flowing rippling waving surging streaming fingering. He is standing there with his damn shoes all wet with the dew and he feels he himself is swaying, the pulsation of his blood is moving him on his own axis (that's the sensation) as it seems to do to accommodate the human body to the movement of a ship. A high earth running beneath his feet. All this softness of grasses is the susurration of a slight dizziness, hissing in the head.
>
> Fair and lovely place. From where does the phrase come to him? It comes back, tum-te-tum-te-tum, as only something learned by rote survives. It's not his vocabulary. Fair and lovely. A place in a child's primer where nothing ugly could possibly be imagined to happen; as if such places exist. No wound to be seen; and simply shovelled under. He looks out over this domain almost with fascination, to think that, somewhere, that particular spot exists, overgrown. No one'll remember where you are buried. (p. 174)

Mehring begins by looking at this scene. As the land exercises its power, he resists by labeling his feelings—"(that's the sensation)"— and by viewing the land as something separate from him, a ship beneath his feet. And when the hissing enters his head, he tries to escape simply experiencing it by searching for the derivation of the phrase, "fair and lovely place," it calls up. These attempts to keep the landscape "out there" fail, as Mehring yields to the fascination of the shallow grave—the wound of the man is transferred to the landscape—and he finally identifies with the dead man when he recalls his mistress' claim that "No one'll remember where you are buried." Clearly, despite his strong efforts to remain detached, Mehring is claimed by the landscape.

He attempts to escape its power by taking to the road, where the tread of other vehicles and his Mercedes "criss-cross again and again the experience he has just left behind him . . . quickly it is covered by a kind of grid. On its tracks are laid down automatic responses to everyday situations of no importance and one of these is that he does not see people who thumb lifts" (p. 175). But even the road's stable pattern has been disrupted by his reveries on the farm. On this trip he does see hitchhikers, indeed gives a ride to the "Colored" girl. And it is through his complete loss of a sense of pattern on the road that his disorientation following the unearthing of the African, after a fire on the farm and the flood, is most overtly revealed:

> A stink to high heaven: the burned willows have grown again and the reeds have become thickets of birds, the mealies have stored sweetness of lymph, human milk and semen, all the farm has flowered and burgeoned from him, sucking his strength like nectar from a grass straw—
> *An awful moment looking at a green light and not knowing what it means.*
> Jeers of horns are prodding at him. Blank.
> A shudder of tremor comes up the back of his neck to his jaw and he jerks to engage the gear. Unnerving; but it happens to everyone now and then. The single syllable chatters away crazily at his clenched jaw. No no. No no. Back to town. (p. 237)

Despite Mehring's attempt to cover over the third pasture with the road's grid, his attempts to remain detached have failed. The reference to Mehring's jaw derives from the prognathous jaw, the feature which most distinguished the unearthed African, and Mehring feels that the farm is sucking his strength metaphorically as it is the African's literally. Even his control of the roads is no longer secure. The horns of the vehicles prod him as if he were some beast that had strayed from the fields into forbidden territory. When the "Coloured" girl hails the Mercedes, Mehring's view conveys none of the assurance that he manifested when picturing the farm at the novel's outset. Rather he sees in the girl the environment which has come to control his life: "He does not take in the face at all. He sees only that the road and traffic, in miniature but clear, are reflected across her eyeballs as in one of those convex mirrors at amusement halls" (p. 238). He sees in her a reflection of an environment in which one's normal powers of observation are subverted; the usual grid is distorted as one's perception is in a house of mirrors. Mehring knows the remedy is "Back to town," but he is no longer in control of the roads which lead there; they have taken on a strange life of their own. He succumbs to the girl's entreaties and turns off the road to the abandoned mine dumps.

The specific form of the psychic seizure he undergoes at the mine dumps—his perceived exposure of his degenerate sexual desires—has its roots in Mehring's attitude toward the landscape. From early on in his stay at the farm, Mehring conceives of sexuality in terms of the landscape. He thinks during his visit to his Afrikaner neighbors that "to go into one of those women must be like using the fleshy succulent plant men in the Foreign Legion have to resort to," and he will later describe his penis as "exactly like the middle of a banana flower. Even the purplish colour and the slight moist shine" (pp. 48, 235). But Mehring's sexual landscape is much more extensive. He describes sex as a "territory" the mistress had visited with him a few times. He views Namibia as a place where "the dunes of the desert lie alongside the road between Swakopmund and Walvis Bay. Golden reclining nudes. Torso upon torso, hip sweeping from waist" (p. 97). And he uses the same phrase, "golden reclining nudes," to introduce his petting of an adolescent girl as they fly over the desert. In effect, he views the South African protectorate as a woman for whom South Africa has paid, a fact which calls up the old image of the colonist as ravisher (evident in such phrases as "colonial intrusion") of a feminine Africa.

More specifically, Mehring equates possession of the farm with sexual possession. His very purchase of it, as he often recalls, was as "a place to take a woman," his liberal mistress. But neither she nor any other woman has relations with Mehring at the farm, and his sexual fantasies become bound up with his only companion there, the dead African. The African and the women Mehring desires are initially linked by the one trait they have in common: relations with them are threatening or forbidden. Mehring is aroused by being forced to meet his mistress clandestinely because of her black friends and underground connections. His petting of the girl on the plane excites him primarily because her guardians are nearby and the penalties are severe should he be apprehended. The relationships with both women have racial overtones; the mistress, Mehring likes to think, has a Jewish, perhaps gypsy, background, and the girl on the plane is Portuguese.

Gradually, Mehring's sexual fantasies become more explicitly connected with the dead African in the third pasture. This linkage begins when Mehring's thoughts of his mistress' "jolly parties with blacks" leads to his feeling "earth in his mouth," his earliest identification with the dead man. This identification is developed as Mehring observes the third pasture after a fire has swept through it. He begins by conceiving it as a picture detached from himself: "Dust has the effect on his distant hills of a pencil sketch gone over by a soft rubber," and some observed guinea fowl appear as "something off the border of a piece of Indian cloth, stylized as the mango pattern on a paisley tie he's got" (pp. 101, 102). But his control, evident in "his hills" and the comparison to his tie, dissipates as he reflects that he is alone here. He realizes that "he would not have his gypsy back" and that an associate's daughter he has desired would never come there; his only companion is "a dead man." He goes on to feel "the stirring of the shameful curiosity, like imagining what goes on behind a bathroom door, about what happens under a covering of earth (however shallow; you can be sure it was done carelessly) when a fire like this one comes over" (p. 104). Mehring has begun to identify his "shameful" attraction to forbidden women—"his gypsy," a young girl—with the dead man beneath the ground.

By Christmas Eve later in the novel, the mistress and the dead African have become one. Mehring begins by thinking how to stop her voice, which torments him even after she has fled the country:

> The only way to shut you up is to establish the other, the only millennium, of the body, invade you with the easy paradise that truly knows no distinction of colour, creed and what-not—she's still talking, somewhere, but for me her mouth is stopped.
> —You'll deal once too often, Mehring.—
> Oh for God's sake. Leave me alone. Touch me.
> The unexpected warmth of the spring evening, a premonition of summer (is it possible the irrigation creates a local humidity, just in this valley of his farm) reaches up his shirtsleeves and down from the neck of his half-buttoned shirt to the navel. He has been sitting so still he has the fanciful feeling that so long as he does not move the farm is as it is when he's not there. He's at one with it as an ancestor at one with his own earth. He is there and not there.
> —What's the final and ultimate price of pig-iron? (p. 154)

The mistress is clearly associated with the dead African: Mehring thinks "her mouth is stopped" as is his. While Mehring reveals the same ambiguous desires for detachment from and involvement with her—"Leave me alone. Touch me."—as for the farm, for which he is at once "not there" and "an ancestor at one with his earth," the tendency toward engagement is dominant. Mehring sees this engagement in terms of his possessing both mistress and land; he conceives of his conquest of her as an "invasion," a term quite appropriate to a colonist's claiming of land. But the passage shows that Mehring has taken possession of neither. Rather, the humidity of the earth seeps sensually under his shirt, invading *him* down to the navel. And the scene ends with the mistress' voice continuing to invade his mind. Clearly, neither's voice is stopped.

As Mehring's disintegration progresses, the dead African, the mistress, and Mehring come to form a strange *ménage-a-trois* in his mind. At one point, for example, Mehring first thinks of himself as the dead African, then equates him with the mistress:

> Those blacks hit me on the head, they stuck a knife in my heart, they threw me away—No moon. You could lie out, down there.

> A quiet sleeper. Turn to her and without making contact with any part of her receive from her open lips, warm breath. Breathe her in as the kiss of life given a dying man. (p. 171)

The "quiet sleeper" is both the African and the mistress. Both are equated as well in Mehring's transfer of his feelings of repulsion from the dead African to the mistress, for he wants to avoid "making contact with any part of her." But, once again, Mehring's urge toward identification is stronger; he needs her life-giving kiss. Throughout, Mehring identifies with the dead African, from his thinking that the blacks had hit him on the head, as they had the dead man, to his picturing himself as a dying man. As his experience on awaking from his afternoon slumber early in the novel presaged, the dead African has become who Mehring thinks he is.

The association of the dead African with Mehring's sex life, which provides the form of his fantasy at the mine dumps, has developed gradually throughout the novel. The setting itself—and the larger cultural associations with which it is endowed—derives from Mehring's trip to Johannesburg when he first gives the "Coloured" girl a lift. Shortly after he makes an avuncular pass at an associate's daughter in the city, he reads of her father's suicide, leading Mehring to equate his shameful sexual desires with death. "The excitation is suffocating; men have died in the act," he thinks, and his reconstruction of the associate's death leads to more practical thoughts—an attempt to detach himself from the fears he is seized by—for committing suicide. In doing so he provides the setting for his future encounter with the "Coloured" girl:

> Cyanide is the stuff that is used in the most effective and cheapest process for extracting gold from the auriferous reef. It is what saved the industry in the early 1900s. It is what makes yellow the waste that is piled up in giant sand-castles and crenellated geometrically-shaped hills where the road first leaves the city. (p. 185)

As South African prosperity has been based on a deathly substance, so is Mehring's personality based on a fascination with death, objectified by his identification with the dead African. The eruption of Mehring's thoughts into consciousness occurs, appropriately, at these mine dumps, where the great sand castles of waste material from below ground serve as an objective correlative for the emergence of his repressed thoughts.

When the dead African is washed up by the flood, what goes on "below ground"—the desire for "shameful" unions with forbidden women which has become identified with the dead man—surfaces for Mehring. The material dredged up from the mines is equated with sexual material rising from his subconscious. The mine dumps' "soft buffed yellow" reminds him of "the tiny snags of hairs when a forearm or backside cheek is brushed against lips" (p. 239). The "Coloured" woman is part of this landscape as well. Mehring thinks, "The grain of [her] skin is gigantic, muddy and coarse. A moon surface. Grey-brown layers of muck that don't cover the blemishes" (p. 246). Her role as a representative of his unconscious desires is supported by her echoes of his thoughts during their encounter. Mehring's conception of suicide in terms of the "cold erection" which hanged men are said to experience is quickly followed, for instance, by her comment that she is "scared stiff" in cars (p. 239).

At the mine dumps not only the setting but the form of Mehring's degradation is appropriate for a man who has attempted to possess his world. He attributes to others the power of observing, and thereby possessing, him. While Mehring begins by observing the landscape, he soon becomes aware "as of a feature of the landscape not noticed before" of thugs looking on at him: "He stands and they gaze at him, caught between the trees as if he were a creature framed in its natural habitat" (p. 248). From this point on, Mehring conceives of himself as a figure "framed"—both unjustly apprehended and seen as a picture—by others. He thinks of his picture appearing in the papers with testimonials to his filthy activities from the Portuguese girl, the associate's daughter, his son, his society friends—framed for all to see. His final image as he runs from the scene is of being observed: "Come. Come and look, they're all saying. What is it? Who is it? It's Mehring. It's Mehring down there" (p. 250). Mehring has finally become what he feared he was all along, the dead African at whom Jacobus had urged him to "Come. Come and look" after the body was unearthed by the flood.

Thus, Mehring's story reveals the consequences of resisting the urge to identify with his world, of remaining detached to enforce his power.

Yet the novel's strength lies not just in the convincing depiction of Mehring's demise but in the exploration of the impulses in him to engage with the African world he confronts on the farm. If Mehring finally sees himself as a dead man, it is to Gordimer's credit that she presents a living man who has unfortunately been too conditioned to conserve power to give rein to his submerged impulse toward engagement with his fellows. This impulse is best revealed on New Year's Eve when he declines the invitations of his suburban friends in order to remain on the farm, where he plans to have a late-night drink with Jacobus. Mehring begins with his defenses well in place. He plans simply to observe his possessions on this night: he chooses a spot with "the best view of the whole farm" and is pleased that "no one is seeing it but him" (pp. 194, 195). Initially, he keeps his distance from Jacobus by thinking they would fraternize "just this once"; indeed, he has unconsciously ensured that they would fail to do so at all by going to a different location than he gave Jacobus.

But his impulse toward identification soon becomes clear; indeed, the scene is developed in terms of Mehring's grappling with his double—his most socially unacceptable self—a process which could lead to the integration of his divided personality. Its divisions are reflected in the fractured world he perceives all around him: Afrikaners party on one side, Africans on the other; a storm is before him, calm behind; the field of lucerne is "cleaved diagonally by a narrow darkness" formed by his passage; and he thinks that "midnight will bisect two years" (p. 195). These divisions are internalized when the lightning-filled sky "cracks like a teacup from top to bottom in a blinding scribble whose running instant (complex as a capillary vein or the topography of a river) is branded upon the dark of eyelids blinked in reaction" (pp. 194–95). Mehring immediately thinks of the companionship he and Jacobus will share:

> We two men sit here where you can keep the whole stretch of reeds and river before you, not so much as a bat can move down there without making a shadow in the moonlight, and we kill the rest of the bottle. From what direction he comes won't be sure, not more than a shadow among shadows. (p. 195)

Since Jacobus is already present in imagination, this shadow self is the dead African who lies in the reeds by the river. Indeed, Mehring will ask Jacobus what the dead man looked like, then imagine him joining them for a drink: "We would give him drink if he were to be here now, poor bastard. We wouldn't ask any questions, eh? Just this once. We drink the whisky and we talk and laugh, he's having the night of his life" (p. 198). Clearly, Mehring is feeling toward "the night of his life," not just through imagining a fellowship his society has forbidden but through seeking out those repressed dark forces which could make his life whole. Mehring wants Jacobus and himself to be just "two men" sitting together; he even has the urge to confront the dark impulses within himself that the dead man has come to represent. But he can do so only within a setting over which he has control, a scene of his own fabrication. When he awakes the next morning, he thinks of the evening as "a narrow escape" and takes refuge in his possession of the farm: "There is absolutely no one. It's his own place. No eyes keep watch on him" (pp. 199, 200). The last sentence introduces those watching eyes which will emerge again at the mine dumps. There, he will need to escape because of his rejection of the urge toward identification on this night.

Through the failure of Mehring's vigorous attempts to possess the land he inhabits, Gordimer makes the strongest assertion of the landscape's power in her fiction. Mehring is simply no match for the dead African who, to call on Gordimer's comment in 1981, undermines the superficial cultural assumptions of Mehring's kind with the tenacity of a mole. That the landscape is the novel's moving force has not been widely apprehended because *The Conservationist* was the first novel in which Gordimer used interior monologue extensively. It is a short jump from Sheila Roberts' assertion that the novel, with Coetzee's *Dusklands*, heralds "a movement away from exterior description to prolonged internalization of character" to Judie Newman's claim that it is about "'that book of unknown signs,' which is within the individual."[8] Such analyses place the locus of attention—and power—too

8 Sheila Roberts, "Character and Meaning in Four Contemporary South African Novels," *World Literature Written in English*, XIX (1980), 20; Judie Newman, "Gordimer's *The Conservationist*: 'That Book of Unknown Signs,'" *Critique*, XXII (1981), 31. South African reviewers often stressed the technical innovation of the novel by comparing Gordimer with the "Sestigers," the innovative writers in Afrikaans in the sixties. But the centrality of the landscape is evident as early as *The Late Bourgeois World*, where Liz Van Den Sandt describes a *Son et Lumière* perfor-

much within the character, too little within the landscape. As Gordimer said quite simply in 1982, "in *The Conservationist*, the landscape is the most important character."[9] If the signs in the landscape remain "unknown" to Mehring—or at best sensed, as they were by Bray—they originate in the "outward" world. It is through depicting the acceptance of the landscape's power by Bray, the rejection of it by Mehring and, after him, the Smales that Gordimer continues to pursue the imperatives of her world.

IV

After some weeks in the village of their former servant July, six hundred kilometers outside Johannesburg, the Bamford Smales are summoned to the village of the chief. While waiting for an audience, they hear a radio broadcast in Portuguese which includes "recurrent mentions of 'Azania Freedom Fighters' in English, a repetition of place-names, Pretoria, Johannesburg" (p. 110). The reclaiming of the land foretold in the African's burial at the close of *The Conservationist* has taken place; South Africa has become Azania, its major cities given the African designation "place-names." While the Smales' situation as city dwellers suddenly placed in the veld appears simply a more radical version of Mehring's experience, the novel develops in a markedly different way, for unlike Mehring, the Smales want to fit in. They try hard. They want to do their share of the work, make friends, be honest about their motivations. Theirs is the most conscious attempt in Gordimer's fiction to make the transition to an alien landscape.

They fail. For all their good will and effort, the Smales remain bound by the conceptual system of the privileged urban world they have been forced to flee, as they come to accept as they look back on their stay after returning from the chief's:

---

mance, in which the intention is to make the landscape come alive through sound and light, as "the real scene of events" (p. 84). The landscape remains "the real scene" through the present; "A Correspondence Course" in *Something Out There* is the best recent example of its invasion of character.

9 Robert Boyers *et al.*, "A Conversation with Nadine Gordimer," *Salmagundi*, LXII (Winter, 1984), 13.

> Pragmatism, that's all, she had said when they first arrived in this dump and she had reproached herself for learning ballet dancing instead of—at least—the despised *Fanagalo*. And he had said, of back there, if it's been lies, it's been lies. He struggled hopelessly for words that were not phrases from back there, words that would make the truth that must be forming here, out of the blacks, out of themselves. He sensed for a moment the great drama hidden in the monotonous days, as she was aware, always, of the yellow bakkie hidden in the sameness of bush. But the words would not come. They were blocked by an old vocabulary, "rural backwardness", "counter-revolutionary pockets", "failure to bring about peaceful change inevitably leading to civil war"— she knew all that, she had heard all that before it happened. (p. 127)

Even two-thirds of the way through the novel, the Smales are unable to find a vocabulary which is not determined by "back there," the city now removed in time and space. Maureen, the central figure in the narrative, will not be able to master the language of the women she moves about; she remains the young ballet dancer even as she flees the village at the novel's close. For both her and Bam "the great drama" remains centered on that yellow bakkie (a safari truck), the only bright spot in the monotonous veld. Indeed, their major interests in the novel are maintaining possession of two items brought from the city, the bakkie and a gun, neither of which is of much use to them now. Their very names reflect this fixation on "back there." "Bamford" is a compound of the sound a gun makes and a vehicle brand name. Maureen's maiden name, Hetherington, derives from "heath," the British counterpart of the veld. Her total inability to relate to the kind of landscape after which she is named is but one of the nasty ironies of their new life.

Nevertheless, the Smales do struggle to come to terms with their new world. Theirs is an often very conscious attempt to find what are variously termed the abstractions, codes, or contexts that define life on the veld. Bam's struggle for words that were not phrases from "back there" is but one of their many attempts to conceptualize their new condition. Even quite early in their stay Maureen realizes that "the absolute nature of intimate relationships," which was part of her "definitive" code, doesn't apply here, that relationships are shaped by the different contexts of a wife's hut and a master bedroom (pp. 64–65). Like the African migrant workers in Johannesburg who, as she thinks, "were able to make the connection between the abstract and the concrete" in their foreign setting, the Smales search for a context in the physical world around them.

The kind of connection of abstract and concrete they seek is revealed very early in the novel in Maureen's reverie of her childhood in a mining community much like Helen Shaw's:

> In the dimness and traced brightness of a tribal hut the equilibrium she regained was that of the room in the shift boss's house on mine property she had had to herself once her elder sister went to boarding-school. Picking them up one by one, she went over the objects of her collection on the bookshelf, the miniature brass coffeepot and tray, the four bone elephants, one with a broken trunk, the khaki pottery bulldog with the Union Jack painted on his back. A lavender-bag trimmed with velvet forget-me-nots hung from the upright hinge of the adjustable mirror of the dressing-table. (p. 3)

This is a world in which concrete objects quite clearly reflect a cultural context: a colonial world with which she can engage. The details indicate how unsuited this context is to their new life. The tourist view of Africa is implied by those elephants; indeed, the bakkie had been purchased for trips to game parks, and the safari mentality will be broadly satirized when Bam later hunts a boar. Even the coffee pot and tray characterizes their old world in a very specific way, for Maureen had awakened at the novel's outset to contrast July's bringing of the morning tray in the suburbs with his entrance into their mud hut. As unsuited as this code is to her new surroundings, it will remain, as the "forget-me-nots" imply, Maureen's "definitive" one.

Preoccupation with their old code is the most obvious reason that the Smales fail to find a new one in the veld. Sitting in their hut after returning from the chief's, "the sounds of July's—the chief's—form of order came to them. The hiccuping wail of a baby being joggled on someone's back, old voices and young shouts in the concourse that was to these people newspaper, library, archives and theatre" (pp. 124–25). This "form of order" seems to them a mishmash of song, baby's wail, and shouts precisely because they persist in viewing it in terms of the archives of their civilization. Often this failure of comprehension is developed in the same way as in *A Guest of Honour* and *The Conserva-*

tionist, through the inefficacy of reading the "outward signs" from a detached perspective. For example, the Smales view the veld from the shelter of the car—a set-piece in Gordimer's fiction—on their way to the chief's village:

> Cows with long, deformed horns drew together to watch the yellow object approach and July wound down the window and put out his arm to bang a warning with the flat of his hand on the body-work. The vehicle passed huts where people were doing what they did where the passengers had come from. The same end-less dragging of wood, chopping of wood, for the same fires; the same backsides bent at washing, squatting picking over maize; the same babies staggering towards mastery of their legs among the old slowly losing it. (p. 106–107)

The South Africa in which Jessie Stilwell could find a continuity in the African kraals on the way back from the Fuecht cottage is clearly gone. The Smales find only a repetition of the same back-breaking labor.

But *July's People* points up the limitations of observation much more explicitly than the earlier novels. Another of Maureen's reveries, which like the first leads her from the dim interior of a hut to "back there," is characteristic of the foregrounding of this issue in the novel. Observing the insignia of a mine worker on a village hut leads her to recall walking home from school with Lydia, the servant in her family's home. The reverie ends with the account of a photographer taking their picture one afternoon, with Maureen's school case on Lydia's head, for

> a *Life* coffee-table book about the country and its policies. White *herrenvolk* attitudes and life-styles; the marvellous photograph of the white schoolgirl and the black woman with the girl's school case on her head.
>
> Why had Lydia carried her case?
>
> Did the photographer know what he saw, when they crossed the road like that, together? Did the book, placing the pair in its con-text, give the reason she and Lydia, in their affection and igno-rance, didn't know? (p. 32–33)

By asking the reader to consider what pictures reveal and how their meanings are related to their contexts, Gordimer questions the usefulness of "picturing" more directly and emphatically than in any of her previous novels. The usefulness of observing and placing in context (the subjects of the final two questions) in determining meaning (the subject of the first) is called into doubt by the photographer's lack of interest in his subjects—he promises to send them a copy of the picture but doesn't even ask for their address—and by the context itself, a "marvellous," glossy *Life* picture. *July's People* develops as Gordimer's most radical renunciation of the knowledge yielded by observation, of which photography is simply the most obvious example. The novel is filled with the attempts, most often Maureen's, to "picture" things through visualizing them as dioramas, maps, museum pieces. It is not simply the fact that these contexts are from "back there" but also her very method of looking for a context by picturing a world she perceives as separate from herself that makes it impossible for her to make the transition to the veld.

The distinctive tone of *July's People* derives from the radical disparity between the Smales' earnest search for a new context and a world where contexts are not the proper issue at all. While there is a certain dignity to being the last colonial, as Mehring was, the Smales' position is, as their name implies, deflated: they are the last tourists of the African veld, whose cameras fail to capture their new surroundings, whose safari vehicle has taken them on an entirely different journey than they expected. They are so clearly at sea—indeed, Gordimer compared them in 1982 to people on a sinking ship who have not done their boat drill—that their attempts to engage with their landscape come to seem preposterous. Maureen's attempt to read the "outward signs" shortly after their arrival seems particularly quixotic when placed in the context of the criticism of "picturing" in the preceding novels:

> Like clouds, the savannah bush formed and re-formed under the changes of light, moved or gave the impression of being moved past by the travelling eye; silent and ashy green as mould spread and always spreading, rolling out under the sky before her. There were hundreds of tracks used since ancient migrations (never ended; her family's was the latest), not seen. There were people, wavering circles of habitation marked by euphorbia and brush

hedges, like this one, fungoid fairy rings on grass—not seen. There were cattle cracking through the undergrowth, and the stillness of wild animals—all not to be seen. Space; so confining in its immensity her children did not know it was there. Royce headed a delegation:—Can't we go to a film today? Or tomorrow?—(The postponement an inkling, the confusion of time with that other dimension, proper to this place.) (pp. 26–27)

Quite clearly, this is a landscape which is "not to be seen." Its immense shapelessness is conveyed not only by Gordimer's comparisons—the bush is like clouds, the hedges like "fairy rings"—but by deliberate obfuscation. She adds muddling modifiers ("moved or gave the impression of being moved") and unnecessarily complicates ("time and that other dimension," instead of simply "space"). Above all, the style creates a sense of formlessness through the elliptical sentences, unorthodox punctuation, and strange tense shifts ("Mould spread and always spreading"). Readers can appreciate the desire of the children for the coherence offered by the world of a film.

Even when Maureen's urge to engage with her new world is most pronounced, there is a relentless demonstration of how her very means of perception sets her apart. When she joins in the gathering of roots and wild vegetables, "At first the women in the fields ignored her, or greeted her with the squinting unfocused smile of those who have their attention fixed on the ground. One or two—the younger ones— perhaps remarked on her to each other as they would of someone come to remark upon them—a photographer or overseer" (p. 91). Maureen is conceived as a photographer or one who "sees over," as opposed to the African women whose "unfocused" smiles cannot be pictured, their attention on the ground. As they continue to gather, it is not simply that Maureen "followed along, watching," but the very way that she conceives of her work that sets her apart: "July's mother, in particular, seemed to have a nose for where her pointed digging-stick would discover certain roots. She herself could not expect to acquire that degree of discernment" (p. 91). It is not just the level of diction which separates the women but their means of perception; having "a nose for" (and the attribution of discovery to the stick) emphasizes the mother's intuition, over against Maureen's rational discrimination. These contrasting approaches are given more explicit form in the depiction of the African women as "marsh birds," acting "individually, yet keeping the pattern of the flock of egrets, that rises and settles now here, now there, where the pickings are best" (p. 92). Their movement may seem random, much like that landscape which could not be seen, but they do keep to a "pattern," which, as the comparison to the birds implies, is achieved through their identification with their world. Once again, it is a "form of order" which is inaccessible to Maureen precisely because she knows only how to exercise "discernment."

If Maureen does not ever fit in to the village world, she nevertheless does change her response to it. The means by which she does is most clearly revealed in two scenes in which bright, city-made objects appear before her in the landscape. The first takes place one night shortly after the Smales' arrival as Maureen stands naked in the rain and sees the yellow bakkie returning after July has appropriated it for the first time:

> She became aware of being able to see; and what she saw was like the reflection of a candle-flame behind a window-pane flowing with rain, far off. The reflection moved or the glassy ripples moved over it. But it existed—the proof was that there was a dimension between her and some element in the rain-hung darkness. Where it was, the rain must have thinned: and now she saw twin faint, needled beams, travelling. They progressed slowly, and because there was no other feature to be made out between her and them, seemed half-way up the sky. Then a sense of direction came to her, from the luminous trace: she stuck a pin where there was no map—there, in the dark and rain, was where the ruined huts were. The vehicle was creeping back. The point placed in her mind went back to darkness. The headlights were out, the engine off, in the roofless hut. (pp. 48–49)

The passage not only opens by emphasizing Maureen's role as an observer but insists on her detachment throughout. Her separation from what is observed is conveyed by the image of glass between her and the bakkie, followed by the more conscious discovery of the "proof" of "a dimension between her" and it. The faint beams in the rain are beautiful, but she remains completely absorbed in assessing their direction and finally in creating a mental map of the scene. At the close, there remain a separate observer, a "mind" left in darkness, and the observed, the bakkie in the hut.

The second scene occurs late in the novel as Maureen sits outside her hut reading Manzoni's *I Promessi Sposi*, which she realizes "would not translate from the page" to the world she now inhabits. Her realization that this European construct offers no assistance in this world is quickly followed by her perception of a red box, which contains a musical amplifier called the *gumba-gumba*, emerging from the direction of the nearby river:

> But this was some sort of trunk or box, bright red. It appeared now as red splinters between the elephant grass on the near side of the river. The man climbed the gradient towards her—not seeing her, there were bushes, there was a great pile of thatch someone had dumped, she felt she was not there—with bowed black shins staggering. The trousers were not shorts but had worn through and been torn off at the knees. The red box was heavy and there were wires looped from it that bothered him. He hailed once, towards the huts. Having announced himself, plodded on. A fix on him, she had felt the bunching of muscles in his neck as he braced himself against rising ground under the red box, the cold tingling in the arm from which the blood receded where it was raised to steady the box; the sweat of his effort melting in the heat of the day was the sweat of her hands' imprint wetting the pages of the book. (p. 139–40)

Though the scene begins with Maureen's observation of the man's trousers and the box, as the man climbs toward her she empathizes with the way the wires bother him, and the sweat of his labor finally becomes the sweat of her hands on the page. The passage is shocking because Maureen's ability to identify with her new world does not develop gradually; it is manifested here for the first time in a very radical way. It is, in short, an event without a context, which is why it proves so threatening to Maureen. She conceives of it not as an identification but a complete effacement of self, which leaves her "not there." Indeed, the scene is approached through contexts, the European novel and the *gumba-gumba*. But, more explicitly, before the incident Maureen thinks that "She was not in possession of any part of her life," for "the background" of her city life "had fallen away." It is her inability to conceive of life in terms other than a context separate from her—as a "background" she can control—that makes her unable to accept the possibilities her empathy for the *gumba-gumba* man holds.

The appeal of the *gumba-gumba* man to Maureen is, no doubt, manifold: he moves easily between city and veld as she would like to do; his location music, unlike her novel, has "translated" to the country world; perhaps in the dull landscape of the village, the bright red of his box reminds her of the only other vivid color, the yellow of the bakkie. The momentary identification with him will determine her behavior for the remainder of the novel—in this sense, the scene can be seen as the climax, the point at which the rest of the action becomes inevitable—but she has not learned at all from it how to relate better to her new world. She still has the need to chart her world when she seeks out July after the theft of their gun by "following in reverse, as if with a finger on a map, the way the *gumba-gumba* man had come towards her" (p. 147). Her urge toward detachment clearly prevails as she names the varieties of thorn trees, knowledge gained from "Roberts' bird book and standard works on indigenous trees and shrubs [which] were the Smales' accommodation of the wilderness to themselves" (p. 147). As she searches for July,

> she had the feeling of not being there, that she had had while the man with the red box was climbing into her vision. The slight rise and fall of her breathing produced no ripple of her counter-existence in the heavy peace. The systole and diastole needed only to cease, and she would be ingested, disappeared in this state of being that needed no witnesses. She was unrecorded in any taxonomy but that of Maureen Hetherington on her points to applause in the Mine Recreation Hall. (p. 148)

The tension she feels sets detachment not against identification but extinction; the terms *taxonomy, recording,* and *witness* are set against *ingested, disappeared,* and a man "climbing into her vision" to erase her. Without seeing the world as separated into herself and a "counter-existence," without an observer and an observed, she has no place. It is not just that she cannot perceive the context which the village holds but, as the strength of "taxonomy" suggests, that she has been part of a world which places a particularly high value on the distinction between individual and context. The African women, moving like birds through the fields, would have no understanding of her problem.

Maureen continues to be defined by her urban context in her final confrontation with July in the veld, in which their bond of fifteen years in the city is irrevocably broken. For all her efforts to fit in to her new world, she has clearly failed to relate to her landscape. Their encounter ends:

> The incredible tenderness of the evening surrounded them as if mistaking them for lovers. She lurched over and posed herself, a grotesque, against the vehicle's hood, her shrunken jeans poked at the knees, sweat-coarsened forehead touched by the moonlight, neglected hair standing out wispy and rough. The death's harpy image she made of herself meant nothing to him, who had never been to a motor show complete with provocative girls. She laughed and slapped the mudguard vulgarly, as he had done to frighten a beast out of the way. The sharp sound flew back to them from the settlement. A little homely fire, the first of those for the evening meal, began to show over there as a match flame grows cupped in a palm. (pp. 153–54)

Maureen's disaffection is revealed partly by the debased context of the urban vamp, itself a parody of beauties at car shows, which she tries to impose on the scene, partly by July's inability to comprehend what she is up to. But, more centrally, the landscape provides an ironic commentary on the failure of them to sustain their bond, mistaking them for lovers at the outset, providing an image of community at the close. Indeed, the final image of the cupped hand is echoed in the last, clearly parodic, panorama of the village:

> At this moment in its span, its seasons, the village coincides with the generic moment of the photographer's village, seen from afar, its circles encircled by the landscape, held in the pantheistic hand, the single community of man-and-nature-in-Africa reproduced by skilled photogravure processes in Holland or Switzerland. (p. 156)

The view begins by seeming limited by a context which captures only a part of a more various pattern but becomes increasingly parodic as it develops, until even the reproduction of this one moment rings with clichés of the Europeans' made-to-order Africa. The "seen from afar" becomes not a bird's-eye view, as it initially appears, but a view from Europe which is perceptually impeded by a distant cultural construct. This picture would fit nicely in that *Life* book containing the photograph of Lydia and Maureen, the young dancer on the mine.

This panorama of the European photographer's "man-and-nature-in-Africa" provides an ironic context for the frenzied state of Maureen, urban vamp in Africa, as the novel closes. As disoriented as Mehring at the mine dumps, she becomes entranced by the sound of a machine, a helicopter, whether of the white or black forces she seems not to care. Her very method of movement as she heads for the river, following the *gumba-gumba* man's path in reverse, reveals the context in which she still operates:

> She walks out of the hut. The pace quickens, stalks past the stack of thatch and the wattle fowl-cage, jolts down the incline, leaps stones, breaks into another rhythm. She is running through the elephant grass, dodging the slaps of branches, stooping through thickets of thorn. . . . She makes straight for the ford, and pulling off her shoes balances and jumps from boulder to boulder . . . holds her arms (the shoes in one hand) high for balance. (p. 159)

Even as she undertakes her intrepid venture into the veld, her rhythm and balancing mark her as the ballet dancer from the mine. As she runs, she continues to accommodate nature to herself; she finds "orderly clumps of Barberton daisies and drifts of nemesia belong to the artful nature of a public park" (p. 160). Her impulse to create an orderly, urban world persists alongside a landscape which suggests that she will be "disappeared." The novel closes as she seeks the helicopter: "She can still hear the beat, beyond those trees and those, and she runs towards it. She runs" (p. 160). "Those trees and those" come closer, ready to ingest her. Her end is appropriate: a combination of urban contexts and the ingesting veld, of "back there" and "not there."

Maureen's failure to make the transition to the world of the veld is simply the most prominent of many such failures in the novel. The other major figures are also disoriented; in the words of the epigraph, they display "a great diversity of morbid symptoms." For the Smales, those symptoms are preeminently the attempt to hold on to the symbols of power—the car and the gun—from their old world and to apply their Cartesian structures to a world that refuses to reflect them. For the chief, the symptom is his allegiance to the whites; he continues to believe that, as the white government has told him, those from Soweto, Russia, and Mozambique would take his land. And while the Smales had seen July as a "frog prince," a figure who had undergone a splendid transformation, his position is much more problematical than they realize. He might take his name from Julius Caesar, but in an interregnum there are no kings; in this one there aren't even princes.

July rules over neither of the two groups, neither the Smales nor his extended family, which are "his people." He has the responsibility of supporting them both, while being only grudgingly accepted and incompletely understood. "Back there," where he has lived his entire adult life except for brief visits home, is incomprehensible, even ludicrous, to his family, and their life only partly accessible to him. This estrangement is most clearly reflected in a scene composed of two juxtaposed pictures, which, as elsewhere in Gordimer's fiction, reveal separation. One is a photograph of July among the Smales' servants in Johannesburg. The wife is interested in learning about his relationship with one of the women in it, but the picture provides "too scanty a trail for her to follow him by" (p. 84). The other is the scene, conceived as a picture, through which Gordimer conveys his alienation from the women as the discussion of the photograph ends. When the wife asks what happened to the town woman,

> He sat down on the small low bench placed inside the hut against the wall, where male strangers sat when they came to visit. The single source of light, from the doorway, axed the interior diagonally; on one side, women, the planes of the bay of mud plaster behind them lifted into ginger-gold, richly-moted relief like the texture of their faces, on the other, the man in darkness. His hands were on his knees. They could see his fingernails and his eyes. Perhaps he had shrugged to show he didn't know. (p. 84)

Their faces reflecting their surroundings, radiant in the sunlight, the women clearly feel at peace in this world. Separated from them, sitting in darkness on the seat for male strangers, July is lost in thought about the fate of his town woman during the revolution. As in the photograph, he remains set apart from them, a man of two worlds—and none.

Indeed, throughout the novel July has a more intense relationship with Maureen than with his wife, with whom he exchanged only occasional letters during his town years. Their one substantial engagement during the novel is an argument: he suggests that they return to town when the fighting is over, his wife that he remain to develop a farm near the village. When he feels "complicity growing in the silence" during their talk, he denies it by taking refuge in a reverie about the loss of his savings account when the fighting erupted. July also remains a man of the city in his relations with the village at large. When the *gumba-gumba* begins, "He had the city man's good-natured amusement at country people's diversions" (p. 141). And Maureen knows where to find him when their gun disappears:

> She found him there sitting on one of their home-made stools at the left side of the vehicle—probably because of the shade it had cast; the sun was low enough now for that to be unnecessary. Neither cleaning nor repairing the vehicle; but the *gumba-gumba* and the beer were not for him despite his show of participation. He was writing with an old short lead pencil in a note-book, calculating something as he used to keep his gambling accounts. (p. 148)

July clearly remains a man of the city. Solitary and seemingly preoccupied with accounts from "back there," even in the veld July seeks the shade of the bakkie.

Here, what will be the final confrontation between him and Maureen is fought against a backdrop of the city superimposed on the veld:

> The gauze round of moon had become opaque and polished with the light of the vanished sun; it began gently to reflect, a mirror being adjusted. The shadow of the vehicle fell upon them and reached out in its blown-up detail, roof-rack and spare tyre, over the bright, watery lacings of sunset in grass and bushes. (p. 150)

Their conversation marks the end of their relationship based on this shadow from the past. Maureen accuses July of having assisted in the stealing of the gun and for fancying himself a "big man"—not by implication "the boy" he had been for her—because he can drive a vehicle that will soon become simply another bit of rubbish on the veld. His response shows his renunciation of their past bond. He speaks in his own language, then refuses to acknowledge her further taunts. Her last image of him is of "his eyes white against the dark of the face blurred by the dimness, now, of all things at the earth's level under the highlight of the sky" (p. 153). July is silent, hidden in darkness for her as he had been for his mother and wife. When the bakkie, symbol of life "back there," is finally ingested by the veld, July will no doubt fashion a new life for himself. His alternatives—"back there" and here—are better than Maureen's. But during the interregnum, this man of two worlds, far from being king, prince, or "big man," inhabits neither.

July's People is Gordimer's most self-conscious treatment of a theme which had concerned her since the outset of her career: the kind of perception required to engage with the South African world. Indeed, Maureen's reaction to the arrival of the *gumba-gumba* man contains strikingly specific echoes of the 1949 story "Is There Nowhere Else Where We Can Meet?" In both cases, women begin by perceiving a bright red spot in a landscape which is "out there," then enter that world, the young woman in the story through entering the picture she initially viewed, Maureen through feeling herself labor with the *gumba-gumba* man. Both women find, as Mehring did, this engagement too threatening and run from a world that can no longer be held at bay. If the ability of these protagonists to engage with their world has not changed, it is no small matter that the prospect for the Smales' children to do so is good, nor that James Bray and Rosa Burger do engage, even if his non–South African setting and her radical family background make them special cases. But what is finally a more telling development than these protagonists' engagement is the sense of the author's own increased identification with her world in the later novels, to which I now turn.

5

Detachment and Identification: "The Double Process" of a Mature Style

I

Midway through *A Guest of Honour*, James Bray contemplates with fascination a "distant landscape of reconciliation . . . of attachment and detachment." Here Gordimer articulates for the first time what she would refer to in 1975 as "the double process," that tension between "excessive identification" and "monstrous detachment" which makes a writer. It is appropriate that Bray expresses fascination with their reconciliation, for it is not until *A Guest of Honour* that the tension between these two impulses begins to be achieved in Gordimer's novels. Even though most of *The Lying Days* took place in this landscape, by its close the detachment which was to characterize Gordimer's view of her world for nearly two decades was reflected in Helen Shaw's retreat to her balcony in Johannesburg, where, she writes, "there was only myself, watching everything, the street, the workmen, life below; a spectator" (p. 332). In her early novels, Gordimer also looks on, watching and recording the details of a world separate from herself. By the late fifties she was functioning, to use the term Balzac applied to himself, as a "secretary" of her society. But whereas he could go on to describe French society as the historian, Gordimer could discern no history in her own. When she could not translate Forsterian liberalism to the South African situation—it is sadly appropriate that Bray's "distant landscape" is England—Gordimer could find no native historical vision to replace it. The effect was a growing alienation from her society; by the sixties, detachment had become her major theme, frustration her distinctive tone.

Gordimer's detachment is most obviously reflected in her characters' preoccupation with their distance from their worlds. Early Gordimer characters are intensely sensitive analysts of their own points of view. When they recognize their detachment—or even suspect it—they register their distress. Toby Hood fears he will become a voyeur of the world's social perversions, and Helen Shaw most often describes her depression in the closing sections of *The Lying Days* by picturing herself as an observer. "I might have been looking down upon [the veld] from a plane," she thinks after the final confrontation with her mother, and as she withdraws to the balcony of her Johannesburg flat, the feeling that assails her is of "being in a cage suspended from the invisible ceiling of the sky" (pp. 313, 283). That view from the balcony remains a gauge of a character's, or a society's, condition in subsequent novels. The late bourgeois world is defined while Liz Van Den Sandt and Graham watch the nuclear sunset from her balcony. By contrast, Rosa Burger renounces the European world for engagement with her own after imagining the Paris apartment—its most salient feature a tiny balcony—she would occupy with Chabalier. When Gordimer's protagonists aren't concerned with observing, they are concerned with being observed. As the Davises are about to arrive at the Stilwell house, Jessie tells Tom, "I don't want any observers," and Rosa Burger's first words, italicized and set on a separate page of the text, are "*When they saw me outside the prison, what did they see?*" (p. 13). Through the characters' preoccupation with observation, the problems of detached examination are kept in the foreground of the reader's vision.

Observation is given the most explicit attention in the novels of the sixties, as Gordimer's position as a spectator became increasingly frustrating. Both Jessie Stilwell and Liz Van Den Sandt observe the central events of their narratives. Jessie's concern with being observed becomes ironic as she herself becomes the observer of the Ann Boaz–Gideon Shibalo affair. Although Jessie does become involved in the relationship she initially observes, her alienation from Gideon at the close makes her identification with the lovers but an occasion. Liz observes the lives of two men, her ex-husband Max and Luke Fokase, who expressed their urge to identify with their society. Even though Liz's attention shifts from the futile kind of identification attempted by Max to the quite possibly effective kind of Luke's, not only is she unlikely to assist him but she will remain a distant accessory should she do so.

The very self-conscious searching of the protagonists for ways to identify with their worlds is the most overt sign of Gordimer's desire to achieve the tension which makes the writer. But the feel of the novelist's detachment in the early novels, her radically increased identification in the later ones is conveyed in three less explicit, but finally more telling, ways. The most immediately evident is through Gordimer's use of references to other writers and texts in her narratives. Her growing identification with her world is seen partly in her decreasing reliance on metropolitan literature, her increased use of African literature to posit a context through which her own work can be evaluated. More significantly, beginning with *A Guest of Honour* the novels cease to be defined so thoroughly by such external literary constructs as epigraphs and other literary works, which provided clear guides to reading the early novels. Rather, the novels explore the tension between two contexts for cultural identification and self-definition, what Gordimer terms "the life of books" and "the life of reality." Gordimer's detachment in the early novels is also conveyed formally through elaborate networks of imagery, discussion of codes by authorial spokesmen, and particularly, neat summary endings. Where these call attention to a detached author fashioning a coherent world, the later novels provide a greater sense of a fluid, even disjunct world envisioned from within the novel's fabric. They capture, in a favorite Gordimer term, the "gaps" so characteristic of her society. Gordimer's early detachment from her world was most fundamentally due to the frustrations posed by what she described in 1972 as "the deeply and calculatedly compartmentalized" structure of South African society, which posed "unscalable limitations" for the writer.[1] Since *A Guest of Honour* Gordimer has gone far toward scaling these barriers, largely through identifying with an African historical tradition, but also, paradoxically, through accepting that the integration of white and black worlds is not possible. It

1 Nadine Gordimer, "1972 Appendix" to "The Novel and the Nation in South Africa," in G. D. Killam (ed.), *African Writers on African Writing* (Evanston, 1973), 52.

was by juxtaposing these two separate worlds, rather than continuing to seek a liberal connection of them, that she was finally able to create in South Africa what Bray perceived in England: the tension between identification and detachment which makes a writer.

II

Gordimer's changing perception of her world is most obviously evident in her redefinition of her literary heritage over the first two decades of her career. In the fifties the literary context in her novels is almost exclusively British. Gordimer refers repeatedly to Lawrence, Yeats, Hopkins, Dickens, and Forster, only occasionally to Continental and never to African writers. But she was increasingly uncomfortable with this British tradition, for in the South Africa of the fifties it was assumed to be the province of whites. Indeed, this assumption received a kind of official sanction in 1959 with the publication of *The Oxford Book of South African Verse*, in which all the contributors were white. In 1954 Gordimer could confidently echo Gertrude Stein's assertion, "I know writing belongs to me, I am quite certain," in the essay "Writing Belongs to Us All." But even here the signs of the tensions which would finally lead Gordimer to renounce that British tradition are evident, for the comment of an African friend that Africans don't have the time to write leads to her lament, "Is this something else to remember, yet another twist that must have a particular horror for me, as a writer? Is even *this* true? It is, of course, but it is certain that white writers in South Africa don't want it, recoil from it. We do not want the only voice. Writing does not belong to the whites. Please, please, I want to say to my African friends, writing belongs to us all."[2] While unusually sympathetic for its time, her perspective remains essentially colonial. White writers "belong"; Gordimer wants to share the bounty they have already claimed with Africans.

By the sixties Gordimer was quite consciously exploring the tradition in which her fiction belonged. Her preoccupation with her literary

2 Nadine Gordimer, "Writing Belongs to Us All," *Forum*, III (September, 1954), 9–10.

heritage builds to a climax in *A Guest of Honour*, which contains what amounts to a catalog of her literary interests. But they are explored as well not only in the preceding novels but numerous short stories, a concern singularly lacking, by contrast, in the stories of the fifties and seventies. Two show her paying homage to important influences, Katherine Mansfield in "Otherwise Birds Fly In" and Olive Schreiner in "The Bride of Christ."[3] The attention to these two colonials, who never quite felt at ease in the British world they joined early in their careers, is but one indication of Gordimer's concern with her relationship to the metropolitan culture. Unlike them, she declared her freedom from it. In the 1964 essay "Notes of an Expropriator," she stressed the advantages of not belonging to the established British tradition:

> One of the freedoms of expropriating a literature from six thousand miles away is that you do not take along with it any of the deadweight of a traditional approach—I was not coerced in my tastes by the kind of education, libraries, journals, conversations, class distinctions and even ancient buildings which surround a literature in the country and among the people of its origin.[4]

Gordimer's literary tastes in this period are quite varied, but she "expropriates" increasingly from two sources. One, broadly socialist, is reflected in her use of epigraphs from Camus and Guevara and, most markedly, in the central place of Fanon's *The Wretched of the Earth* in *A Guest of Honour*. In 1973, she would define her place more precisely by claiming the tradition of "critical realism," as formulated by Georg Lukács, as her own. The other is an African tradition, which Gordimer places herself in quite emphatically at the outset of *The Black Interpreters*. There she claims an "African-centered consciousness" and provides a definition of African literature which, unorthodoxly, encompasses her own work. "African writing," she argues, "is writing done in any language by Africans themselves and by others of what-

---

3 Both stories appear in *Livingston's Companions* (London, 1972). "Otherwise Birds Fly In" contains a visit by two women to southern France, where they come upon a commemoration of the writing of "Bliss" at Bandol; the central character of "The Bride of Christ" is named Lyndall after Shreiner's heroine in *The Story of an African Farm*.

4 Gordimer, "Notes of an Expropriator," 484.

ever skin colour who share with Africans the experience of having been shaped, mentally and spiritually, by Africa rather than anywhere else in the world." Gordimer's conception of her literary heritage had come full circle: the writing which "belongs to us all" is now defined as a native, not a metropolitan, tradition. The African writers clearly "belong"; she claims the right to join them.

Gordimer's "African-centered consciousness" finds especially clear expression in the use of allusions to African literature in the later novels. The ending of *A Guest of Honour*, for example, parallels quite specifically the ending of Chinua Achebe's *Things Fall Apart*. Achebe's novel ends with a postscript in which the life of the protagonist Okonkwo is fatuously summarized by an English district commissioner who plans to give it perhaps a paragraph in his planned book, *The Pacification of the Primitive Tribes of the Lower Niger*. In the final paragraphs of *A Guest of Honour*, Bray's case, like Okonkwo's, is "discussed as an interesting case in point" by the historian intent on applying an English perspective—quite appropriately, an English liberal perspective. He, like the commissioner, finds a primitive quality in his subject's acceptance of "wading through blood" to bring "apocalyptic change." Through this parallel Gordimer places her novel in the developing body of African literature in English in a very specific way: where Achebe pointed up how uninformed an English perspective was in assessing Africa near the outset of British rule, Gordimer does so near its close. Both authors emphasize the African-centered consciousness of their heroes through underscoring the limitations of Eurocentric views.

Identification with an African tradition is much more explicit in *The Conservationist*. It is most overtly present in ten excerpts from *The Religious System of the Amazulu*, which are interpolated between segments of the narrative to provide a cultural context for the Africans' symbolic reclaiming of the land in the burial of the dead man at the novel's close. In the narrative itself there is only one reference to a work of literature, but it comes at a critical point in the narrative, as Mehring leaves the farm following the unearthing of the dead African. He thinks of his liberal girl friend's taunt that the Africans will "plough down palaces and thrones and towers," a reference to "The Serf," a sonnet by the South African Roy Campbell. (He ends the poem by affirming "the timeless, surly patience of the serf," which "ploughs down palaces, and thrones, and towers.") The allusion has a direct application to the landscape Mehring perceives; the struts of the water tower near the farm have been undermined by the flood, and Mehring will view the mine dumps as "a pyramid" and "a monument" to white rule (pp. 238–39). The serf's means of destroying those palaces, thrones, and towers—through patience—reinforces this point in the narrative, for the African farm laborers do nothing to bring about Mehring's relinquishment of the farm; they simply wait for his strength, like the water tower's, to be undermined by the forces of the environment in which he moves.

In the following novels, by contrast, references to a native literature are singularly lacking. The two significant references are European: to Raskolnikov's dream of a horse being beaten in *Crime and Punishment* when Rosa Burger observes the mule beating and to Manzoni's *I Promessi Sposi*, which Maureen cannot make translate to the world of July's village. The lack of attention to a native tradition in these works, however, is part of a more pervasive transformation in Gordimer's fiction: to definition in terms of the life one lives rather than through the world of literature. As Gordimer said of colonials in a 1963 interview, "in common with people like Dan Jacobson and others" she had found "a very curious thing: we had one life which we lived in books and another life that we lived in reality."[5] This distinction is not simply the kind made in *The Lying Days* between the life of European books and the native world with which Helen Shaw was so concerned; Gordimer uses "reality" in the same way Lukács does, as the imperatives of the historical situation in which one lives. Literature is useful, but not in itself sufficient, in helping us to examine those imperatives, for, as Lukács has written, "People are only transformed when they participate in the transformation of reality."[6] The tension between examining

5 Studs Terkel, "Nadine Gordimer," *Perspective on Ideas and the Arts*, XII (May, 1963), 43. Jacobson finds that the disjunction between the world the colonial inhabits and the one reflected in books causes an "almost metaphysical preoccupation with reality" (*Time of Arrival*, 159–60). The distinction between these two "lives" was accentuated in Gordimer's case by her private situation. "I was twelve or thirteen, and leading the odd kind of life I did, living in books," is how Gordimer described her enforced seclusion in 1980 (Hurwitt, "The Art of Fiction LXXVII," 92).

6 Georg Lukács, *Realism in Our Time: Literature and the Class Struggle*, trans. John and Necke Mander (New York, 1971), 105.

life through books and participating in reality becomes increasingly pronounced in the novels through *A Guest of Honour*, in which Bray's learning to participate in the new reality of the African state leads him to become the first of Gordimer's protagonists to be transformed. Only with this and the following novels is the identification with the life "lived in reality" given sufficient weight to counterbalance the detachment implied by the life "lived in books."

In the novels through *A Guest of Honour* this tension takes the same form. On the one hand, definition through the life lived in books finds clear expression in the use of epigraphs to posit a particular kind of reading of the text. The epigraph from Yeats in *The Lying Days* supports Helen's assertion at the close that she has emerged from "the lying days of my youth" and will now "wither into the truth." In *A World of Strangers*, Lorca's poem promising that a black boy will announce "the reign of the ear of corn" prepares for the focus on Toby's political commitment at the close. In the novels of the sixties the epigraphs bear even more weight; *Occasion for Loving* has three, each pointing up a central theme of the novel, and in *The Late Bourgeois World* both epigraphs are referred to in the text, the one from Kafka repeatedly, sometimes italicized and set off from the narrative. In *A Guest of Honour* the same technique is used only slightly less explicitly. Bray thinks of the Turgenev epigraph—"An honourable man will end by not knowing where to live"—shortly before his death, and in an allusion to the epigraph from Che Guevara, he is described as an adventurer who risks his life to prove his platitudes, in contrast to Rebecca Edwards' adventurer husband who does not. These novels reveal, then, not just a continuing but a growing reliance on literary contexts external to the text.

Running counter to this development, however, is one which shows a rejection of such external contexts and an affirmation of the life "lived in reality." All of the novels through *A Guest of Honour* reveal a growing criticism of the life lived through books. In the novels of the fifties it is made implicitly, through the protagonists' renouncing literature as a means of self-definition. Helen's references to literature are almost entirely in the first third of the novel; after she moves to Johannesburg, literature not only ceases to serve as a guide to her life but becomes a barrier to living it. She gives up her last job because it involved simply "selling novels to leisured women," after which references to literature virtually disappear from the text. This progression is even more pronounced for Toby Hood. He realizes at the outset that he knew only faces "shaped by books," and his features mark him as something "straight out of Dickens and nowhere else" (pp. 7, 10). Again, such references occur mainly in the opening sections; those made later are to insipid tourist pamphlets and potboilers like *White Cain, Black Abel*, a best seller on the failure of Christianity to influence white racial views.

The use of literature as a substitute for the life of reality is introduced as a subject more explicitly in the late fifties story "The Night the Favorite Came Home." A young woman, thrown by chance into a drunken celebration, takes refuge in the room provided for her, only to realize that her favorite books are in the living room where the party is going on. She takes solace in writing "MY BOOKS" in her diary and propping it next to her bed. The radical distinction between the worlds of books and life is enforced by the works she thinks of; "her *Georgics*, a book of poems and a missionary's chronicle of early travels in Africa" represent worlds divorced in space, temperament, and time from the one in which she is confined.[7] Where this woman might be able to escape to this life of books, Jessie Stilwell clearly cannot. Only once during the novel, while seeking a private existence at the South Coast cottage, does she find time to read. The books—*Victory!*, *The Magic Mountain*, something by a West Indian writer—strongly permeate her world. Once, on a morning "so quiet that her book actually seemed to sound aloud," she looks up through the "dreamy daze" caused by her reading to see a figure approaching, "then felt the pull of its attention on her" (p. 198). The pull of this figure is clearly more powerful than her books, for it is Ann, who is seeking shelter with Gideon. Their arrival pulls Jessie back into the reality of the South African world for the rest of the novel.

Except for one passage in which Max Van Den Sandt's quixotic behavior is defined by his inability to separate the worlds of books and life—"he knew all the rest of us as he knew Raskolnikov and Emma Bovary, Dr. Copeland and Torless"—the distinction between the two

7 Gordimer, *Selected Stories*, 154–55.

worlds is not developed in *The Late Bourgeois World* (p. 52). *A Guest of Honour*, however, presents a strong case for the life of reality. It is affirmed, most emphatically, at the novel's close where Bray's commitment to acting in his chosen world is juxtaposed with two unseemly documents—the English writer's glib assessment of his transformation and "The Bray Report," a gradualist approach to the country's problems which Bray renounced for action in Shinza's behalf. But the life of books is criticized more pervasively; throughout the novel, books are associated with a colorless death-in-life. When Bray thinks of Mme. Guermantes' red shoes from Proust's *Remembrance of Things Past*, for instance, he realizes that the pleasures of such reading were the kind Olivia offered back in Wiltshire, "exactly the sort of treat retirement promises to compatibility beyond passion" (p. 397). And when he fixes on a line from Graham Greene to describe the insidious effect of place on one's behavior, he questions, "Why do I keep turning to other people's opinions, lately, leaving myself out" (p. 187). The kind of life in which one relies on the opinions of others, of books, is epitomized in the novel by Hjalmar Wentz, who is an aging liberal, the sort of man Bray could have become. Wentz has carted his library with him after escaping Nazi Germany, lacking, as Bray thinks, "the strength of mind ever to leave it behind" (p. 50). Having sought refuge with Bray just before the trip that leads to his death, Wentz asks if Bray wants to take a book of Orwell's; Bray responds, "Good lord, keep the books"—an apt summary of his choice of the life of reality. It is worth noting that the books in this novel—indeed, in all of Gordimer's works—are by authors for whom she has expressed particular admiration: here, Camus, Greene, Proust, Dostoevski; in earlier novels, Carson McCullers, Mann, Conrad, and Forster. Even the most exemplary books offer a different kind of life—and by *A Guest of Honour* one clearly less authentic—than the life of reality. The use of Orwell in the final exchange between Bray and Wentz makes this point exceptionally well; Orwell is clearly the kind of adventurer who risked his life to prove—more accurately, test—his platitudes, but a record of his experience is still an encumbrance. Perhaps the clearest expression of the proper relationship of the lives of books and reality in the novel comes in Bray's choice of "La Fille au Yeux d'Or," the title of an early Balzac novel, as the password for reclaiming his money in Switzerland after his planned departure with Rebecca. Books become useful, finally, in the service of the life of reality.

A Guest of Honour is Gordimer's most conscious criticism of the misuses of literature and, as the subsequent novels reveal, heralded the resolution of the tension between the life of books and the life of reality. Henceforth, literature plays a much reduced role. Most obviously, none of the epigraphs provide the guidance toward meaning so pronounced before; rather, they simply posit issues. The fragment from Richard Skelton's poem "The Tatooed Desert" which serves as the epigraph to *The Conservationist* alludes to central images and issues in the novel—a bicycle (the antithesis of the car), exploration of a foreign environment, and self-destructiveness—but the lines are ambiguous and cannot be applied in any easy way. The Levi-Strauss and Antonio Gramsci epigraphs to *Burger's Daughter* and *July's People* indicate that "place" and "morbid symptoms" during an interregnum are central issues, but provide no attitude toward them. "I am the place in which something has occurred" is, for example, less directing than the Turgenev epigraph to *A Guest of Honour*, "An honourable man will end by not knowing where to live," or than Mann's to *Occasion for Loving*, "In our time the destiny of man presents its meaning in political terms."

This is not to say that literature is completely rejected in Gordimer's later novels, for she is striving, after all, for the tension between the sense of detachment that references to literature outside the text enforce and the involvement that their absence, by contrast, implies. If the epigraphs are less directing and reduced to one per novel, Gordimer still chooses to use them. If the references to literature are markedly fewer, they are still significant. The Amazulu religious excerpts, a kind of extended epigraph, and Campbell's poem do develop the central theme of *The Conservationist*. The parallels between Raskolnikov's dream and Rosa Burger's witnessing of the mule beating serve to heighten the impact of what a number of commentators, perhaps partly by virtue of the allusion, have seen as the most powerful scene in the novel.

It is in *July's People* that the single work of literature, Manzoni's *I Promessi Sposi*, best reveals a conflation of Gordimer's attitudes to-

ward the lives of books and reality. At first glance the novel appears to
be a simple rejection of the life of books in favor of the life of reality. It
seems a vicious irony, for example, that Manzoni's novel is in transla-
tion, in a novel which centers on the inability of the Smales, the chief,
or even July to "translate" from one era to another. And the narrative
turns on the superior attraction of the *gumba-gumba* as Maureen sits
holding the novel. Even early in Maureen's stay, "the transport of a
novel, the false awareness of being within another time, place and life
that was the pleasure of reading for her, was not possible. . . . No fiction could compete with what she was finding she did not know, could
not have imagined or discovered through imagination" (p. 29). For
Maureen, at least, literature provides not just an escape, but a "false
awareness." But the passage calls up Maureen's misuse of literature as
something which must "compete with," not assist in the understanding of reality. Had she been able to read the novel, she would have seen
how it not only translates to her world but is, in essential ways, the
same "time, place and life." Manzoni's novel is set during the Thirty
Years' War, clearly another interregnum such as South Africa is entering. It shows a young couple eventually overcoming the "morbid symptoms" of their time, most notably the evil designs of a prince, through
identifying with the sufferings of the poor, something Maureen attempts but cannot achieve. Indeed, the ending of *July's People* contains
a clearly ironic parallel with *I Promessi Sposi's.* Where the young
lovers are reunited after crossing the Alba River, Maureen, crossing the
river near July's village, becomes "like a solitary animal at the season
when animals neither seek a mate nor take care of young, existing only
for their lone survival" (p. 160). The ends of the protagonists during
these interregnums derive from their different attitudes toward their
social roles: in Maureen's case, probable death through concern with
her lone survival; in the lovers', a promising life represented by their
acceptance of the responsibilities of marriage and, by extension, to
children and society at large. *July's People* suggests that if reading a
novel may be the quintessential example of the solitary life fostered by
bourgeois society, novels may also be used, in a way more complex
than Bray's use of Balzac's novel, in the service of the life of reality.

Through the use of *I Promessi Sposi* Gordimer calls attention, moreover, to the tradition in which she wishes *July's People* to be placed. Gordimer, who has praised Lukács as one of the three or four most important literary critics of our time, is surely aware of his high estimation of Manzoni's novel. In *The Historical Novel* Lukács describes it as "a general tragedy of the Italian people in a state of national degradation and fragmentation." *July's People* warrants the same designation for South Africa. The use of Manzoni's novel is at once Gordimer's most subtle means of providing her readers with a context through which to approach her work and an affirmation that the life of books and life of reality may translate each into the other.

III

Gordimer's detachment from the world of her early novels is reflected more broadly in the formal means by which she shapes her texts. The novels of the fifties and sixties provide the sense of an author imposing a coherent pattern from without through intrusive image patterns, discussion of codes by characters in the text, and, especially, endings in which themes are underscored. It is telling that in 1972, in the midst of the period when these tendencies were dissipating, Gordimer herself emphasized that the author's shaping presence should be unobtrusive. In a review of Carson McCullers' *The Mortgaged Heart* Gordimer found that her subject's journals revealed an "aspect of her genius (perhaps the key one) by demonstrating the skill with which she concealed the wires of cerebration, carrying the societal ideas of her work in the living subconscious of her characters, transmuted into totally implicit actions and words."[8] In Gordimer's own early fiction these "wires of cerebration" are visible; not only the societal ideas but the complex fates of her protagonists are too often provided by an author who can be seen pulling those wires. The motivations for the highly ordered structure of these works are no doubt manifold, but important among them is the substitution of a formal

8 Nadine Gordimer, "A Private Apprenticeship," *London Magazine*, XII (October/November, 1972), 135.

order for Gordimer's failure to discern one in her society itself. Not until *The Conservationist*, and especially the following novels, when she had claimed a new African cultural order as her own, would her narratives reflect what Gordimer has variously termed the discontinuities, gaps, and silences which characterize the South African world.

Gordimer's primary stylistic excess in her early novels was the image pattern. There are easily a score of allusions in *The Lying Days* to leaves (a reference to the epigraph), to children, and to sea changes; in *A World of Strangers*, a consistent chain of references to canines (which are associated with Steven Sitole's death) and to descending through the cultural assumptions of the South African world to the realities beneath; in *Occasion for Loving*, to childish behavior and to the sheltered world of gardens; and in *The Late Bourgeois World*, to the contact of hands and to knives (an allusion to "The Spear of the Nation," an African resistance group). The sense of authorial intrusion these patterns create is evident, in brief, in two scenes conceived as seascapes in the early novels. When Helen Shaw and a friend become engulfed in a riot in an African location late in *The Lying Days*, they see a mass of people as "solid and writhing as a bark of fish in a net," the police come "like a tidal wave churning through the crowd," a stone in the air is a "watery zigzag," a man crouches to pick up debris like "a child on a beach gathering shells," and after their escape, they sit in a bar smiling at each other "like people who have just been dragged up out of the water" (pp. 324–27). The very attempt to capture their confusion and terror is, of course, undercut by the heavy patterning of the imagery here, as it is in Toby Hood's description of the party where he first meets Steven Sitole:

> The party formed, broke apart and reformed, like a shoal of fish; Steven was the one that darts about, in and out the body of the shoal at different points; the hostess, Sylvia, burst into the room at intervals, as a wave washes out the formation of a shoal, breaking up a conversation, dragging someone off to talk to someone else, begging another to help her with some kitchen mystery, and withdrew again, as a wave recedes over the bodies of fish, and they gently float back into their order of suspension in calm water. (p. 82)

The references to Steven's darting and Sylvia's bursting into the room indicate the intention to create a sense of disjunct movement within a larger pattern, but the image, while a good one, is too consistently imposed. By calling attention to the scene's structure, this technique keeps the reader from feeling its movement; instead of identifying with the flow of the party, we watch its pattern being described. These two passages are extreme cases, but they create an accurate sense of how the texture of the work is brought to our attention as numerous allusions to gardens, leaves, knives build up in the course of the early novels.

Intrusive image patterns do not completely disappear in Gordimer's later fiction, but she far more often transmits images into "implicit words." This is most notably the case in *The Conservationist*, in which the central images are phrases: "one of them," Mehring's depictions of the Africans; and "Come. Come and look" and "Something happen," Jacobus' references to the dead man which achieve an incantatory power over Mehring after the African is unearthed. The novel's major image pattern, the various manifestations of "pale freckled eggs," which reveal Mehring's concern with possessing, develops less intrusively as well. He might perceive those eggs anywhere, say, on the peace symbol painted on the water tower near his farm. Or eggs might suddenly cluster when his defenses weaken, as they do when he enters the mine dumps with the "Coloured" woman. As she eats an egg sandwich, a marble which Mehring kept for his son Terry falls to the floor:

> She's dived for it. A glass marble. It has been lying there as it lay in the dust and fluff (smell of cat) where I found it for you; it lies in the stranger's hand that was on my thigh but did not touch me, an egg stolen from a nest, as you showed a brown agate egg in a stranger's adolescent hand, a whole clutch of pale, freckled eggs that will never hatch. (p. 243)

The marble, which was an indication of Mehring's fatherly affection for his son, becomes an egg stolen by the farm children, transmutes to an egg-shaped stone Terry gave his mother, then reverts to the guinea-fowl eggs. The eggs, a reflection of Mehring's linked obsession with possession and sexuality (raised here by the hand on his thigh), bring us into his world as much as they allow us to see its shape.

In the following novels key phrases remain more instrumental than image patterns in giving the narratives form. In *Burger's Daughter*, the most important is "one of us," the designation of those committed to the anti-apartheid struggle. It becomes associated, like "the Future," as much with the restraints Rosa feels as with her pride in belonging—a more ambiguous usage than in Conrad or Hemingway. In *July's People*, "back there" and its variant "not there" come to epitomize Maureen's failure to leave the past, engage in the present. All are societal images transmuted into totally implicit words.

Only slightly less intrusive than the image patterns are the discussions which clarify events in the early narratives: the criticism of the country's peculiar institutions by Helen Shaw's liberal-bohemian friends; the numerous dinner party arguments involving Tom Stilwell, Boaz Davis, and Gideon Shibalo; the appraisal of the South African condition by Liz and Graham as they watch the super-sunset. All are very conscious, and often portentous, commentaries on the forces implicit in the narrative. In these discussions the society may be seen from a detached perspective largely because certain of the characters are what William Plomer in *Turbott Wolfe* called "intellectual researchers," characters interested in social analysis. Paul Clark in *The Lying Days* is a doctoral candidate in sociology, Tom Stilwell an historian engaged in a history of South Africa from an African perspective, and Boaz Davis an ethno-musicologist collecting African instruments. Only in *The Late Bourgeois World* is there a touch of irony in these highly serious discussions when Liz realizes that she and Graham are having what he calls an "undergraduate conversation."

In the later novels such conversations are carried "in the living subconscious" of the characters, most markedly in Mehring's disjunct thoughts about the mining industry, his relationship to the laborers, and the political activities of his mistress. When "intellectual researchers" figure in the later novels, rather than summarizing key aspects of the narrative, their theories are obsessions, their detachment a mark of callousness. The long scene in which one of Lionel Burger's biographers questions Rosa is characteristic. He wants to check the "documentation available" against her recollections. He runs through "information gleaned" from "documents unearthed," and finally becomes "eager to expatiate upon his theory, somewhat second hand" that a certain trial was "a watershed" in South African political history. His perspective throughout is clearly not only "second-hand" but reveals a gross insensitivity to his interlocutor, as the end of their interview emphasizes. All the developments which support his pet theory,

> hindsight told the biographer, began when the indictment against her father and his associates in the miners' strike case was quashed, May 1948. It was the month when the first Afrikaner nationalist government took office; that would round off a chapter with a perfect touch of foreboding.
> It was the month and year that Rosemarie Burger, hearing him out, was born. (p. 94)

The episode criticizes at once the kind of continuity detached observers create—"hindsight" allows this one to provide "a touch of foreboding"—and their failure to identify with their subjects, in this case with Rosa who, with her characteristic stoicism, endures "hearing him out."

In the earlier novels the limitations of detached biographical study could well have been the topic at a Stilwell dinner party; in *Burger's Daughter* it is transmuted into the dramatic structure of the novel. The movement from telling to presenting over the course of Gordimer's career is best seen in the means by which she treats the discontinuities of South African history. In the early novels, we are told that discontinuities exist. In *The Lying Days*, for instance, Helen observes that "we were presented to visitors in our own home as creatures without continuity," and Joel Aaron, Gordimer's first intellectual researcher, describes the first generation of urban Africans as "pressed into a sort of ghetto vacuum between the tribal life that is forgotten and the white man's life that is guessed at" (pp. 80, 133). Not only Jessie's description of the continuity she sees in the African kraals but Bray's acceptance of life's discontinuity are stated, not revealed. He may realize that "there was a growing gap between his feelings and his actions, and in that gap—which was not a void, but somehow a new state of being, unexpected, never entered, unsuspected—the meaning lay" (p. 244), but no matter how elliptical the sentence, how many Conradian adjectives Gordimer employs, we still do not experience it.

Not until *The Conservationist* do such "gaps" cease to be a topic of discussion and find expression in the structure of the novels. Through the novel's two-score narrative fragments, the interpolated excerpts about the Amazulu religious system, and the sudden transformation brought on by the flood, we come to feel those gaps. A similar effect is achieved in *Burger's Daughter*. Events without contexts lead to the two radical changes Rosa undergoes. At the close of Book One, the mule beating occurs in one of those "'places' that don't appear on any of the city environs"; at the close of Book Two, Baasie's middle-of-the-night phone call rouses Rosa out of the "vertigo of sleep" (pp. 207, 318). But Rosa's acceptance of the gaps in her world is seen most clearly in the novel's closing section. It is not so much that the event which brings about the denouement—the Soweto children's revolt—was totally unforeseen, or that this upheaval places Rosa in detention. More important is the sense of discontinuity carried by the narrative, which creates the sense of a world split open. We feel, in Rosa's phrase, that the old cracks and "meaning shakes out wet and new" (p. 348). The narrative becomes a series of brief, unconnected fragments: Rosa's depiction of the lady and the unicorn tapestry, her talk with a distraught African friend of the older generation, and a Soweto Students Representative Council handbill follow in succession. The narrative cracks open; what is shaken out at us captures the feel of the South African interregnum.

So clearly are the fracturing of the old, the disjunct morbid symptoms of the new reflected in the structure of *July's People* that they scarcely require treatment. The harsh irony of Bamford Smales's life's work as an architect is immediately clear in the juxtaposed settings shaken out of Maureen's consciousness at the novel's outset:

> The knock on the door. Seven o'clock. In governors' residences, commercial hotel rooms, shift bosses' company bungalows, master bedrooms *en suite*—the tea-tray in black hands smelling of Lifebuoy soap.
> The knock on the door
> no door, an aperture in thick mud walls, and the sack that hung over it looped back for air, sometime during the short night. *Bam, I'm stifling; her voice raising him from the dead, he staggering up from his exhausted sleep.*
> No knock . . . . (p. 1)

Using the same structure of brief, unconnected episodes as in *The Conservationist* and at the close of *Burger's Daughter*, Gordimer leads us staggering through the new world in which the Smales learn that nothing is what it appears; doors are not doors, knocks not knocks, landscapes "not to be seen." We identify with Maureen's feeling of "not being there" largely because not only the landscape but the novel's structure, "the wires of cerebration," are "not to be seen."

In the early novels the author is seen most clearly in the means she uses to provide a sense of an ending. As Helen Shaw looks out from the balcony of her Durban hotel room at the close of *The Lying Days*, she summarizes her experience:

> My mind was working with great practicalness, and I thought to myself: Now it's all right. I'm not practicing any sort of self-deception any longer. And I'm not running away. Whatever it was I was running away from—the risk of love? the guilt of being white? the danger of putting ideals into practice?—I'm not running away from now because I know I'm coming back here. (p. 367)

Helen's thoughts do indeed display a "great practicalness" in her careful listing of the issues which confronted her and the self-confident claim that they have been resolved. Although an essentially picaresque tale like Helen's often has a summarizing coda, the summary is usually provided through a symbolic landscape or an implied contrast with an earlier condition, rarely in so bald a form as this. Even if we reject Helen's assessment of her progress and choose to see the novel's title as a pun, a reference to her self-deception rather than her "withering into the truth," we are quite emphatically asked to stand back and appraise her progress. Like her, we look back—and look on—at her life.

If Helen's summation does not have the finality of a wedding or funeral, it still marks the end of a discrete period in her life. Only the reference to the future raises the prospect of a life continuing to unfold. To be sure, Helen's future piqued the interest of reviewers from magazines as diverse as the *TLS* and the South African Communist *Fighting Talk*.[9] But this impulse toward an ending leading into an uncertain future would not be given free rein until *Burger's Daughter* and, most

9 A. O. D., Review of Nadine Gordimer's *The Lying Days*, in *Fighting Talk*, X (April, 1954), 13; "Defying Convention," *TLS*, October 30, 1953, p. 689.

emphatically, *July's People* when Maureen stumbles toward the helicopter at the close:

> She runs: trusting herself with all the suppressed trust of a life-
> time, alert, like a solitary animal at the season when animals nei-
> ther seek a mate nor take care of young, existing only for their
> lone survival, the enemy of all that would make claims of respon-
> sibility. She can still hear the beat, beyond those trees and those,
> and she runs towards it. She runs. (p. 160)

The subject, running from one's world, remains the same. But the
sense is altogether different. The running sentence pattern, emphasized by the participles, contrasts with Helen's careful listing of issues;
the movement closer to the world, to "those trees and those," is the
opposite of Helen's balcony view; the lack of resolution, as Maureen
runs toward what may be friend or foe, is in contrast with Helen's cer-
tainy. As the novels close, Helen's world is appraised from without,
Maureen's felt from within.

It took Gordimer a quarter century to make this transition—to
moderate the sense of detachment in Helen's end, to accentuate the
feeling of immersion in Maureen's. Indeed, the novels from *A World of
Strangers* through *The Conservationist* reveal the tension between
these two impulses in the same way: all have double endings. One, like
Helen's, provides a summation of themes. The other, like Maureen's,
attempts with increasing success to create a sense of involvement in
the novel's world through focusing on the gaps that epitomize it.

A World of Strangers concludes as Toby Hood, accompanied by Sam
Mofokenzazi, departs on a business trip to Cape Town. In the midst of
the rush to leave, he summarizes what he has come to understand during his year's stay in South Africa:

> In my pocket were two newspaper cuttings; and a letter. The cut-
> tings came from the same week-old issue of the morning paper;
> the issue of the day on which the paper had broken suddenly out
> of its accepted place in the ritual of shaving at breakfast, for there,
> in it, was a list of black and white people arrested on a treason
> charge, and half-way down the list was Anna Louw's name. (p. 253)

This event happens "suddenly," during one of the gaps in the routines
of everyday life. But it is a strikingly orderly gap, as Toby goes on to

explain, for this clipping and the other, a picture of Toby's old girl friend Cecil in the social column, "rested in my wallet in polarity. In a curious way, they set me at peace" (p. 254). The very retention of these documents, the neatness of their having appeared in the same day's paper, and Toby's easy decision, given in the letter, that he would stay on indefinitely in South Africa make for a conclusion much like Helen's.

The second ending appears to undercut Toby's certainties. As they head for the train platform, Sam questions whether Toby really can remain his friend given the separate worlds South African society enforces:

> We disappeared from each other down our separate stairways. But at the bottom of the steps, where the train was waiting, he was there before me, laughing and gasping, and we held each other by the arms, too short of breath to speak, and laughing too much to catch our breath, while a young policeman with an innocent face, on which suspicion was like the serious frown wrinkling the brow of a puppy, watched us. (p. 254)

This concluding passage seems to reveal a polarity not of peace but of strangers. The bond with Sam is called into question by those separate stairways and, especially, the onlooking policeman. Yet the details do not, on closer inspection, make Toby's position more ambiguous but, rather, reinforce the first ending. Descent, as down the stairways here, has been associated throughout the novel with identification with a more authentic, fulfilling African world, and the expansive laughter of Toby and Sam is set against the constrained Cecil, who "hunched her shoulders in laughter" in the newspaper clipping. Toby's commitment to Sam's world is most clearly indicated by the young policeman, who is much like Toby at the start of the novel—an innocent who observes. Here, Toby participates freely and expansively for the first time in the novel. The second ending serves, finally, to underscore the easy certainty of the first.

The first ending of *Occasion for Loving* is the "silver spoon" passage, in which commentators have been quick to find a summation of the novel's theme: that, as Jessie thinks, there could be no integrity to personal relationships until the laws were changed. The scene, however, presents one complication, namely Jessie's reaction; she might blow up a power station "perhaps, in time." The second ending seems to add to this ambiguity by raising questions about Gideon's future as well as Jessie's. This ending centers on a gap, Gideon's calling Jessie a "white bitch" when he is drunk at a party. Jessie's uncertainty about Gideon's future after Ann's leaving is accentuated by the contrast with Tom Stilwell's easy comment, "He'll be all right. He'll go back and fight; there's nothing else" (p. 288). And the novel's final sentence is an implied question about both Gideon's and Jessie's futures—"So long as Gideon did not remember, Jessie could not forget." The answer, however, is clear: Gideon will not remember, as his failure to broach the subject of his drunken comment in their numerous visits together since the party indicates; Jessie will not be able to forget—or even confront him—because in his drunkenness, "perhaps it was not her" he addressed. "Perhaps," in short, no longer raises questions about Jessie's future; it determines it. Jessie ends not indecisive but paralyzed, stifled by a "perhaps" which does not raise the possibility of, but rather deters, action in the future.

As its title indicates, *The Late Bourgeois World* is about the decline of a cultural order. The novel's conclusion, Gordimer's most overt attempt to create an open ending, is actually a compendium of world orders, which at once underscores the novel's historical focus and clearly reveals Liz to be a creature of her "dead" world. As in the preceding two novels, the conclusion centers on a gap. Not knowing what time it is, Liz awakes to reflect on Max's death and the American astronauts who walked in space for the first time that day. Her reverie leads to a tentative summation of her world, that the astronauts represent "a yearning for God," if in a lunatic form appropriate to the age: "That's what's up there, behind the horsing around and the dehydrated hamburgers and the televised blood tests. If it's the moon, that's why . . . that's why . . ." (p. 117). She drifts off to sleep, and on awaking her thoughts shift to whether or not she should assist Luke Fokase. The novel concludes with what is seemingly a more ambiguous reflection of her condition:

> It's so quiet I could almost believe I can hear the stars in their courses—a vibrant, infinitely high-pitched hum, what used to be referred to as "the music of the spheres." Probably it's the passage of the Americans, up there, making their own search, going round in the biggest circle of them all.

> I've been lying awake a long time, now. There is no clock in the room since the red travelling clock that Bobo gave me went out of order, but the slow, even beats of my heart repeat to me, like a clock; afraid, alive, afraid, alive, afraid, alive . . . (p. 119)

But which impulse will prevail—her fear of the consequences of assisting Luke or the life-giving sense of purpose aiding him would produce—is quite evident in this conclusion. The mechanistic image of the clock she applies to herself places Liz firmly in her dead world. Given the references to world views in the closing sections—the Renaissance "music of the spheres" here and the astronauts whom Liz had earlier seen as the representatives of a new search for a God—Liz's reference to the clock suggests the eighteenth-century deist view that God had started the universe going like a clock, then withdrawn. Like the clock of that universe, the beat of Liz's heart winds down as the novel closes. It is an apt reflection of the world of which she is a part.

A Guest of Honour and *The Conservationist* also employ double endings, in both cases an open ending followed by one that more explicitly points up the novel's themes. *A Guest of Honour* could well end with the murder of Bray as he and Rebecca attempt to leave the country. His final thought, "I've been interrupted, then," is an appropriate close for a man who finally accepted that "there was no finality, while one lived, and when one died it would always be in a sense, an interruption" (pp. 469, 465). Indeed, given this comment shortly before Bray's death, this, the end of Part Five, contains a clear conclusion. Yet the novel continues in a manner which underscores the correctness of Bray's choice. His old friend Roly Dando states that what mattered was Bray's understanding of why he died; Rebecca contrasts Bray with the man drawing the picture of remembered happiness in Mozambique and with her husband, the kind of adventurer who doesn't risk his neck to prove his platitudes. The novel, in short, goes on to explain the gap in which Bray died.

The Conservationist repeats the pattern of *A Guest of Honour* in a more ambiguous fashion. The novel's first climax at the mine dumps ends in uncertainty: does Mehring run or, since his disordered mental state makes it unclear whether he acts or imagines, only desire to do so? At the conclusion of the episode, he might well be locked in a psychotic seizure or apprehended by those he perceives in the landscape around him. The final chapter resolves these uncertainties. Mehring has escaped, for Jacobus has received instructions from Mehring to attend to the farm. But if the pattern is the same as in *A Guest of Honour*, the effect, at least for some critics, has been different. Sheila Roberts finds the novel's ending "obscure." Valentine Cunningham, the *TLS* reviewer of the novel, and even Abdul R. JanMohamed in a lengthy analysis, assume that Mehring, not the dead African, is buried at the close.[10] All of them—even the two who fail to read closely—call up important points. So powerful is the sense of Mehring's disorientation that his situation strikes us as obscure, and so strong is his identification with the dead African that his own spiritual death is imaged in the burial at the close. And if the second ending of the novel makes too clear a case for a new South African order, the first makes by far the stronger impact. With Bray dead, Mehring is the first Gordimer protagonist since Helen Shaw about whom readers might wonder—and care—where he runs to.

Burger's Daughter and *July's People* have endings which quite specifically recapitulate those of the two preceding novels, but without the second explanatory endings. Rosa, like Bray, ends by not being understood; the two visitors to her cell are Brandt Vermeulen and Flora Donaldson, an enlightened Afrikaner and a liberal English-speaker, who have been roundly satirized in the novel for dabbling in the kind of activity the Burgers and their kind risk their necks for. A second parallel is more telling. Where Bray ended in mid-thought, Rosa ends literally in mid-sentence; her letter to Madame Bagnelli concludes with a deletion by the prison censor which the woman in France is never able to make out. Rosa's story, like Bray's, ends with a gap, but in *Burger's Daughter* there is no following section to explain that her not being understood doesn't matter, that her commitment to act does. For the first time in Gordimer's novels, the gaps and silences of the novel's world speak for themselves.

From the preceding novels, it could be predicted that the ending of

10 Roberts, "Character and Meaning in Four Contemporary South African Novels," 28; Valentine Cunningham, "Kinds of Colonialism," *TLS*, November 1, 1974, p. 1217; JanMohamed, *Manichean Aesthetics*, 123–24.

July's People would appear, perhaps, in time. For it is, in a very specific way, the ending Gordimer had long sought but could not quite allow in her fiction. Helen Shaw ends by running, but claims not to; Toby Hood leaves for Cape Town but promises to return; Mehring runs, but escapes to another country. *July's People* ends, "She runs." What Maureen runs to, what she seeks in running, are questions that truly are obscure. Moreover, the means by which the novel ends is abrupt, totally left to chance—an interruption of the narrative not articulated as Bray's is. The sound of a helicopter is heard in the village; the machine appears above, out of the blue. Maureen, associating it with the *gumba-gumba*, runs toward it, and the novel is suddenly over. Gordimer has provided a patently arbitrary ending: this machine from the sky is a *deus ex machina* appropriate for a world in which there can be no resolution. During the time of morbid symptoms, there can be no clear ending, summation of intentions, promises of commitment to come. In *July's People* these conditions are finally reflected, implicitly, in the novel's ending.

IV

From the start of her career Gordimer confronted the "unscalable limitations" posed by her "deeply and calculatedly compartmentalized" society. She faced, in short, the problem of identifying with Africans, over three-quarters of her countrymen, whose life was largely inaccessible to her. As she wrote in 1959, after describing the conditions under which Africans live, "What it means to live like this, from the day you are born until the day you die, I cannot tell you. No white person can." She would reiterate this view again in 1975 in speaking of "the dilemma of a literature in a country like South Africa, where the law effectively prevents any real identification of the writer with his society as a whole, so that ultimately he can identify only with his colour."[11] Gordimer and her contemporaries have, from the time of the Witwatersrand Conference to the present, returned to prob-

11 Nadine Gordimer, "Apartheid," *Holiday*, XXV (April, 1959), 95; Gordimer, "English Language Literature and Politics in South Africa," in Christopher Heywood (ed.), *Aspects of South African Literature* (London, 1976), 107.

lems which would seem strange in any country where racial division was not so severely maintained: how to see people from that other world as individuals rather than the types infrequent contact makes them seem; how, more broadly, to create a sense of that other world's social fabric; how to present a feeling of identification with a world which is radically divided. Gordimer would return again and again to those problems throughout her career.

Both the early difficulties she had in responding to them and the first signs of how she would effectively address them are evident in the visit of Luke Fokase to Liz Van Den Sandt's apartment near the close of *The Late Bourgeois World*. Like Gordimer's earlier African characters, Luke is confined to a highly romantic stereotype. To Liz, "He is immensely *there*—one of those people whose clothes move audibly, cloth on cloth, with the movement of muscle, whose breathing is something one is as comfortably aware of as a cat's purr in the room, and whose body warmth leaves fingerprints on his glass" (p. 95). No white man in Gordimer's fiction gives off this body warmth or moves like that, but Gideon Shibalo does, and even Steven Sitole, seen from Toby's perspective, is so sensual that Robert F. Haugh found that their relationship suggested an "unmistakable homosexuality."

Yet the scene reveals, in Liz's franker expression of feelings, that the often exalted, nearly always gentler, treatment of Africans in the early novels is dissipating. She complains to Luke, for example, that Max wouldn't have had to commit suicide after turning state's evidence if he had been black, for "If he'd been one of your chaps he wouldn't have needed to do it himself, ay?—someone else would have stuck a knife in him and thrown him in the harbor" (p. 100). Even the timid Rosa Burger will give as good as she gets in her midnight telephone exchange with Baasie, and Maureen Smales will use every device at her disposal to make July suffer the same sense of powerlessness she comes to feel in the interregnum. Such give-and-take among whites and Africans is in marked contrast with Toby's acceptance of Steven's rudeness in not showing up for a luncheon date as due to an African way of doing things he doesn't understand or Jessie's inability to confront Gideon for perhaps calling her a white bitch, where she certainly would confront a white man in a comparable situation. After *The Late Bourgeois World*, contact will be less restrained; there will be a more open expression of feeling on both sides, more treatment, in short, of Africans as individuals.

The major reason that Africans will be accorded less deferential treatment is raised during Luke's visit as well: he is Gordimer's first African character who is not defined as a creature—indeed, as a victim—of white society. The surprisingly few Africans in the early novels—Luke alone is given anything more than casual treatment in this one—are lonely figures in white-controlled areas. Partly because Gordimer's liberal white protagonists have limited access to most parts of the African world, Africans are seen moving mainly in the small area where liberal whites and urban Africans meet—generally in white houses, only occasionally in African shebeens. Luke's will be the last visit of an African to the white house; indeed, the sense of power that operating on one's own territory provides is already gone, for Liz quickly realizes "I am the outsider" (p. 100). Henceforth, the world of Gordimer's novels will be African: Bray is a guest in Gala, the Smales in July's village, Mehring a brief colonizer of his farm, Lionel Burger's house a memory from Rosa's past.

But the most fundamental change is reflected when Liz is surprised to find herself mentioning Max's death shortly after Luke arrives, for "it had no connection with the visit; the visit had no connection with anything else in my life" (p. 99). Where all the earlier protagonists had relentlessly sought connection, Liz accepts that there is none. This acceptance finds its clearest expression in *The Conservationist* and *July's People*, where the narratives, composed of numerous fragments generally treating white and African life separately, allow a more concerted treatment of African life as the largely separate entity it is in South Africa. Through accepting this lack of connection Gordimer would, paradoxically, be able to create a fuller sense of identification with the African world.

While the attention to connecting the separate white and black worlds is immediately clear in the early novels—indeed, it is the central subject of the narratives—the perspectives of the first-person narrators in the fifties and even the dominance of Jessie's in *Occasion for Loving* tend to obscure how little the African world figures. Although these white narrators are often preoccupied with thoughts of Africans, it is striking how few Africans appear in the novels, how these are con-

fined to a narrow range of types, how persistently they serve as vehicles for reflections of white attitudes, how consistently they are victims. The five who have more than cameo roles are confined to two
urban types. The first is shy, studious, and above all, intent on finding a
place in the white world. The purest case is Mary Seswayo in *The
Lying Days*, who seems almost frozen by the foreign environment she
is attempting to enter. She stands "like a neat schoolgirl, feet together," remains silent when Helen and a friend give her a ride to her
location home, and listens with "painful intentness" to lectures that
she can place in no cultural context. Like her, Sam Mofokenzazi in *A
World of Strangers* has worked hard to cultivate a European life. When
Toby and Stephen visit him for dinner, "Sam's wife, Ella, pretty and
shy, served a roast lamb and potato dinner with a bottle of wine, and
afterwards the four of us listened to a Beethoven quartet and then to
Sam, playing some songs of his own composition" (p. 124). As Toby
notes, the blinds of this European outpost are drawn to block the world
of the location outside. Len Mofolo in *Occasion for Loving* is, by contrast, interested in developing a caravan of traveling African art and
sculpture, but he is still more at ease in white surroundings. He is
"quiet, studious" and "not much of a dancer, but he liked to talk"
(pp. 97, 93). Ann Boaz captures his nature well when she admonishes,
"Don't be so limp, Len" (p. 94).

Sam and Len are mainly foils for the more active presences of Steven
Sitole and Gideon Shibalo, who move more easily in both African and
European worlds than their studious counterparts. Steven has been to
Europe, and though Gideon's passport to study art in Italy was denied,
he fits comfortably into the Stilwell's circle. Both men remain part of
their African worlds as well, Steven as one of the liveliest party givers,
Gideon through his continued interest until late in the novel in the
political activities of the African National Congress. Both are perceived by the white protagonists as romantic figures senselessly destroyed by the white world. Steven, the soul of the passionate shebeen
world, is "buried like a king"; for a time Jessie sees Gideon possessing
"a new kind of magic," which links the old and new African worlds.

Helen Shaw's comment that "getting to know Mary Seswayo was
like gently coaxing a little shy animal to the edge of your hand" indicates well the problems in both the characterization and attitude to-

ward the Africans in these early novels. They are so persistently reserved in the white society in which they move that even Steven and Gideon lack the vitality of the white characters. Their reserve around the whites who have the privileges and power is natural, indeed a large part of the reason that, even in the liberal circles where interaction is sought, it fails to occur. But the African characters seem of consequence only when their bitterness breaks through their shy façades: when Steven perversely emphasizes his equality with Toby by asking for a drink in the presence of his secretary or refuses a liberal girl a cigarette because it turns out to be the last one in his pack; when even Len Mofalo snubs Ann after she expresses interest in the mine dances (although he is quickly confused by his own snub); and when Gideon calls Jessie a white bitch in the drunkenness brought on by Ann's departure.

But the more fundamental problem is that Gordimer is too gentle with these Africans, particularly by contrast with the trenchant satire she directs toward the white community. As Lionel Abrahams noted, her fiction seems "emotionally bonded" because it reveals an excess of cynicism for "people with whom she can more readily identify herself," the privileged whites, an excess of compassion for the dispossessed.[12] Only in brief portraits of minor black characters does she occasionally exercise her often mordant satire on blacks as she does on whites. One is Mr. Thabo, "a fat, pompous teacher-priest 'continuing his studies,'" who is the other black student in Helen Shaw's class. Where Mary Seswayo's situation is consistently treated tragically, Mr. Thabo's blatherings on "Thackeray's discursive muse" are placed in the same category of "irrelevancies and idiocies" as the other students' (pp. 128–29). And it is refreshing to find Gideon's brother-in-law assessing his incompetent shop worker in this fashion: "Half Nyasa. . . . At least that's my explanation. Dumb as he's black, that's all I can tell you. Don't you know somebody for me? They can't even measure out a shilling sugar without spilling. You could start operations for the recovery of waste sugar on this damned floor" (p. 171). These are two of the rare cases in which black foibles, limitations, prejudices are given the same treatment as whites, cases in which the

12 Abrahams, "Nadine Gordimer: The Transparent Ego," 149.

author identifies in the same way with both groups. These examples point to the less gentle, more human, portrayals of Adamson Mweta, whose youthful affability is diminished to a reflex smile that James Bray likens to those found in European toothpaste advertisements; of a black college student in *Burger's Daughter* who, confident in the power and truth of a black cause he has not risked his neck to advance, is arrogant enough to reject even Lionel Burger, who died for it; of the lack of empathy of July's family for the outcast Smales.

In the early novels, moreover, no clear sense of the African world emerges. This might be seen as a consequence of the limitations of the first-person narrators of the fifties—Helen's inability to "reconstruct" Mary's world, Toby's romanticizing of Steven's—except that no different picture emerges when Gideon Shibalo is left to enter the location on his own in *Occasion for Loving*. He goes, like the white protagonists, as a visitor from the white world. Gordimer makes the transition to Gideon's perspective when Jessie visits him one day in his flat in a white area where he does his painting. When she departs, we are left to follow his trip to the location, during which he thinks about his liaison with Callie Stow, a radical Scotswoman. Thoughts of the end of their affair turn him to the location world he enters:

> After he had turned away from Callie Stow, like a man who goes out for an evening stroll and never comes back, he had come to see his own old view of his home was as inaccurate as hers: she thought of the townships as places exalted by struggle; like treasure saved from the rest of the plundering world in a remote cave, she believed the Africans kept love alive. He went about the townships again now almost as he had worn the coating of streets there as a child, without any moral or spiritual conception of them. He went in from the white world like an explorer who, many times bitten and many times laid low with fever, can go back unthinkingly into territory whose hazards mean no more to him than crossing a city street. (p. 126)

Gideon is positioned to observe with the detachment of Toby Hood—he has no preconceived "moral and spiritual conception" of the township—but without Toby's romantic attitude, which is criticized here in Stow's similar view that "the Africans kept love alive." But Gideon takes the white world as his reference point; he comes to the location "like an explorer." Indeed, the passage is not so much a provision of his own view as a criticism of two prevalent white approaches to African life here: as plunderers, economically or emotionally, or as explorers trying to fathom the African world.

The journey may be Gideon's but the perspective is consistently the narrator's. Gordimer does provide at one point a relatively unmediated reflection of Gideon's thoughts; as he reads on the bus, he notices the woolly heads ahead of him and thinks, "If you saw us from high enough we would populate the earth like the furry patch spreading on a bit of cheese" (p. 125). But this elevated perspective serves only as a transition to the omniscient view which follows:

> As he walked through the township he called out to people he knew, stopped to talk, and, as the home-comers dispersed along the streets, passed for whole stretches, before houses, boarded-up shops, a church with uneven windows, a dry-cleaner's, a coffin-maker's, a men's hairdresser's, the insurance agent and the herbalist, without seeing what he passed, though he avoided surely the sudden ditches that sagged down beside the streets, the zig-zag of brats and dogs and the occasional mule. He did not see all this, but he could have sat down in a room anywhere on earth and drawn it. If it were to be pulled down, bulldozed and smoothed flat for other occupants, he would not see it any less clearly, or forget a single letter of the writing on the hairdresser's sign that got smaller as space on the board ran out. (p. 125)

It is natural, of course, that Gideon does not notice the stores he passes in this environment so natural to him. But Gordimer calls attention to the narrator's intrusion by repeating that he did not see, in order to prepare for the discursion, clearly not his, on his ability to reproduce it should it disappear. The narrator's commentary is directed toward an historical allusion which, as in the novels of the fifties, can be read in the landscape: townships like Gideon's were being bulldozed out of existence to make way for whites under the Separate Areas Act. Not only allusion to this event but the narrator's careful selection of details calls attention to her recording of the "outward signs" in this environment; the boarded-up shops and uneven windows show the location's decay, and of the half-dozen concerns mentioned, two deal with provision against distress, two with the next world. The journey, in short, provides more of the signs that the white protagonists recorded in the fifties. The narrator leads Gideon deftly back to the white world. After he visits a friend's house, the chapter closes with a reference to his African girl friend finding a streak of paint on his shirt, a detail which recalls the art studio with which the chapter opened. During his journey, then, Gideon remains consistently under the narrator's control as she calls attention to her intrusions and guides him through a smooth exit and reentry to the white world.

Gideon's case reveals that more than a narrative technique which allowed Africans to move in their own worlds was needed to allow for a sense of identification with the African world. Indeed, while the point of view remains Bray's with only a few exceptions throughout *A Guest of Honour*, the sense of an African world permeates the novel. Particularly by contrast with the limited scope of Gordimer's earlier African communities, the novel is a forceful indication of Gordimer's desire to portray a large and heterogeneous African world. There are scores of well-drawn African characters from the full range of the country's groups: the exploited fish-factory workers, the pitiful semieducated class which is still trying to satisfy what are to them hopelessly obscure British standards, rural and urban youths lining up in support of the Shinza and Mweta political factions, and the new political elites. Not only is there a larger variety of types, but Gordimer manages to individualize these characters with a deftness not often present in her earlier work, as in this description of the radio broadcaster Ras Asahe, whom Bray sees shortly after his arrival:

> His clothes, watch, cufflinks were those of a man who feels he must buy the best for himself, he had the Mussolini-jaw quite common among the people in the part of the country he came from but those hands were the lyrical, delicately strong, African ones that escaped the international blandness of businessmen's hands as Bray had marvelled to see them escape the brutalizing of physical hardship. Convicts broke stones with hands like that, here. (p. 23)

Gordimer not only puts Asahe in the contexts of the group from which he came and the businessmen's class he has recently entered but implies his future political activities; he will be involved in a right-wing coup and narrowly escape imprisonment at the novel's close. He is individualized as well; the truculence implied by the Mussolini jaw and the sensitivity evident in the hands are both facets of Asahe's character. It will be easy to pick him out, as it is the other supporting characters, in the novel's numerous crowd scenes.

The creation of Asahe and the other African characters is especially striking considering the presence of only a limited range of urban Africans in the earlier novels. But the most important sign of Gordimer's identification with this world is the treatment of Edward Shinza, her first African character to be accorded the same full, unromanticized treatment as her major white figures. Shinza develops from the stereotype of the older African socialist spanning the pre- and post-independence periods. He might be a Julius Nyerere or Kenneth Kaunda who never assumed power. A wily man of the country, entirely identified with those who have not rushed to join the new elite, Shinza quotes Fanon and speaks in terms of the education of the masses. He has been abroad for independence deliberations in England and has the cosmopolitan man's taste for a good cigar. But while he is entirely credible in his political role—Gordimer does not hesitate to show his bitterness at being out of power or his willingness to use others, like Bray, in his cause—his effect on Bray takes a private form. Unlike the earlier black protagonists, who influenced the white characters because they represented a particular kind of black life, Shinza influences Bray as a man. For what most impresses Bray is that Shinza, in his fifties like Bray, has fathered a child. Bray, who thinks recurrently of his affair with Rebecca as "one last kick of the prostate," is influenced most by the example of Shinza's continued virility. Bray thinks of Shinza during his first love-making with Rebecca, and he muses at the party congress where he finally agrees to renounce Mweta and assist Shinza that seeing him with "the boy-child he had begotten on a young girl, feeble in his hand" had sparked a "moment of pure sexual jealousy." Bray wonders, "was that when it began—when *he* was holding his son?" (p. 353). For the first time in Gordimer's novels, a black character's influence is primarily due to his personal qualities: Steven Sitole exercised his power as a creature of the shebeen world, Gideon Shibalo affected Jessie largely because of the sexual associations white South African society imposes on black men, and Luke Fokase, for Liz, offers not just the prospect of a lover, but a black lover. Shinza is not confined by such thoughts; his sexual vitality operates independent of his race.

A Guest of Honour is, of course, a special case among Gordimer's novels. While it depicts a large and various African world and liberates Africans from the stereotypes of Gordimer's earlier novels, it is not the world of the deeply compartmentalized South Africa. *The Conservationist* is the first of Gordimer's novels to reflect this division in a narrative which treats Mehring's and the farm laborers' worlds separately. The sense of identification with the African world is profound. It is created partly, as in *A Guest of Honour*, through depicting a more various black population, not only Jacobus and the younger farm workers Solomon and Izak but, for the first time in Gordimer's novels, an Indian community as well. But the strength of the African world is mainly achieved through counterpointing the developing power in African society with Mehring's decline. Indeed, this combination creates too strong a sense of identification with the African world, a perhaps natural overreaction to the insufficient identification in the earlier novels. Nevertheless, the impression created is decidedly different from that of the more fluid, less compartmentalized world of *A Guest of Honour*. Where it created, in the phrase Bray used in describing the effect of Shinza on him, the feel of a genie escaping from a bottle, in *The Conservationist* the bottle contains a message.

This message is clearest in the ten brief excerpts from *The Religious System of the Amazulu*, which not only underscore the resurgent power of the farm laborers but provide a series of very specific contrasts with Mehring's lack of a belief system. The first of them, for example, is a call during a drought for divine aid—"I pray for corn, that many people may come to this village of yours and make a noise, and glorify you"—counterpointing Mehring's focus on negative aspects of the drought, such as the hippos "aborting their foetuses in dried-up pools" (pp. 35, 36). Most of the passages provide a view of death that contrasts with Mehring's and reflect on one event in the farm community. Solomon, a young farm worker, is taken one night to the field where the dead man lies by two men from the neighboring location. He is stabbed and left to die, but is found and unexpectedly recovers. Solomon has, in fact, suffered the fate Mehring fears, but unlike Mehring, whose only religion is "The Baal of Development," the Africans have means of revitalizing Solomon after his traumatic experience (p. 75). They do so by calling on their traditions, detailed in the religious passages, which have been weakened but not destroyed during the period of white domination. A ceremony is held with the assistance of Phineas' wife, who suddenly feels she can maintain contact with the dead:

> They owned no cattle: not a single beast between the lot of them. That woman who thought she was going to be a diviner, she was dreaming back somewhere in the old days, somewhere in the Reserves, where you killed a beast from your herd for a wedding, a funeral, a thanksgiving, or to put things right—cleanse the kraal, they used to call it. (p. 161)

Phineas' wife is initially scorned by the laborers for believing in the old ways of the Reserves, but gradually there is a resurgence in the old beliefs, evident both in the religious passages, which indicate continued faith in the ancestors, and in the narrative. While the religious sections initially question if "the *Amatongo*, they who are beneath . . . buried beneath the earth," are "an intimation of an old faith in a Hades or Tartarus, which has become lost and is no longer understood," the final section is an assertion of continuing belief in the ancestors (p. 155). An old man, questioned about the beginnings of the Zulu people, replies:

> 'Uthlanga begat Unsondo: Unsondo begat the ancestors; the ancestors begat the great grandfathers; the great grandfathers begat the grandfathers; and the grandfathers begat our fathers; and our fathers begat us'—'Are there any who are called Uthlanga now?'—'Yes.'—'Are you married?'—'Yes.'—'And have children?'—'Yêbo. U mina e ngi uthlanga.' (Yes. It is I myself who am an uthlanga.) (p. 233)

Similarly, in the narrative there is the vivid reclaiming of the ancestral heritage as the dead man, initially feared by the farm workers, is accepted and given a proper burial when washed up by the flood.

It is at the burial which concludes the novel that the identification with the Africans is most excessive. There is too thorough an affirmation of their culture, too little detachment from the scene to create the tension which makes the artist. It is not surprising, perhaps, that the affirmation in this scene should be so marked, for Gordimer had been trying to get this African properly buried since the early fifties story "Six Feet of the Country," in which African farm laborers find that the authorities had placed the wrong body in the coffin they carry. Where that burial ended in despair, this one proceeds from a participant's drumbeat to a smooth close:

> He struck the drum softly once or twice: the sound of a sigh in space, the great sun-lit afternoon that surrounded the gathering. There was a moment of absolute silence when everyone was still, perhaps there was no need of speech, no one knew what to say, and then the one with the staff began to declaim and harangue, sometimes lifting a foot in the air as if to climb some invisible step, waving his staff. The women of his group, round white hats starched and ironed into the shape of four-petalled flower-bells, sang a hymn. He prayed aloud again and once more they sang, and Thomas's voice joined them in thin but perfect harmony. The eyes of the children moved with the spade. Phineas's wife's face was at peace, there was no burden of spirits on her shoulders as she watched Witbooi, Izak, Solomon and Jacobus sink the decent wooden box, and her husband shovel the heavy splatter of soil, soft and thick. (p. 252)

The details are clearly chosen to enforce a reverential attitude toward a community with a firm sense of its traditions; not just the surrounding sun-lit afternoon and the "sigh in space" of the drum, but the adjectival insistence of "absolute silence," "perfect harmony," and "decent" box elevate this ceremony. Its effect is also heightened, of course, by the contrast with Mehring's experience at the mine dumps which immediately precedes it: the enclosure of the mine refuse, the constant jabbering of voices within his mind, the *indecency* which he feels pervading the whole scene. By contrast with Phineas' wife here, Mehring is clearly not "at peace."

This excessive identification with the Africans through the use of the Amazulu religious passages and the strong affirmation of their reclaiming the land is most likely motivated by the restraints Gordimer continued to feel in portraying African life. While she will show Africans alone in their farm community, she still will not enter their consciousness, as she does Mehring's so consistently. The phrase "perhaps there was no need of speech" is telling; *perhaps* or a variant comes up time and again in the African sections, for Gordimer is still hesitant to presume too much about that African life which, as she wrote, no white person can tell about. Where *The Conservationist* provides her fullest view to its date of African life, it is developed as too strong a counterpose to the lively interior life of her white protagonist, the only figure in the novel she feels no constraint in telling about.

As in *A Guest of Honour*, Gordimer avoids through her choice of subject and situation in *Burger's Daughter* many of the problems posed by her divided society. In the Burger family identification with African aspirations was assumed, Africans and whites in the struggle treated in the same way. Yet so strong is the effect of the deeply compartmentalized society that even Rosa Burger must undergo a long education to overcome the romantic image of Africans which affects her perception. Inasmuch as the background from which Rosa comes allows her to acknowledge these tendencies much more consciously than the earlier protagonists, *Burger's Daughter* contains a more sophisticated treatment of the barriers to identifying with African life. More than that, however, by coming to terms with her idealized images of Marisa Kgosana and her "step-brother" Baasie, after her parents the two most important figures in Rosa's life, she is finally able to identify completely with her society.

Marisa Kgosana, the wife of one of Lionel Burger's compatriots imprisoned on Robben Island, is perceived by Rosa as the only woman in her world who offers a bond which is not tainted by a motherly possessiveness. Rosa finds in Marisa a strong, sensuous womanhood with which she can identify. As Rosa says after their first meeting in the novel,

> To touch in women's token embrace against the live, night cheek of Marisa, seeing huge for a second the lake-flash of her eye, the lilac-pink of her inner lip against the translucent-edged teeth, to enter for a moment the invisible magnetic field of the body of a beautiful creature and receive on oneself its imprint—breath misting and quickly fading on a glass pane—this was to immerse

in another mode of perception. As near as a woman can get to the transformation of the world a man seeks in the beauty of a woman. (pp. 134–35)

Rosa's opening of this passage by calling it a "token embrace" serves to accentuate how far from being token it is; Rosa enters Marisa's orbit, which at first seems to leave an imprint, then gives her the feeling of being immersed in another's world. Rosa's excessive identification here is only partly balanced by her going on to question whether she is falling prey to the use of blackness as "a sensuous-redemptive means of perception."

Rosa's excessive identification with Marisa is called into question by her monstrous detachment from Claire Terblanche, a young white woman who is also "one of us." The one scene in which they are alone together centers, as in the one with Marisa, on Rosa's perception of the other woman's femininity. "As a female she has no vision of herself," Rosa thinks. Claire, standing "as if someone plonked down a tripod," provokes Rosa's active hostility and finally shame; their visit concludes with their embarrassment on finding a used sanitary towel, which Claire guiltily places in the trash. Rosa, of course, overreacts in both cases. The slight, timid girl seeks redemption through identifying with the vivacious black woman of almost Amazonian proportions; she is repelled by Claire, a girl of her own age, on whom she projects her own feelings of sexual inadequacy. Only after having achieved a sense of herself as a woman through her affair with Bernard Chabalier is Rosa able to cease glorifying the black woman, rejecting the white. When all three women sit together in prison at the novel's close, they are peers. Here, as Rosa says, her "sense of sorority" is clear; more than that, for the first time in Gordimer's fiction, it is racially indiscriminate.

The same demystification of blackness is revealed in Rosa's changing perceptions of Baasie. Rosa realizes during her first meeting with Marisa, "I felt it in Marisa's presence, after so long; the comfort of Baasie in the same bed when the dark made that house creak with threats" (p. 155). Indeed, the "immersion" Rosa experienced in Marisa's presence is objectified in her recurrent recollections of "sputtering the same water together in the same pool" with Baasie during their early years (p. 172). This easy identification ends abruptly during their acrimonious exchange, centering on their different backgrounds, when Baasie telephones Rosa in London. If their love remains, it must do so in tension with the animosity enforced by the conditions of the land which molded them. Baasie's surname means "Suffering Land"; his father died unremembered in prison. Rosa's means "solid citizen"; her father died a celebrated martyr. She shows her acceptance of a different bond between them as their taunts reach their nastiest pitch. They seem to be "poking with a stick at some creature writhing between them," an image which recalls the brutal mule beating that led Rosa to leave the country. Her conversation with Baasie prompts her return by calling up the brutality inherent in any relationship between privileged whites and dispossessed blacks. Rosa's acceptance of hate as well as love—monstrous detachment and excessive identification—in her bond with Baasie makes the woman we see at the close of *Burger's Daughter.*

July's People deals with African life in much the same way as *The Conservationist,* through treating it in sections which are largely separate from those about the whites. But the underscoring of the African culture's sustaining rituals, so evident in the earlier novel, is almost absent here. Such emphasis is not necessary because the African world need no longer be asserted; it is now dominant. Moreover, the Smales' inner lives, being less vital than Mehring's, require less of a counterbalance. But perhaps most importantly, Gordimer has the confidence to treat the white and black worlds equally, with the impartiality of the historian. The societies have found a strange balance: the whites are losing control with the destruction of "back there"; the blacks have yet to assume power. The novel takes as its period an interregnum when no culture is sure of its foundations, a time of tension between the old and new when there are simply "morbid symptoms." Indeed, the place of the whites now is viewed as a reversal of the Africans' prior to the revolution. Where the Africans journeyed to the mines, Maureen, a product of the mine world, now leaves for the veld. There are aspects of the interim society that neither group can comprehend. For instance, the comments of July's wife Martha that the urban world of separate rooms, shelves of books, and water closets, "all these things I've never seen, my children have never seen," are juxtaposed with the passage in which Maureen looks at a veld which is "not to be seen" (p. 19).

The means of describing African life is consistent with the underlying assumption of an historical situation marking the transfer of power. The narrative voice will often be that of the detached historian as in the description of Martha's life while July was away:

> Across the seasons was laid the diuturnal one of being without a man; it overlaid sowing and harvesting, rainy summers and dry winters, and at different times, although at roughly the same intervals for all, changed for each for the short season when her man came home. For that season, although she worked and lived among the others as usual, the woman was not within the same stage of the cycle maintained for all by imperatives that outdid the authority of nature. The sun rises, the moon sets; the money must come, the man must go. (p. 83)

Terms like "diuturnal" and "imperatives" mark the passage as that of a rather dry historian, but they are set in tension with Gordimer's identification with Martha, evident here in the use of her kind of language—a concrete listing of activities and seasons and, especially, the proverbial quality of everyday speech in the final sentence.

In the narrative there is a gradual movement toward presenting the experience of the Africans not just in their own language but, if very carefully and transiently, through their own thoughts. This developing identification with them is heightened by contrasting, roughly parallel scenes, given first from the Smales', then from an African perspective. The gathering of roots in the field in which Maureen looks on as a photographer might is set against the later cutting of grass for a new house roof, seen from the perspective of July's mother:

> July had told his mother again and again, the white woman was different at home. He meant that place that had a white china room to do your business in, even he had one in the yard. She had never worked for whites—only in wedding parties on their farms, and there in the lands they didn't tell her where to go and do it. She wouldn't be told that by whites!
>
> The grass was the correct height, the weather neither too damp nor too hot and dry—exactly right for cutting thatching grass, and she, who knew the best sources for all the materials she used for her brooms and her roofs, was on her way to a stretch up-river she had been watching for weeks. Since before her son brought his

white people. She grinned with top lip pursed rubbery down over her empty gums and pointed a first finger as if to prod the white woman in the chest: You, yes you. (p. 131)

This passage differs from those like the closing burial in *The Conservationist* not only in the absence of ennobling adjectives (this is a simple description of a woman doing a competent job), but in the deft movement closer to the mother in each paragraph. In the first, Gordimer moves from July's statement to her perspective in her designation of the toilet as "the place that had a white china room" and from there to the closing exclamation which is her thought. Similarly, the second paragraph moves from the description of the grass to a close-up of her and, again, her thought as she gestures toward Maureen. The writer remains cautious about presuming to know what African life is like, but she can here move within the mind of even the character most outside her own experience in the novel, without the qualification of a single "perhaps."

July's People shows, then, that Gordimer has indeed scaled many of the limitations enforced by her compartmentalized society. She treats both whites and blacks with the same detachment—as an historian of a period in which the rise and fall of power is at an equilibrium. And if she identifies more consistently with her white protagonists, she still moves farther toward looking from an African perspective than in any of her previous works. But *July's People* is, as *A Guest of Honour* and *Burger's Daughter* were in their different ways, a special case. The novel is set in a South African world which does not yet exist, one which allows an interaction of blacks and whites not possible in the world Gordimer now inhabits. In this sense the novel is the antithesis of the apocalyptic view that it is often seen to be; rather, it reflects the wish-fulfillment of a novelist who has been constrained by the barriers of her society for over three decades. For in *July's People* those barriers break; the former servant talks to the former missus in ways that would be unimaginable "back there," affording the development of an understanding Gordimer's society does not presently allow. And the novel shows the identification of children, in whom Gordimer has always placed the greatest hope, with an emerging order in which those barriers might well not exist.

But for the present they do. As Gordimer said in the mid-seventies, "The white writer is cut off from the greater part of the life of the society in which he lives; the life of the proletariat, the ordinary people, the nineteen millions whose potential of experience he does not share, from the day he is born *baas* to the day *he* is buried in *his* segregated cemetery."[13] In these conditions, which Gordimer defined as the 98th, unlisted kind of censorship in South Africa, a full identification with her society remains impossible. *July's People* is her fullest attempt at that broader identification, except perhaps for the only novel she was never able to finish because its major figure, a young Soweto black, was, as Gordimer has stated, too much outside the potential of her experience.[14] The novel became the story "Not For Publication." This title is a comment on the continuing frustrations to identification with a whole society posed by the 98th, the most pernicious, kind of censorship in Gordimer's world.

V

In a 1969 interview, Gordimer said that "we all write one book, but we write it piecemeal and from very different points of view throughout our lives. You move on, you change, and your writing changes with this advancement. . . . But in the end, for a writer, your work is your life and it's a totality."[15] Gordimer's "one book" has had an unusually distinct set of concerns from the outset of her career. Indeed, her major themes are present in Helen Shaw's visit to the concessions with which her first novel opens. Helen stands

> in this unfamiliar part of my own world knowing and flatly accepting it as the real world because it was ugly and did not exist in books (if this was the beginning of disillusion, it was also the beginning of Colonialism: the identification of the unattainable distant with the beautiful, the substitution of "overseas" for "fairy-

13 Gordimer, "98 Kinds of Censorship in South Africa," 117.
14 Morris, "A Visit with Nadine Gordimer," 26. The story "Not for Publication" appears in the collection of that name and in *Selected Stories*.
15 "Nadine Gordimer Talks to Andrew Salkey," *Listener*, August 7, 1969, p. 185.

land") I felt for the first time something of the tingling fascination of the gingerbread house before Hansel and Gretel, anonymous, nobody's children, in the woods. (p. 21)

Not only Helen but Gordimer's later protagonists might well find a parallel with their own experiences in the Grimm fairy tale containing not one, but two, evil mother figures—and take solace in their dispatch. Gordimer's "private apprenticeship" would begin with the attempts of her protagonists to escape them, to become "nobody's children." Only in the later novels would they be able to return to a house in which they could fit in; Rosa finds a "sense of sorority" and the Smales' children are freed of the mother's warping love through identifying with the African world. Gordimer's major public theme is raised during Helen's brief trip as well. She sees not only the cause of her dissociation from her world, her colonial background, but the remedy to it Gordimer's protagonists would take: examining the "unfamiliar part[s] of my own world" through its "outward signs." The identification of Gordimer's later protagonists—and, more pervasively, of the author—with their world requires the renunciation of the "unattainable distant" metropolitan world. Indeed, the growing power of the "real world" they inhabit, the diminished power of the life of books, which shapes Helen's response to the concessions, is conveyed at the close of *July's People* through the same metaphor with which Helen's passage ends, for Maureen finds that "the real fantasies of the bush delude more inventively than the romantic forests of Grimm" (p. 160).

What now stands as Gordimer's "one book" has often been viewed as simply a record of such deluded whites in a foreign landscape. Jane Kramer finds in the ends of Maureen, Rosa Burger, and Mehring only the prospect of annihilation. And "X" found in a 1982 *New York Review of Books* article that "Perhaps, for white South Africans, there are indeed no defections, only flight; no 'liberal' choices or responsibilities, only panic, finally, and primitive response to unknown but inevitable disaster."[16] There is flight and panic; Mehring and Maureen—and, for that matter, Liz Van Den Sandt and Jessie Stilwell—will not be saved. Gordimer's novels are the most complete record we have of the "morbid

16 "X" [pseud.], "Fall of a House," *New York Review of Books*, August 13, 1981, p. 18.

symptoms" of the current conditions of South Africa and the suffering those like Rosa Burger must undergo to identify with their land. But what is, in the phrase from *July's People*, "not to be seen" in this view is Gordimer's broader identification with her society over the past decade. She stressed the need for this broader identification, specifically for accommodating "very different points of view," in a 1981 interview: "In a country like this it's become the fashion to say that whites can't write about blacks, and vice versa. To you or me a white character in a black novel might seem like a caricature, or simply crude and inaccurate. Nevertheless *that's how they see us*. We must try to see them with equal clarity. If there is to be a true South African culture. . . ."[17] The conditional clause with which Gordimer's comment trails off indicates that the fashioning of a true South African culture is an uncertain prospect. But she looks to that true culture of the future here as she has in all her novels since *The Late Bourgeois World*. This focus on a future after the current interregnum in Gordimer's later "inspirational" novels is the most telling refutation of the apocalypse those like Kramer and "X" see prefigured in their endings.

It was to the "true South African culture" of the future that Gordimer turned in 1982 when defining the present role of the South African writer. Characteristically, she did so in terms of the landscape, in which she has sought her land's cultural foundation over the three decades that her one book has developed. "Only as apprentices of freedom," she wrote, "may we perhaps look out for, coming over the Hex river mountains of the Cape, or the Drakensberg of Natal, that 'guest of the future'—the artist as prophet of the resolution of divided cultures."[18] Gordimer has been an apprentice of her land's freedom since her first published collection of short stories. It is to the *I Corinthians* passage from which she took its title, not to the Apocalypse, that we should look in defining her art. In Gordimer's later novels the resolution of divided cultures can be seen, if through a glass darkly. In these novels we can already discern the "guest of the future" carrying an image of the true South African culture over the mountains.

---

17 Morris, "A Visit with Nadine Gordimer," 27.
18 Gordimer, "Apprentices of Freedom," 22.

Bibliography

I. Primary Sources

A. Novels

Burger's Daughter. New York, 1979; London, 1979; rpr. Harmondsworth, 1980. (The New York, 1979 edition is cited herein.)

The Conservationist. New York, 1975; London, 1974; rpr. New York, 1977; Harmondsworth, 1978, 1983. (The New York, 1974 edition is cited herein.)

A Guest of Honour. New York, 1970; London, 1971; rpr. Harmondsworth, 1973, 1982. (The New York, 1970 edition is cited herein.)

July's People. New York, 1981; London, 1981; rpr. Harmondsworth, 1982. (The New York, 1981 edition is cited herein.)

The Late Bourgeois World. New York, 1966; London, 1966; rpr. London, 1976; Harmondsworth, 1982. (The New York, 1966 edition is cited herein.)

The Lying Days. New York, 1953; London, 1954; rpr. New York, 1955; London, 1978. (The London, 1978 edition is cited herein.)

Occasion for Loving. New York, 1963; London, 1963; rpr. London, 1978. (The London, 1978 edition is cited herein.)

A World of Strangers. New York, 1958; London, 1958; rpr. Harmondsworth, 1962; London, 1976; Harmondsworth, 1981. (The London, 1976 edition is cited herein.)

B. Short Story Collections

Face to Face. Johannesburg, 1949.

Friday's Footprint. New York, 1960; London, 1960.

Livingston's Companions. New York, 1971; London, 1972; rpr. London, 1975.

Not for Publication. New York, 1965; London, 1965.

Selected Stories. New York, 1976; London, 1975; rpr. as *No Place Like: Selected Stories,* London, 1978; rpr. as *Selected Stories,* London, 1983.

Six Feet of the Country. New York, 1956; London, 1956.
The Soft Voice of the Serpent. New York, 1952; rpr. London, 1954; New York, 1956.
Some Monday for Sure. African Writer's Series, No. 177. London, 1976.
Something Out There. New York, 1984; London, 1984.
A Soldier's Embrace. New York, 1980; London, 1980; rpr. Harmondsworth, 1982.

C. Essays and Criticism

"Apartheid." *Holiday,* XXV (April, 1959), 133–34ff.
"Apartheid and Censorship." In *The Gray Ones,* edited by Stephen Gray. Johannesburg, 1973.
"Apartheid and the Primary Homeland." *Index on Censorship,* I (1972), 25–29.
"Apprentices of Freedom." *New Society,* December 24/31, 1981, pp. ii–v; rpr. *In These Times,* January 27–February 2, 1982, pp. 12–13.
The Black Interpreters: Notes on African Writing. Johannesburg, 1972.
"Boycott: A Matter of Personal Taste or Public Principle?" *Index on Censorship,* IV (1975), 21–22.
"Catalogue of the Ridiculous." London *Times,* July 2, 1975, p. 11.
"Censored, Banned, Gagged." *Encounter,* XX (June, 1963), 59–63.
"Censorship and the Primary Homeland." *Reality: A Journal of Liberal and Radical Opinion,* I (1970), 81–83.
"Censorship and the Word." *Bloody Horse,* I (1980), 20–24.
"Chief Luthuli." *Atlantic,* CCIII (April, 1960), 34–39.
"The Congo River." *Holiday,* XXIX (May, 1961), 74–79.
"Egypt Revisited." *National and English Review,* CLII (February, 1959), 47–53.
"The Fischer Case." *London Magazine,* V (March, 1966), 21–30.
"From Apartheid to Afrocentrism." *English in Africa,* VII (1980), 45–50.
"How Not To Know the African." *Contrast,* XV (March, 1967), 44–49.
"In a World They Never Made." *Playboy,* May, 1972, pp. 166–69.
"The International Symposium on the Short Story: South Africa." *Kenyon Review,* XXX (1968), 457–63.
"The Interpreters: Some Themes and Directions in African Literature." *Kenyon Review,* XXXII (1970), 9–26.
"Johannesburg." *Holiday,* XVIII (August, 1955), 46–51ff.
"Leaving School—II: Nadine Gordimer." *London Magazine,* III (May, 1963), 58–65; rpr. as "The Bolter and the Invincible Summer," *Antaeus,* XLV/XLVI (Spring/Summer, 1982), 105–14.
"Letter from the 53rd State." *New York Review of Books,* November 6, 1980, pp. 12ff.

"Letter from South Africa." *New York Review of Books,* December 9, 1976, pp. 3–10.

"The Life of Accra, the Flowers of Abidjan." *Atlantic,* CCXXVIII (May, 1971), 85–87.

"Literature and Politics in South Africa." *Southern Review: An Australian Journal of Literary Studies,* VII (1974), 205–27; rpr. as "English Language Literature and Politics in South Africa," in *Aspects of South African Literature,* edited by Christopher Heywood. London, 1976.

"Living in the Interregnum." *New York Review of Books,* January 20, 1983, pp. 21–23.

"A Morning in the Library." *Quarry* (1976), 27–35.

"New Forms of Strategy—No Change of Heart." *Critical Arts,* I (1980), 27–33.

"98 Kinds of Censorship in South Africa." *American Pen,* V (1973), 16–21; rpr. *Hekima* (Nairobi), I (December, 1980), 115–19.

"Notes of an Expropriator." *TLS,* June 4, 1964, p. 484.

"The Novel and the Nation in South Africa." *TLS,* August 11, 1961, pp. 520–23; rpr. *African Writers on African Writing,* edited by G. D. Killam. Evanston, 1973.

"One Man Living It Through." *The Classic,* II (1966), 11–16.

"Party of One." *Holiday,* XXXIV (July, 1963), 12–17.

"Plays and Piracy." *Contrast,* XII (July, 1965), 53–55.

"Politics: A Dirtier Word Than Sex!" *Solidarity,* III (1968), 69–71.

Reply to "The Politics of Commitment," by N. Z. *African Communist,* LXXX (1980), 109.

"Pula." *London Magazine,* XII (February/March, 1973), 90–103.

"Report and Comment: Tanzania." *Atlantic,* CCXXXI (May, 1973), 8–18.

"Some Notes on African Writing." *South African Outlook,* C (1970), 172–74.

Foreword to *The Sound of a Cowhide Drum,* by Oswald Mtshali. New York, 1972.

"The South African Censor: No Change." *Index on Censorship,* X (1981), 4–9.

"A South African Childhood: Allusions in a Landscape." *New Yorker,* October 16, 1954, pp. 121–43.

"South African Riviera." *Holiday,* XXII (December, 1957), 166ff.

"South African Writers Talking: Nadine Gordimer, Es'kia Mphahlele, André Brink." *English in Africa,* VI (September, 1979), 1–23.

"South Africa: Towards a Desk-Drawer Literature." *The Classic,* II (1968), 64–74.

"Themes and Attitudes in Modern African Writing." *Michigan Quarterly Review,* IX (Fall, 1970), 221–31; rpr. as "Modern African Writing" in *The Writer's Craft: Hopwood Lectures, 1965–81,* edited by Robert A. Martin. Ann Arbor, 1982.

"What Being a South African Means to Me." *South African Outlook,* CVII (1977), 87–89ff.

What Happened to "Burger's Daughter," or How South African Censorship Works. Emmarentia, S.A., 1980.

"What Makes Us Write?" *Writer,* LXXXIX (October, 1976), 23–24.

"Where Do Whites Fit In?" *Twentieth Century,* CLXV (1959), 23–24.

"White Proctorship and Black Disinvolvement." *Reality,* III (1972), 14–16.

"Why Did Bram Fischer Choose Jail?" *New York Times Magazine,* August 14, 1966, pp. 30–31ff.

"The Witwatersrand: A Time of Tailings." *Optima,* XVIII (January, 1968), 22–26; rpr. *On the Mines* (with David Goldbatt, photographer). Cape Town, 1973.

"A Writer's Freedom." *New Classic,* III (1975), 11–16; rpr. *English in Africa,* II (September, 1975), 45–49.

"Writers in South Africa: The New Black Poets." *Dalhousie Review,* LIII (1973–74), 645–64.

"Writing Belongs to Us All." *Forum,* III (September, 1954), 9–10.

"Zambia." *Holiday,* XXXIX (June, 1966), 38–47.

D. Reviews

"Alberto Moravia's Africa" (Review of his *Which Tribe Do You Belong To?*). *London Magazine,* XIV (October/November, 1974), 53–56.

"The Child Is the Man" (Review of *Aké: The Years of Childhood,* by Wole Soyinka). *New York Review of Books,* October 21, 1982, pp. 3–6.

"Color of Want" (Review of *The Race War,* by Ronald Segal). *Nation,* CCIV (1967), 313–15.

"At the Crossroads of Cultures" (Review of *Morning Yet on Creation Day,* by Chinua Achebe). *TLS,* October 17, 1975, p. 1227.

"Death, Love, and the Fruit Basket on Carmen Miranda's Head" (Review of *Sergeant Getúlio,* by João Ribeiro, and *Sol,* by Mario Satz). *London Magazine,* XX (June, 1980), 91–93.

Review of *The Habit of Loving,* by Doris Lessing. *Africa South,* II (July/September, 1958), 124–26.

"The Idea of Gardening" (Review of *The Life and Times of Michael K,* by J. M. Coetzee). *New York Review of Books,* January 2, 1984, pp. 3–6.

"The Last Colonial Poet?" (Review of *Lyric and Polemic: The Literary Personality of Roy Campbell,* by Rowland Smith). *London Magazine,* XIV (April/May, 1974), 115–18.

"The Metaphor of Exile" (Review of *Thoughts Abroad,* by John Bruin [pseud. Dennis Brutus]). *South African Outlook,* CI (December, 1971), 12.

"The Onlooker and the Insider" (Review of *The Separated People,* by

Ellison Kahn, and *The Long View*, by Alan Paton). *Nation*, CCVII (1968), 21–22, 24–25. — MFILM . N.S. 3554

"Path and Not Goal" (Review of *The Literature and Thought of Modern Africa*, by Claude Wauthier). *Nation*, CCIV (1967), 822–23.

"A Private Apprenticeship" (Review of *The Mortgaged Heart*, by Carson McCullers). *London Magazine*, XII (October/November, 1972), 134–37.

"Taking into Account" (Review of *Force of Circumstance*, by Simone de Beauvoir). *London Magazine*, V (January, 1966), 73–77.

"A Wilder Fowl" (Review of *Turbott Wolfe*, by William Plomer). *London Magazine*, V (June, 1975), 90–92.

E. Films

The Gordimer Series (seven films based on Gordimer's short stories; various directors; marketed by Teleculture, Inc.). New York, 1984.

F. Interviews

Boyers, Robert, *et al.* "A Conversation with Nadine Gordimer." *Salmagundi*, LXII (Winter, 1984), 3–31.

Bragg, Melvyn. "The Solitude of a White Writer." *Listener*, October 21, 1976, p. 514. — 808.2805. L773 - Green

Burrows, E. G. "An Interview with Nadine Gordimer." *Michigan Quarterly Review*, IX (Fall, 1970), 231–34.

deBeer, Mona. "Nadine Writes from a Position of Involvement." London *Times*, April 9, 1969, p. 7.

Gardner, Susan. "'A Story for This Place and Time': An Interview with Nadine Gordimer about *Burger's Daughter*." *Kunapipi*, III (Fall, 1981), 99–112.

Gray, Stephen. "An Interview with Nadine Gordimer." *Contemporary Literature*, XXII (Summer, 1981), 263–71.

———. "Landmark in Fiction." *Contrast*, XXX (April, 1973), 78–83.

———. "Writing in South Africa: Nadine Gordimer Interviewed." *New Nation*, September, 1972, pp. 2–3.

Hurwitt, Jannika. "The Art of Fiction LXXVII: Nadine Gordimer." *Paris Review*, LXXXVIII (Summer, 1983), 83–127.

Kakutani, Michiko. "Nadine Gordimer, South African Witness." New York *Times*, December 28, 1981, Sec. C-11.

Morris, Edmund. "A Visit with Nadine Gordimer." *New York Times Book Review*, June 7, 1981, pp. 26–27.

Ravenscroft, Arthur. "A Writer in South Africa: Nadine Gordimer." *London Magazine*, V (May, 1965), 20–28.

Riis, Johannes. "Nadine Gordimer." *Kunapipi*, II (1980), 20–26.

Salkey, Andrew. "Nadine Gordimer Talks to Andrew Salkey." *Listener*, August 7, 1969, pp. 184–85.

Servan-Schreiber, C. "Learning to Live with Injustice." *World Press Review*, January, 1980, pp. 30–34.

Terkel, Studs. "Nadine Gordimer." Chicago *Perspective on Ideas and the Arts*, XII (May, 1963), 42–49.

II. Secondary Sources

A. Books

Christie, Sarah, Geoffrey Hutchings, and Don Maclennan. *Perspectives on South African Fiction*. Johannesburg, 1980.

Fiedler, Leslie, and Houston A. Baker, Jr., eds. *English Literature: Opening Up the Canon*. Baltimore, 1981.

Haugh, Robert F. *Nadine Gordimer*. New York, 1974.

Heywood, Christopher, ed. *Aspects of South African Literature*. London, 1976.

Jacobson, Dan. *Time of Arrival and Other Essays*. London, 1962.

JanMohamed, Abdul R. *Manichean Aesthetics: The Politics of Literature in Colonial Africa*. Amherst, 1983.

Lawrence, John. *The Seeds of Disaster: A Guide to the Realities, Race Policies, and World-Wide Propaganda of the Republic of South Africa*. London, 1968.

Lukács, Georg. *The Historical Novel*. Translated by Hannah and Stanley Mitchell. Boston, 1962.

———. *Realism in Our Time: Literature and the Class Struggle*. Translated by John and Necke Mander. New York, 1971.

Mphahlele, Ezekiel (Es'kia). *The African Image*. London, 1962; rev. ed. New York, 1974.

Partridge, A. C., ed. *Proceedings of a Conference of Writers, Publishers, Editors, and University Teachers of English*. Johannesburg, 1957.

Pieterse, Cosmo, and Donald Munro, eds. *Protest and Conflict in African Literature*. London, 1969.

Sachs, Bernard. *South African Personalities and Places*. Johannesburg, 1959.

Sontag, Susan. *On Photography*. New York, 1977.

Wade, Michael. *Nadine Gordimer*. London, 1978.

B. Articles

Abrahams, Lionel. "The Idea of Johannesburg." *Purple Renoster*, VIII (Winter, 1968), 2–4.

————. "Nadine Gordimer: The Transparent Ego." *English Studies in Africa*, III (September, 1960), 146–51.

Abrahams, Lionel, and Ursula A. Barnett. "Does the White Writer Belong?" *Quarry* (1978–79), 167–88.

Abramowitz, Arnold. "Nadine Gordimer and the Impertinent Reader." *Purple Renoster*, I (September, 1956), 13–17.

A. O. D. Review of *The Lying Days*, by Nadine Gordimer. *Fighting Talk*, X (April, 1954), 13.

Bailey, Paul. "Unquiet Graves." *TLS*, July 9, 1976, p. 841.

Balliett, Whitney. Review of *A World of Strangers*, by Nadine Gordimer. *New Yorker*, November 29, 1958, pp. 230–32.

Barkham, John. "South Africa: Perplexities, Brutalities, Absurdities." *Saturday Review*, January 12, 1963, p. 63.

Boyers, Robert, ed. *Nadine Gordimer: Politics and the Order of Art. Salmagundi*, LXII (Winter, 1984). Microtext MFILM. USI, 5:44 1807-08

Brink, André. Review of *Nadine Gordimer*, by Robert F. Haugh. *Books Abroad*, II (1975), 840.

Brown, Andrew. "A Guest of Honour." *South African Outlook*, CI (December, 1970), 187–88.

Cooke, John. "African Landscapes: The World of Nadine Gordimer." *World Literature Today*, LII (1978), 533–38. 028.88725 SI Green

————. "Out of the Garden: Nadine Gordimer's Novels." In *Design and Intent in African Literature*, edited by David Dorsey, *et al.* Washington, 1982.

————. Review of *Nadine Gordimer*, by Robert F. Haugh. *Research in African Literatures*, VIII (1977), 147–49.

Cunningham, Valentine. "Kinds of Colonialism." *TLS*, November 1, 1974, p. 1217.

Daymond, Margaret. "Disintegration, Isolation, Compassion." *Bloody Horse*, IV (March/April, 1981), 91–94.

Driver, Dorothy. Review of *Nadine Gordimer*, by Michael Wade. *English in Africa*, V (March, 1978), 77–80.

Fido, Elaine. "*A Guest of Honour*: A Feminine View of Masculinity." *World Literature Written in English*, XVII (1978), 30–37.

Gardner, Colin. "Nadine's World of Strangers." *Reality: A Journal of Liberal and Radical Opinion*, VIII (1977), 13–15.

Gerver, Elizabeth. "Women Revolutionaries in the Novels of Nadine Gordimer and Doris Lessing." *World Literature Written in English*, XVII (1978), 38–50.

Gill, Brendan. "New Old World." *New Yorker*, November 21, 1953, pp. 217–18.

Girling, H. K. "Compassion and Detachment in the Novels of Dan Jacobson." *Purple Renoster*, II (Spring, 1957), 16–23.

————. "Provincial and Continental: Writers in South Africa." *English Studies in Africa*, III (September, 1960), 113–18.

————. "South African Novelists and Short Story Writers." *English Studies in Africa*, IV (March, 1961), 80–86.

Gordon, David J. "Some Recent Novels: Connoisseurs of Chaos." *Yale Review*, LX (1971), 428–37.

Green, Robert. "Nadine Gordimer's *A World of Strangers*: Strains in South African Liberalism." *English Studies in Africa*, XXII (1979), 45–54.

Hayes, Richard. Review of *The Soft Voice of the Serpent*, by Nadine Gordimer. *Commonweal*, LVI (May, 1952), 204.

Hendricks, David. Review of *Friday's Footprint*, by Nadine Gordimer. *Purple Renoster*, IV (Summer, 1960), 85–87.

Hope, Christopher. "Out of the Picture: The Novels of Nadine Gordimer." *London Magazine*, XV (April/May, 1975), 49–55.

Hynes, Samuel. "The Power of Hatred." *Commonweal*, LXXVII (1963), 667–68.

Jacobson, Dan. Introduction to *The Story of an African Farm*, by Olive Schreiner. London, 1971.

Jacoby, Tamar. "Harsh and Unforgiving Vision." *Nation*, June 6, 1981, pp. 705–706.

King, Bruce. "Keneally, Stow, Gordimer, and the New Literatures." *Sewanee Review*, LXXXIX (1981), 461–69.

Kramer, Jane. "In the Garrison." *New York Review of Books*, December 2, 1982, pp. 8–12.

Laredo, Ursula. "African Mosaic: The Novels of Nadine Gordimer." *Journal of Commonwealth Literature*, VIII (June, 1973), 42–53.

Libra [pseud.]. "Beyond the Fiction of Fact." *Purple Renoster*, VII (Winter, 1967), 30–34.

Lomberg, Alan. "Withering into the Truth: The Romantic Realism of Nadine Gordimer." *English in Africa* III (March, 1976), 1–12.

Maclennan, Don. "The South African Short Story." *English Studies in Africa*, XIII (March, 1970), 112–19.

Marquard, Jean. "The Farm: A Concept in the Writing of Olive Schreiner, Pauline Smith, Doris Lessing, Nadine Gordimer, and Bessie Head." *Dalhousie Review*, LIX (1979), 293–307.

McGuinness, Frank. "The Novels of Nadine Gordimer." *London Magazine*, V (June, 1965), 97–102.

Nakasa, Nat. "Writing in South Africa." *The Classic*, I (1963), 56–63.

Newman, Judie. "Gordimer's *The Conservationist*: 'That Book of Unknown Signs.'" *Critique*, XXII (1981), 31–44.

Nkosi, Lewis. "Les Grandes Dames." *New African*, IV (September, 1965), 163.

N. Z. "The Politics of Commitment." *African Communist*, LXXX (1980), 100–101.

Ogungbesan, Kolawole. "The Way Out of South Africa: Nadine Gordimer's *The Lying Days.*" *Ba Shiru*, IX, (1978), 48–62.

Parker, Kenneth. "Nadine Gordimer and the Pitfalls of Liberalism." In *The South African Novel in English: Essays in Criticism and Society*, edited by Kenneth Parker. New York, 1978.

Paton, Alan. "Gordimer's South Africa." *Saturday Review*, May, 1981, p. 67.

Plomer, William. "Several Revolutions." *Twentieth Century*, CLXV (1959), 385–96.

Ricks, Christopher. "Fathers and Children." *New York Review of Books*, June 26, 1975, pp. 13–14.

Roberts, Sheila. "Character and Meaning in Four Contemporary South African Novels." *World Literature Written in English*, XIX (1980), 19–36.

Sands, Raymond. "The South African Novel: Some Observations." *English Studies in Africa*, XIII (March, 1970), 89–104.

Smith, Rowland. "Living for the Future: Nadine Gordimer's *Burger's Daughter.*" *World Literature Written in English*, XIX (1980), 163–73.

Staniland, Martin. "Apartheid and the Novel: Desperation and Stoicism in a Situation Which Frustrates." *New African*, IV (March, 1965), 15–17.

Theroux, Paul. "The Conservationist." *New York Times Book Review*, April 13, 1975, p. 4.

Tuohy, Frank. "Breaths of Change." *TLS*, April 25, 1980, p. 462.

Voss, A. E. "The Conservationist." *Reality*, VII (May, 1975), 15–17.

Webster, Mary Morrison. "Trends in South African Literature." *Forum*, September, 1954, pp. 19–20.

Woodward, Anthony G. "South African Writing." *Contrast*, II (Autumn, 1962), 45–50.

———. "Nadine Gordimer." *Theoria*, XVI (1961), 1–12.

"X." "Fall of a House." *New York Review of Books*, August 13, 1981, pp. 14–18.

Index